The Persistent
Poppy

The Persistent Poppy

A Computer-Aided Search for Heroin Policy

Gilbert Levin
*Albert Einstein College
of Medicine*

Edward B. Roberts
*Alfred P. Sloan School
of Management,* M.I.T.

Gary B. Hirsch
Pugh-Roberts Associates, Inc.

with a foreword by
John F. Collins

Ballinger Publishing Company ● Cambridge, Mass.
A Subsidiary of J.B. Lippincott Company

This book is printed on recycled paper.

International Standard Book Number: 0-88410-031-6

Library of Congress Catalog Card Number: 75-4656

Printed in the United States of America

Library of Congress Cataloging in Publication Data

Levin, Gilbert.
    The persistent poppy.

    Includes bibliographical references.
    1. Heroin habit. 2. Narcotics, Control of—United States. 3. System analysis. I. Roberts, Edward Baer, joint author. II. Hirsch, Gary B., joint author. III. Title. [DNLM: 1. Computers. 2. Heroin addiction. 3. System analysis. 4. Research design. WM288 L665p]
    HV5822.H4L48   363.4'5   75-4656
    ISBN 0-88410-031-6

To
Elizabeth, Nancy, and Linda

Contents

vii

List of Figures

List of Tables

Foreword

The general public views the drug problem most graphically in terms of the heroin addict who commits crimes to support his habit. While but another in the long list of seemingly intractable urban problems, heroin addiction is, however, one problem which has attained great visibility. The increase in violent crimes and theft, the agony of families and associates of the usually youthful addicts, and the increased fear of addiction or even contact with addicts have combined to hasten the flight of more mobile families from center city to suburb. But the migration of the drug culture into the suburbs, with attendant crime growth, has spawned an alliance between suburbanites and city dwellers. The alliance aims to cope with the effects of drug-related problems which until recently had been regarded as a central city monopoly. The drug problem, in its many dimensions, now pervades our society.

The slow early growth of heroin addiction, followed by rapid expansion, is typical of many socio-economic problems highly resistant to change. The public gradually becomes frustrated and fearful. Greater sums of money for police, courts, and prisons produce no discernible improvement in abating violence or street crime. Fear of the public streets, while formerly nocturnal, in many areas has now become a 24-hour-a-day phenomenon attributed by the public to a "heroin menace."

Demands to identify and eliminate the root causes of addiction—an endeavor which has so far been unsuccessful and time-consuming—are matched by equally fruitless clamor for eradication of the heroin flow into this country.

The legal and health authorities have pursued several well-intentioned programs to conclusions far below the anticipated benefits. For example, methadone maintenance or even free heroin have been suggested as antidotes to heroin-related crime. Clearly, proponents argue, if the drug supply is free, violence is not necessary to finance its purchase. Intuition and good intentions persuade us that we shall overcome.

This book provides a framework for examining the system of forces that encourages and discourages the growth of heroin use in our cities and suburbs. The authors have developed and been aided by a mathematical model that embodies the generally agreed-upon facts about the problem, as well as informed opinions of social scientists, treatment-program directors, enforcement officials, addicts, and victims. They have analyzed the social and economic causes of addiction, and evaluated the whole array of corrective strategies and the trade-offs among them.

The Persistent Poppy fulfills the great promise of *Urban Dynamics* and *The Limits to Growth,* two earlier applications of system dynamics to important societal problems. While the problem addressed here is narrower in scope, the analysis is fuller, better documented, and more accessible.

The language of system dynamics provides a powerful tool for stating in precise terms the assumptions behind our actions and decisions. Some causal relationships in a system dynamics model are drawn from the observations of policy-makers; others, from the world of academia. The authors move within and between these diverse worlds, drawing wisdom from each into a coherent whole.

The book is important not only to professionals in the field of drug-abuse treatment and enforcement, but to anyone concerned with public policy and the practical solution of complex social problems. Social scientists will be interested in the computer model as a rare example of a rigorous social theory complex enough and rich enough to do justice to its subject matter. Without compromising the highest standards of technical excellence, the book's step-by-step exposition makes it an ideal introduction to computer simulation for the lay reader.

John F. Collins
Former Mayor of Boston, 1960–67
Past President of National League of Cities
Consulting Professor of
Urban Affairs, M.I.T.

Acknowledgments

We could not have carried out this task without the active particpation of many individuals, organizations and governmental agencies.

At the Sound View-Throgs Neck Community Mental Health Center, a series of seminars in 1970 and 1971 helped immeasurably to sharpen our thinking about the heroin system. Melvin Roman, Aaron Schmais, Erlene Collins, and Deborah Kligler attended regularly and criticized most generously. Luis Diaz led us into the neighborhoods of the Southeast Bronx and helped to get us in touch with the drug scene there. The management of the Center as represented by Jack Wilder and Sutherland Miller supported our efforts in every possible way, as did the Center's community advisory groups.

Albert Warner, David Laskowitz, Richard Brotman, Jerome Jaffe and Robert Lee stand out among those scholars who shared freely their knowledge of the field with us, and without whose contributions this work would not have been possible. John Langrod has been especially helpful to us. His involvement began early in our work and has continued to the present time.

We were fortunate to have had the opportunity to present earlier versions of our model of the heroin system to various governmental agencies and task forces. Their feedback greatly facilitated our task and it may be that we have contributed in a small way to their efforts. The Addiction Services Agency and the Mayor's Narcotics Coordinating Committee in New York City, the New York State Narcotics Addiction Control Commission, the U.S. Bureau of Narcotics and Dangerous Drugs, the White House Office of Science and Technology, and the Executive Committee of the Club of Rome are among those organizations that heard us and in most cases answered back. We are grateful to Graham Finney, who while director of the Addiction Services Agency guided and encouraged us in New York and again to Dr. Jaffe who performed a similar role in Washington.

We thank Andrew Weiss and Linda Hirsch for their research assistance that aided us in formulating and documenting the model.

The National Institute of Mental Health provided the financial support for our research under Grant #16586 to the Albert Einstein College of Medicine and also provided guidance and emotional support through Harold Halpert, who has done so much to encourage the systems point of view in mental health.

Part I

Overview

Chapter One

The Persistent Poppy

Fears of a continually rising heroin tide are abating as we enter the second half of the seventies. Evidence accumulates, though not without contradiction, that the heroin system is producing addicts at a slower rate than when the decade began.[1]

Heroin, methadone and other narcotic drugs nevertheless remain a central preoccupation in the lives of many thousands of Americans. Narcotic addiction reached its peak, in both relative and absolute terms, at the beginning of this century. Terry and Pellens suggest that as many as one million persons were addicted to opiates before 1920.[2] The most alarmed recent estimates fall far short of this figure, against a much larger population base.

That the late 1960s and early 1970s saw a rapid increase in the incidence of narcotic addiction is demonstrated vividly in Figure 1.1. Narcotic-related deaths in New York City increased in only two years from about 650 in 1968 to well over 1200 in 1970. In recent years a relatively fixed percentage of the addict population, perhaps 1 percent, is widely believed to die each year from narcotic-related causes. Hence the recent annual death rate is a reasonable index of prevalence. (Opiate usage in the early part of the century did not consist of injections and so was less dangerous.)

Equally striking is the evidence that growth of the heroin problem dates back to the 1950s. For more than two decades an increasingly severe problem was confined to the slums of our large cities. Middle-class consciousness of the narcotics problem arose suddenly in the late sixties as the problem proliferated past the boundaries of the ethnically segregated inner city.

This new consciousness was heightened by a trend toward increasing involvement of youth. During the past quarter-century the average age of the heroin addict has declined. One study showed an increase in the percentage of persons aged 16–20 charged with narcotics violations from less than 0.5 percent in 1938 to more than 13 percent in 1951.[3] More recent statistics reveal a continuation of this trend. Leslie reported that the percentage of newly reported

3

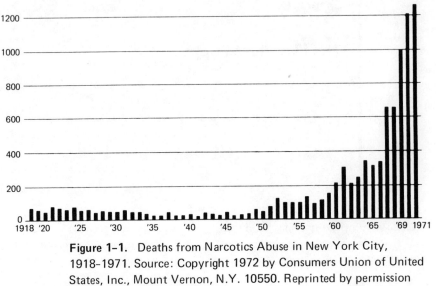

Figure 1-1. Deaths from Narcotics Abuse in New York City, 1918–1971. Source: Copyright 1972 by Consumers Union of United States, Inc., Mount Vernon, N.Y. 10550. Reprinted by permission from *Licit and Illicit Drugs*.

heroin abusers in the under-20 age group in New York City increased from about 7 percent in 1964 to 23 percent in 1968.[4]

The subsiding of hysterical media coverage of narcotics is a welcome event. The undesired legacy of the past decade, however, is a large addict population base, which, reviewed in historical perspective, represents the potential for future exacerbations of the problem. While the opium poppy no longer preoccupies us, it persists in our society.

1.1 WHY MODEL?

This book brings to the heroin problem the outlook and methods of computer-based systems analysis, and in particular the system dynamics perspective.[5] The development of this philosophy and associated methodology has been progressing at M.I.T. under Jay W. Forrester and his colleagues since 1957. System dynamics was created as an integration of: (1) developments in computer technology and simulation; (2) new recognitions about decision-making processes; and (3) insights gained from the application of feedback-control principles to complex systems. The initial ten years of work in this field emphasized the dynamic behavior of industrial systems, while the period since then has seen a shift primarily to the problems of complex social and economic systems.

The system dynamics approach begins with an effort to understand the system of forces that has created a problem and continues to sustain it. Relevant data are gathered from a variety of sources, including literature, informed persons (experts, practitioners, victims, perpetrators) and specific quantitative studies. As soon as a rudimentary measure of understanding has been achieved, a formal model is developed. This model is initially in the format of a set of logical diagrams showing cause-and-effect relationships. As soon as feasible the visual model is translated into a mathematical version. The model is exposed to criticism, revised, exposed again and so on in an iterative process that continues as long as it proves to be useful. Just as the model is improved as a result of successive exposures to critics, a successively better understanding of the problem is achieved by the people who participate in the process. Their intuition about the probable consequences of proposed policies frequently proves to be less reliable than the model's meticulous mathematical approach.

This is not as surprising as it may first appear. Socioeconomic systems contain as many as 100 or more variables that are known to be relevant and believed to be related to one another in various nonlinear fashions. The behavior of such a system is complex far beyond the capacity of intuition. Computer simulation is one of the most effective means available for supplementing and correcting human intuition.

A computer simulation model of the kind described here is a powerful conceptual device that can increase the role of reason at the expense of rhetoric in the determination of policy. A model is not, as is sometimes supposed, a perfectly accurate representation of reality that can be trusted to make better decisions than people. It is a flexible tool that forces the people who use it to think harder and to confront one another, their common problems and themselves, directly and factually.

A computer model differs principally in complexity, precision and explicitness from the informal subjective explanation or "mental model" that men ordinarily construct to guide their actions toward a goal. It is an account of the total set of forces that are believed to have caused and to sustain some problematic state of affairs. Like the informal mental model, it is derived from a variety of data sources including facts, theories and educated guesses. Unlike the mental model, it is comprehensive, unambiguous, flexible and subject to rigorous logical manipulation and testing.

The flexibility of a model is its least understood virtue. If you and I disagree about some aspect of the causal structure of a problem, we can usually in a matter of minutes run the model twice and observe its behavior under each set of assumptions. I may on the basis of its behavior be forced to admit you were correct. Very often, however, we will both discover that our argument was trifling, since the phenomenon of interest to us may be unchanged by a change in assumptions.

A computer model constructed and used by a policymaking group has the following advantages:

1.   It requires policymakers to improve and complete fully the rough mental sketch of the causes of the problem that they inevitably have in their heads.

2.   In the process of formal model-building the builders discover and resolve various self-contradictions and ambiguities among their implicit assumptions about the problem.

3.   Once the model is running, even in a rudimentary fashion, logical "bootstrapping" becomes possible. The consequences of promising but tentative formulations are tested in the model. Observation of model behavior gives rise to new hypotheses about structure.

4.   Once an acceptable standard of validity has been achieved formal policy experiments reveal quickly the probable outcomes of many policy alternatives; novel policies may be discovered.

5.   An operating model is always complete, though in a sense never completed. Unlike many planning aids, which tend to be episodic and terminal (they provide assistance only at the moment the "report" is presented, not before or after), a model is organic and iterative. At any moment the model contains in readily accessed form the present best understanding of the problem.

6.   Sensitivity analysis of the model reveals the areas in which genuine debate (rather than caviling) is needed and guides empirical investigation to important questions. If the true values of many parameters are unknown (which is generally the case in social planning), the ones that most affect model behavior need to be investigated first.

7.   An operating model can be used to communicate with people who were not involved in building the model. By experimenting with changes in policies and model parameters and observing the effects of these changes on behavior, these people can be helped to better understand the dynamic forces at work in the real-world system.

1.1.1 A Way of Thinking.

1.1.1 **A Way of Thinking.**   Without dwelling on them it is necessary to introduce a few basic system dynamics ideas. Our examples are not hypothetical. They are drawn from basic relationships in the heroin system.

Despite striking differences among policy advocates, almost everyone agrees that the social problem of heroin consists of the presence of too many addicts and of the crimes they commit to support their addiction. Nearly everyone also agrees that the supply of heroin that enters this country illegally is a principal source of the problem. These beliefs can be constructed as shown in Figure 1.2. The structure describes believed cause-and-effect linkages: an increase in the heroin supply leads to an increase in the number of addicts, thereby increasing addict-related crime. Alternatively, a decrease in heroin supply decreases the number of addicts, thus effecting a decrease in addict crime.

With this simplistic structure we shall now do two things: (1) enlarge

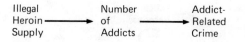

Figure 1-2. Visual Structure: General Beliefs

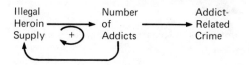

Figure 1-3. Positive Feedback in Addiction

the visual structure to "close" the now open system; and (2) use it to evaluate proposed policies aimed at coping with the narcotics problem. First let us recognize that the illegal supply of heroin does not merely appear in a community from mid-air, as perhaps is suggested by Figure 1.2. The presence of addicts in a community creates a market for the "pushing" of heroin, attracting pushing activities that bring illegal supplies into greater availability. The greater supply, according to general beliefs, generates further increase in the number of addicts in the community, attracting still more heroin supply, as is indicated in Figure 1.3. This now-closed relation between heroin supply and the number of addicts is called a "closed loop", or a "feedback loop", in that a change in any one factor eventually "feeds back" through the other factors in the loop to affect itself. For example, if the number of addicts in a community were sharply increased by an influx of migrant addicts, this would soon lead to an enlarged heroin supply being attracted to the area, thus enabling more potential addicts to become addicted. In this particular case, the loop is a "positive feedback" loop, defined by the fact that an initial change in any factor eventually induces further self-change in the original direction. That is, an increase in supply leads to more addicts, inducing further increase in supply. This change would produce continuous exponentially increasing growth of the addiction problem, including its associated crime, unless and until other constraining factors were brought to bear. Such continual exponentially changing behavior characterizes all positive feedback loops.

But every positive feedback loop tends to set in motion counterforces that seek to control the exponential growth behavior. In our example, the growing positive loop of heroin supply and addicts induces marked growth of addict-related crime. As this occurs the crime generates responses aimed at controlling and reducing crime, in general consisting of increased police activities, initially against addict-criminals.

The new feedback loop that is formed is shown in Figure 1.4. As addicts increase, crime rises, leading to an increase in the community's responsive use of police, which if effective reduces the number of addicts "on

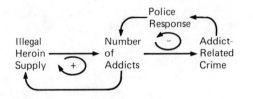

Figure 1-4.   Positive and Negative Feedback Loops in Addiction

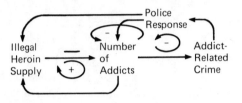

Figure 1-5.   A Simple Overview of Heroin Addiction Control

the street". Notice that the influence of this feedback loop is to control or decrease the force that sets it into motion. The increase of crime leads to a police response aimed at decreasing crime. A feedback loop that tries to behave in this controlling or reversing manner is called a "negative feedback" loop.

All complicated social systems are composed of interrelated positive and negative feedbacks, the "positives" tending to amplify changes or disturbances, the "negatives" tending to counter or control changes. When several such loops interconnect, consequences of any change become difficult to predict, especially as each loop takes its toll over different periods of time. For example, the increase of addicts may quickly produce more drug pushing and induce greater heroin availability. But it may be a much longer time before a community reacts to increased crime by increasing resources devoted to crime fighting and control.

Adding a second effect to police response will further illustrate the importance of this time dimension. Usually long after a community adds to its police force to combat increased shoplifting and breaking-and-entering, people will note the relation between the crime and drug use. This often leads to overt attempts to use some of the police resources to search out, seize, and attempt to lessen the drug supply. To the extent that such efforts have any success, another longer-time-delayed negative feedback loop is closed, as shown in Figure 1.5. The police effort directed toward controlling narcotics supply is inevitably slower in being initiated and slower in having impact. The structure as now developed permits a simple overview of the heroin addiction control process. The positive feedback loop of drug supply operates the vicious circle of addiction growth, while the negative feedbacks of police response attempt to contrain the number of addicts and the supply of heroin. The interplay among these loops over a period of years can be hypothesized as explaining much of the overall problem behavior of heroin addiction in a community, with the negative loops seeming to struggle against the positive growth forces for domination.

Although the examples of positive and negative feedback loops cited here are instructive, and although they do describe fundamental aspects of the heroin scene, the resulting overview is still too simplistic. Attempts to prescribe policy from so simple a representation would be misleading and possibly dangerous. Let us further elaborate the structure and consider two often proposed "solutions" to the heroin problem:

Proposed Policy #1. Eliminate the source of heroin supply. The rationale is clear. If there is no heroin, there will be no heroin addicts, and obviously no addict-related crime.

Proposed Policy #2. Provide a legal supply of heroin to all addicts. This policy accepts the continued presence of a population of addicts and aims at eliminating all addict-related crime.

Consider first the policy of eliminating the source of illegal heroin. While this appears almost impossible to achieve, it indeed would lead toward elimination of addiction in the long run, if accomplished. But the short-run effects of achieving a drastic reduction in the supply of heroin, which would drive up its price, could cause an increase in addict-related crime of unprecedented proportions. Society may be unwilling to pay the short-term cost to gain the long-run advantage, especially if the short-term condition were to last several years as a minimum.

To visualize these consequences of an implemented policy to shut off supply, we must recognize explicitly what would happen to the price of heroin as a result of the policy. Price, as added in Figure 1.6 to the basic visual

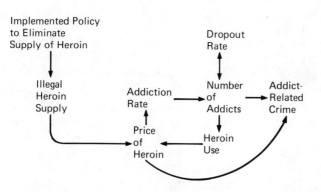

Figure 1-6. Price Consideration Added to Basic Structure

structure, is shown as dependent upon the illegal heroin supply and the illegal use, as determined by the number of addicts. A reduction in the supply of heroin per addict would therefore increase the price. The price of heroin plays two important mediating roles omitted from Figure 1.5. First, price affects the rate at which potential addicts become addicted. When the price of heroin is low the drug is more accessible to the discretionary (nonaddicted) user, and vice versa. Price does not have much effect on the habits of present addicts, or on their dropout rate. Secondly, the price of heroin determines the amount of crime each addict must commit to support his habit. If the price is higher, more crime is induced. The more detailed structure of Figure 1.6 now suggests that to the extent a supply reduction approach works in the short run, it tends to drive up the price of heroin. This may dampen the rate at which new prospects become addicts, but it does not have much impact on addict dropout and therefore on heroin use. As more of the present addicts find themselves unable legally to support their habits and so turn to crime, and as already criminal addicts experience the need to commit more crime, crime in the community mushrooms.

These circumstances may cause further changes to occur. With crime rising, the media might communicate the scarcity of heroin that induced the increased crime, leading to waning public support of antisupply activities. A policy aimed at crime reduction can thus produce a counter-intuitive increase in crime, with abandonment of the original policy as the probable consequence.

Let us examine Proposed Policy #2, the policy of providing heroin legally to addicts. This proposal, growing largely out of observations and interpretations of the British experience with heroin maintenance programs, can also be seen to produce another set of undesirable counter-intuitive consequences. The intention of this policy is to destroy the illegal heroin production-distribution system through competition. If all addicts can obtain all the heroin they need through legal channels at zero or nominal cost, it is reasoned, illegal competitors are driven out of business. There is a serious flaw in this policy.

The previous diagram of Figure 1.6 must be augmented to take account of the contemplated legal supply of heroin that the proposed policy would introduce. As Figure 1.7 indicates, the extent of legal heroin supply determines the number of addicts whose habits can be supported on legal doses. As the legal supply grows, illegal addicts begin to fall in number, having a price-reducing effect on the market price for illegal heroin. The heroin in the illegal pipeline when the policy goes into effect will not dry up, and most of it eventually reaches the market. Further, addicted customers who previously consumed the lion's share of the illegal drug are the most likely ones to turn to the legal supply. As heroin prices fall, many individual operators are driven out of business, as the policy intends. But those remaining are likely to seek buyers among nonaddicts with increased vigor. The structure shown in Figure 1.7

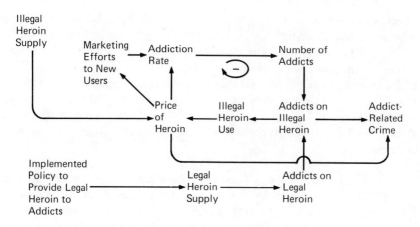

Figure 1-7.   Consideration of Legal Heroin Supply

suggests that low heroin prices and more aggressive marketing would result in a significant increase in the number of new addicts.

This postulate can be supported by important evidence. First is the fact that each addict who turns to the legal supply frees up enough illegal heroin to addict four or five new users. The buildup of drug tolerance in the long-term addict causes him to use as many as five to ten bags per day. Yet a high is easily caused in the nonaddict, and narcotic dependence can occur at the rate of only one or two bags per day. Thus, from a supply-demand perspective, every addict converted to legal supply enables the illegal system to enlist four or five new customers. Second is the evidence that such intense marketing indeed takes place. For example, numerous reports indicate that street pushers lowered the price of heroin, and sold it mixed with marijuana and hashish, in order to increase their market during the federal government's 1969 Operation Intercept, in which the flow of cannabis was severely restricted at the Mexican border.

Under the assumptions diagrammed in Figure 1.7 the illegal supply of heroin, originally intended primarily to satisfy the needs of existing addicts and only secondarily to increase their number, is diverted substantially to the latter purpose. Thus, while legal heroin might reduce addict-related crime, it would probably significantly increase the total number of addicts. Note that Figure 1.7 indicates the presence of another negative feedback loop, one that leads to the undesired policy consequence. The increase of addicts on legal heroin quickly reduces the number of addicts on illegal supply; this diminishes illegal heroin use, decreases heroin price, and induces an increased rate of new addictions. The increased flow of new addicts adds to the total addict pool, increasing those on illegal heroin. The loop is initiated by a force aimed at decreasing illegal heroin addiction, but ends on an up-beat of increased illegal addiction. Each time more legal heroin supply is added to the system, the same negative feedback loop behavior would result.

The visual structures displayed in these two policy evaluations have permitted the explication of the believed cause-and-effect issues underlying policy design. Though only illustrative thus far, diagramming demands the talking through of the issues involved. The diagrams are subject to change as new evidence appears and as new arguments are made. But visual representation alone is inadequate for predicting precisely the effects or the costs of the considered policies.

1.1.2 **A Computer Scenario**. To advance toward policy prescription we first constructed an initial visual representation of the important system relationships and then translated it into a comprehensive computer model of heroin in the community. The computer model shows the alarming potential for growth of the problem, while providing a tool for its analysis and for the evaluation of corrective policies. Figure 1.8 traces the growth of the problem in a hypothetical urban community of 200,000 persons. A twenty-five-year projected history is plotted starting in about 1965.

As the computer run begins, the number of addicts on the street (plotted by the computer in Figure 1.8 using the letter A) is rising at a steady rate. With no program response by the community, not even police directed at addict criminals, the positive feedback loops that enlarge the addiction problem are dominant in the community. Addict and drug-user populations expand due to concurrent and ever-increasing growth of drug culture, exposure to addicts, and increasing availability of heroin. The rapid unimpeded growth of the addict population makes pushing very attractive, bringing more drugs into the community, enabling even more rapid escalation of addiction. With the growth of the street addict population, the community experiences a concomitant development of addict crime necessitated by the addicts' need for income to support their drug habits.

By the end of the twenty-five-year simulated future, the number of street addicts has risen to 8300 and is still growing. Crime has risen to about 10,000 incidents per month and is still on the increase.

The underlying assumption behind this computer-generated future is that no effective actions are taken to combat the problem. The assumption is of course not realistic, given public concern about the problem. Various steps are actually being taken, many others have been advocated. Other computer simulations will be presented later to explore the probable outcomes of these alternatives.

1.2 A PESSIMISTIC OUTLOOK

A wide range of attempts to correct the situation is possible. According to our analyses, no single measure or combination of measures fully solves the problem.

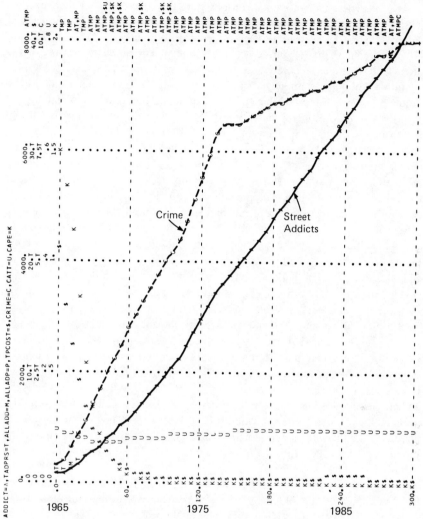

Figure 1-8. Heroin Addiction: No Community Response

Even at unrealistically high levels of effort and expenditure, efforts at solution yield one of three kinds of results:

1. They wash out. Over time, the self-corrective structure of the identified heroin system overwhelms the attempted policy.
2. They make the problem worse.
3. One aspect of the heroin problem is solved, but in the process another of its aspects is aggravated.

These frustrating conclusions stem from the fact that there are two heroin problems, not just one. In thinking about the problem at the level of policy design, it is necessary to keep this constantly in mind.

First, the heroin addict is a criminal. His purchase and use of the drug, while criminal acts, are secondary in importance to the crimes he must commit to obtain the money to pay for this supply. The criminal side of the problem is the one most visible to and most impactful upon the community. In addition to loss of property and the cost of crime control, community sensitivity to the presence of the addict-criminal helps to reduce the quality of urban life and has contributed to the flight of the middle class from city to suburb and from there to exurbia.

The addict is also a victim—of his drug, and of society's attitude toward it and toward him. The pursuit of heroin dominates all facets of his life: economic, social, psychological and biological. Ironically, he pays this terrible price not for the ecstasy experienced in his early contacts with the drug, but to avoid the discomfort he feels whenever it is absent from his body. His body rapidly and almost indefinitely increases its tolerance toward the drug. The addict hustles, with remarkable industry, not to get high but to stay straight. Once addicted, he is committed, without the experience of any choice in the matter, to a single-minded pursuit of the drug; a path through discomfort, ostracism, exploitation, harassment and imprisonment, to early death.

It is remarkably instructive to contrast the addict with the alcoholic. Both are victims of drugs; both are prone to commit crimes and cause pain to others. Beyond this essential similarity, differences are dominant. The alcoholic is responsible for more crime and for crimes of a more violent nature than is the addict. Death, personal injury and property loss due to accident and assault by persons under the influence of alcohol are significant problems of our society. In contrast, the heroin user is docile, compliant and content when under the influence of his drug. When high the alcoholic might beat his wife but the addict will doze sedately in the corner.

The addict commits practical, economically motivated crime to get his drug. Once he has obtained it he is a problem to no one but himself and those who care personally about him. The alcoholic commits senseless crime and causes accidents after he has obtained his drug. He is generally harmless when sober.

The harmful consequences of alcohol result directly from its chemical action in the body. Most of the harmful consequences of heroin derive not from the drug itself, but from society's attitudes toward those who use it. Even the direct hazards to health are greater for the user of alcohol than for the user of heroin. Cirrhosis of the liver and chronic brain damage are caused by alcohol. Pure heroin, properly administered, has not been demonstrated to cause any illness more serious than irregularities in bowel movements. We have some measure of social control over how much harm heroin does to its users. The harmfulness of alcohol is basically biochemical in nature.

Nevertheless the addict is seen and portrayed almost exclusively as a fiendish criminal, while the alcoholic is most often the helpless, perhaps comic, victim. As we shall see later, this view of the addict contributes to the problem of heroin and may be modifiable.

The two problems of heroin interact in a perverse fashion. Effective present actions, guided by policies aimed at reduction in numbers of the addict-criminal or the addict-victim, may exert an unintended and undesired impact upon the number of addicts who will constitute the future problem. For example, the criminal problem could be solved simply by providing free heroin to addicts. Unsupported by an economic incentive, many addicts would stop stealing. However, the introduction of additional quantities of the drug would exert a downward pressure on the street price of illicit heroin. Lower prices and a modified marketing strategy (selling smaller quantities to a larger market) could greatly increase the growth rate of the addict population. (This causal mechanism would further reduce the already declining age of the average addict.)

Conversely, a significant reduction or elimination of the heroin supply, if it could be accomplished through improved enforcement procedures, would result ultimately in the solution of the problem of the addict as victim. No heroin could be used, if none were present. However, scarce heroin would sell at a higher price and in the short term could cause a significant increase in addict crime. The size of this increase and its duration are unknown but critical variables, since they would determine whether such a strategy has any promise; so is the question of whether the public would tolerate the short-term discomfort of the policy long enough to gain its long-term benefits.

Another possible consequence of effective supply reduction is worth noting. As the costs and risks of importing botanical opium increase, incentives for the illicit domestic production of methadone and other synthetic opiates would grow correspondingly. A resultant decentralized production-distribution system would probably represent a more difficult task for law enforcement than its present one.

1.3 STRUCTURE OF THE BOOK

The following chapters develop a perspective on the heroin problem that is sufficiently comprehensive to encompass all of the symptoms described above. First, Chapter 2 presents a macroscopic view of the identified heroin system. The two heroin problems cited above are linked to one another through a causal feedback structure. At this stage the reader will be able to grasp the essential features of our analysis.

Chapter 3–5 examine the microstructure of the heroin system. Each structural component is analyzed and evaluated against the available evidence. The results of methodologically valid investigations are employed whenever possible. Often hard evidence simply does not exist. In such cases the authors have relied upon the estimates and judgments of persons generally believed to be qualified observers. While this procedure is less than perfect, there is at present and in the foreseeable future no better alternative. Social planning is an imperfect art. The present analysis shares these generic imperfections with other analyses. Its unique advantage is that all questionable assumptions are explicit and therefore open to the influence of debate and further investigations.

Based on the structure presented in Chapter 2, and the details provided in Chapters 3-5, a detailed computer model of the heroin system has been built (documented and explained in the Appendix). This computer model permits experimental manipulation of the parameters and variables of the system which, as presented in Chapter 6, are the primary raw materials used in our search for rational heroin policy.

The specific policies advocated in Chapter 7 are the authors' present conclusions, taking account of the available facts, theories and educated guesses about the heroin problem and subjecting them to the rigorous, often ruthless, logic of the computer model. While our conviction about these policies stems in large part from the model, the reader can join the dialog without any special technical education beyond the capacity to read critically and reason logically.

We have forewarned the reader of our principal conclusion that in the short term the heroin problem cannot be solved, at least not in the sense desired by us all. It may be possible to bring it under control and over a period of time to manage it effectively, steadily reducing its destructive consequences. To accomplish even this limited goal will require more careful planning, more cooperation among agencies and political constituencies, more changes in attitudes, and more flexibility and patience than is characteristic of our society and its government.

Many well-informed persons will disagree with our conclusions. Our hope is that they will join us in debate and dialogue. We suggest the present model, and others that might be constructed, as a vehicle for facilitating that process. While it may turn out that our model is wrong in some or many respects, it is not sufficient merely to assert this. Any criticism carries the implication that some alternate causal formulation is a better one. We acknowledge this possibility and hope that mechanisms can be found to make alternate views explicit, to realize them in a model and subject them to logical analysis. The result of such a process would be improved policy, not merely a dispute among scholars and politicians.

REFERENCES

1. *Annual Report of the Special Action Office for Drug Abuse Prevention 1973* (Washington, D.C.: U.S. Government Printing Office, 1973), pp. 51–58; Lucia Mouat, "Heroin Abuse Reaches Small Towns", *Christian Science Monitor,* October 8, 1974, p. 1.

2. C. E. Terry and M. Pellens, *The Opium Problem* (New York: Bureau of Social Hygiene, 1928).

3. H. Finestone, "Narcotics and Criminality", *Law and Contemporary Problems* 22 (1957): 69–85.

4. Alan C. Leslie, *A Benefit/Cost Analysis of New York City's Heroin Addiction Problems and Programs* (City of New York, Health Services Administration, Office of Program Analysis, March 1971), Appendix Table III.

5. The initial text in the field is Jay W. Forrester, *Industrial Dynamics* (Cambridge: M.I.T. Press, 1961).

Chapter Two

The Heroin System in Brief

The focus of this work is on the dynamics of growth of heroin addiction in an urban community, its consequences, and the attempts to cope with it. The investigatory field work that accompanied the analysis of the problem drew substantially from consideration of a specific ethnically and economically heterogeneous geographic region in New York City—the Sound View—Throg's Neck section of the Bronx—an area of eight square miles with a population of 180,000 persons. But the data were extended to include considerations of experiences with drug addiction in a wider array of urban and suburban environments. Confidence in the generation of the analysis has been gained from careful study of the research literature, interviews and consultation with numerous social scientists and medical and enforcement experts as enumerated in the preface to the book, and widespread public presentations of the analytical framework and tentative conclusions prior to publication of this book.

Our thinking has been dominated by our active work in a mixed income, but mostly blue-collar/middle-class, neighborhood undergoing transition. Lower income blacks and Puerto Ricans now constitute 20 percent of the local population of the area in which we worked, with this percentage steadily increasing. But we believe that what we have found about the underlying processes of heroin addiction applies to all large cities in the United States, nearly all medium-sized cities, and many smaller communities as well. Only at the extremes of exceptional wealth or exceptional poverty do we balk at applicability of the analyses.

This chapter conveys our general understanding of the dynamics of the heroin addiction process. Figure 2.1 is a flow chart that accounts for the people of interest to us as they participate in the heroin system. On the right-hand side of the figure, the category Potential Drug Users refers to 80 percent of the people in the community in the vulnerable range between the ages of ten and thirty, who are not currently involved in the illegal use of drugs. Drug

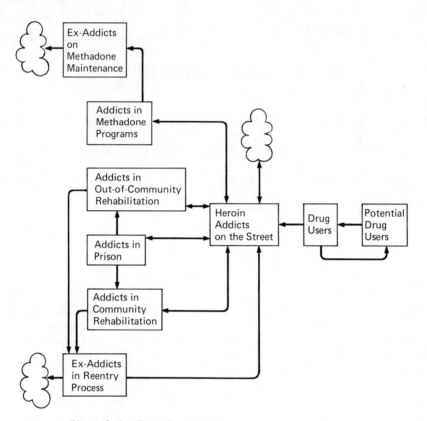

Figure 2-1. Total Person Flow

Users encompasses all people who indulge in the occasional illegal use of drugs up to and including heroin, but are not addicted to heroin and do not take up the addict's life style. The drugs they use are mainly marijuana and hashish, but also include LSD, barbiturates, glue, and other commonly used substances. Heroin Addicts on the Street refers to the people who live in the community and require at least daily injections of narcotics to prevent withdrawal symptoms. They devote most of their time to procuring and injecting heroin and associating with other addicts. This group includes some people who live with their families and can buy heroin with money obtained from their families or from part-time jobs, without resorting to theft. We are aware that finer conceptual distinctions are usually made between types of drug users, but we have refrained from the practice because it would not affect our overall structure in a significant way. The arrow from Users to Addicts indicates that almost all heroin addicts were previously users of other drugs such as marijuana, but this is not intended to imply a causal relationship.

Addicts remain in the reference community or can migrate into or out of the community depending on the attractiveness of the area for an addict (the outside world being represented by the cloudlike symbol). They can also drop out of the addict population through death or by "burning out", a process that occurs when an addict of many years standing simply becomes tired of all the difficulties involved in being an addict and spontaneously stops taking heroin. Addicts who have been arrested and convicted spend time in prison and are released to the street or to rehabilitation programs if the programs have available capacity. Addicts also enter rehabilitation programs directly from the street. Community rehabilitation refers to therapeutic community programs, usually of a residential nature, that exist within the community itself. The Phoenix Houses in New York are an example of this kind of program. However, the existence of in-community programs depends on the tolerance and support of the neighborhood, usually not forthcoming until the residents view the drug-abuse problem as sociomedical in character. Out-of-community rehabilitation refers to similar therapeutic community programs in nearby areas, assumed to be available to treat addicts even if the modeled community does not regard addiction as a social and medical problem.

Addicts in the reentry process have been deemed rehabilitated by either an in-community or an out-of-community program, and either successfully reenter the community (remain heroin-free for a specified period of time) or return to being addicts. Addicts in methadone programs receive daily doses of methadone and are, for the most part, heroin-free. Those that remain in methadone programs for a period of three years are shown in the diagram as ex-addicts on methadone maintenance. A large proportion of the addicts in the rehabilitation programs and a smaller proportion in the methadone programs return to being active addicts before completion of the programs. The return arrows back to the "street" throughout the diagram indicate the dominance of this path in the heroin experience to date.

We are aware that a variety of other addict dispositions are possible. Detoxification programs and heroin maintenance propositions are prominent among those omitted at the moment for the sake of simplicity. Figure 2.1 contains the most common flow categories of the heroin system. Other alternatives will be considered later.

The principal forces responsible for the induction of potential users into use of the so-called soft drugs are displayed in Figure 2.2. The rate at which potential users become users is a function of the relative balance between the forces creating an appeal to drug use and those acting to deter use, with the growth in use constrained by drug availability. A community's potential drug use is affected by the poverty and ethnic status of the area and the appeal of drug use deriving from drug-associated culture. Some potential users are deterred from drug use by education programs and fear of arrest. A community with a low socioeconomic level has a greater potential for producing drug users than a more affluent community. An affluent community, however, due to alienation of youth from the values of their parents, may have a higher potential for creating drug users than a middle-class community. Widespread use of drugs among youth from all social strata is making this socioeconomic differential of drug use much less important. Drug-associated culture refers to the presence in the community of drug users who are willing to turn on their friends, drugs of various sorts and individuals selling them, and the music, style of dress and appearance and all of the other cultural factors that the youth population tends to associate with drug use. As drug use becomes more pervasive, these cultural factors play an increasingly larger role in enhancing the appeal of drug use to potential users. Drug-associated culture grows with the number of users and is responsible for the further growth of the user population, another positive feedback loop. Fear of police action is likely to deter some but not many potential users from drug use, and pervasiveness of use may render this deterrent even less effective. Education programs are assumed to be ineffective in preventing drug use although credible programs, those that deal honestly with the effects of drugs, deter some youngsters from using drugs with some demonstrable dangers, such as LSD or barbiturates.

The rate at which the number of users grows is partially a function of drug availability. If drugs are relatively plentiful, users have more to share with their friends, and drug use spreads more rapidly. A scarcity of drugs causes

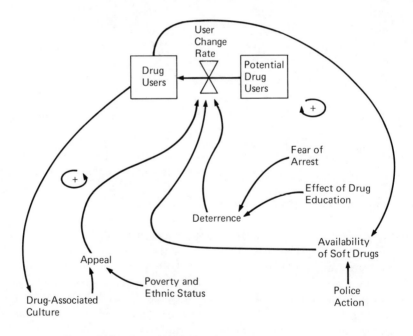

Figure 2-2. Drug Use Induction

users to hoard their supplies, resulting in a longer time required for the drug-user pool to grow. Drug availability is determined largely by the number of users in the community. Thus drug usage and its availability are also linked in a positive feedback loop. The intensity of police action against drugs can also affect drug availability. People drop out of the user category and flow back to the potential user population if police action against users becomes very intense or if education programs effectively communicate the real dangers of certain drugs.

Consideration of the price of soft drugs has been omitted from this diagram. Implicitly, "availability" treats some of the same issues that would relate to drug price; historically soft drug prices have been sufficiently low that their markets seem basically unaffected by reasonably wide price movements.

Figure 2.3 illustrates the forces that control the rate at which drug users become heroin addicts. Again, a set of forces promotes the growth of the addict population and another set of forces retards this growth. The number of potential heroin addicts in a community depends more importantly on its socioeconomic level than does the number of potential drug users. This reflects a complex set of differences in values, alternative life styles, and education about the dangers of addiction among the youth of various socioeconomic groups.

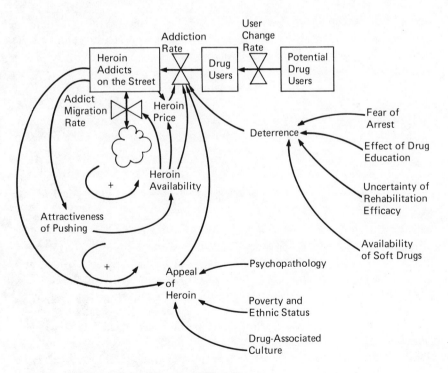

Figure 2-3. Heroin Addiction

The number of addicts already in the community is itself a positive force for more addiction. If the addict life style is seen as appealing, or at least not repulsive, and a number of addicts are available to initiate new addicts, the addict population is likely to grow in a positive feedback manner. Psychopathology is another causal factor implicit in the driving forces of the increase in addiction. This term refers to an individual aberrant personality pattern that responds paradoxically to community attitudes toward addiction. Community disapproval increases the likelihood that such individuals will turn to drugs. Not incidentally, as some degree of psychopathology is inevitable in a community, its manifestation in addiction may be socially less harmful than its expression in more violent alternatives such as rape or murder.

One inducing influence is the drug-associated culture in the community. At high levels of intensity of drug use, patterns of social communication between addicts and nonaddicted drug users reach the point where widespread drug trading and experimentation becomes more likely. Under these conditions increased heroin use seems likely, leading to increased addiction.

Just as soft-drug-related culture is thus seen here as a force increasing the appeal of heroin, its availability in an area may actually provide a deterrent to heroin use and addiction by making it easy to remain a soft-drug user. The suppression of soft-drug supplies could lead to an increase in addiction by depriving users of an alternative to heroin. Thus soft-drug availability simultaneously encourages and discourages heroin addiction, leading to the suspicion of a near-zero net effect.

Education can also act as a deterrent to heroin addiction, but only if it is credible. Credibility may require stress upon the dangers of addiction without making judgments about good versus bad life styles. In contrast, scare tactics employed in the name of education may add to the appeal of heroin as an antisocial and antiestablishment outlet. Fear of arrest also deters some users from become addicts, but heavy-handed police methods can also induce further youthful alienation.

Uncertainty of rehabilitation efficacy and its concomitant, fear of lifelong addiction, remain deterrents to many addict prospects as long as rehabilitation programs are scarce and believed to be ineffective. The existence of successful rehabilitation programs mitigates against this effect. Thus we have the anomolous situation that attractive and effective rehabilitation programs pull some addicts from the street, thereby decreasing addiction. But this leads to less fear of lifelong addiction, thereby increasing the net attraction to new addicts. This is an example of a negative feedback loop in the heroin system.

The rate at which drug users become heroin addicts is strongly dependent on heroin availability. If heroin is abundant, addicts are more likely to sell or even share with others some of their heroin supply. This is less likely to occur if the drug is scarce. When there is only a small addict population in an area, local addicts have to travel to other areas to get heroin and little excess heroin is available in the community of interest. As the addict population increases, so does the attractiveness of pushing to addicts as an alternative way of making money. High volume of sales activities within the community necessitates inventories of heroin that increase its availability in the community and allow the growth of addiction to proceed more rapidly. More addicts thus enhance the attractiveness of pushing, thereby increasing heroin availability and enabling the addict population to grow even more rapidly. This is readily seen to be a positive feedback loop, inducing growth. Though not specifically indicated in Figure 2.3 the attractiveness of pushing is also affected by police action directed against heroin pushers. Police action against addicts and heroin availability are also responsible in part for migration of addicts into and out of the community.

As was pointed out earlier, the price of heroin also affects the rate of which drug users may turn to and become addicted to heroin. The greater the amount of heroin available in the community, relative to its use, the lower the price of heroin. A lower price makes young people, in particular, more able to afford initial access to heroin, with even less need to steal. By removing these barriers the lowered price thereby stimulates a higher rate of new addiction, increasing the total number of addicts. As the new addicts increase their heroin habits, due to the effect of increased physiological tolerance and therefore need for the drug, heroin use rises in the community. This may lead to increased pressure on heroin availability, tending to raise heroin prices in a negative feedback fashion, as illustrated in Figure 2.4's inner loop. But the increased number of addicts also increases the attractiveness of drug pushing, producing increased heroin availability, and tending to restore a lower heroin price. This is the positive feedback loop also shown in Figure 2.4.

This behavior does not have a completely symmetrical counterpart. Reversal of the number of addicts does not set in if heroin price escalates. The key reason is that the addict is indeed addicted, not merely enjoying a pleasure

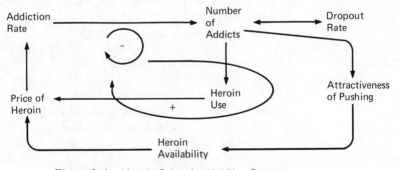

Figure 2-4. Heroin Price-Availability Structure

that he can give up should it become too expensive. Therefore, the rate of addict dropout is rather independent of price effects. Only the rate of growth of new addicts appears to be price-related. In addition, of course, the extent of addict crime does depend on the cost of supporting the addict's habit.

Due to the expense of the heroin habit, growth of the addict population has as a direct consequence the growth of the community's crime rate. Addicts support their habit from available personal and family funds, including welfare support, from consensual crime (such as prostitution and pushing), and from property crimes (such as shoplifting and burglary). The lower the socioeconomic level of the community, the greater the need of the addict to turn to property crime. Because property-related crime thus produces the primary visible impact that addiction has on the community, residents usually define addiction initially as a criminal problem and seek to combat it with a strong police response. The mechanisms underlying this response are diagrammed in Figure 2.5.

The addicts in the community commit crimes that influence the residents' awareness of the drug problem. This awareness is amplified by the pervasiveness of addiction and drug use in the area. When there are few addicts in the community, their presence is not noted, and their crime is not identified as especially drug-related. But many addicts and users in the community become more readily observable in public and even more than their share of the community's crime may be attributed to them. As this awareness grows, the community desires added police protection, oriented more and more toward drugs.

The decision to allocate additional police effort to drug-related problems is also subject to the degree of community alarm. If the crime rate is growing rapidly and is significantly above the residents' standard for crime (the level they are accustomed to), a high degree of community alarm is generated and a large fraction of the police effort needed tends to be budgeted. On the other hand, if crime is growing slowly or if residents quickly tolerate increased crime, community alarm is low and only a small fraction is budgeted. Poor cities or low-income sections of larger cities usually lack financial and political resources to get the police effort they desire.

Police effort against drugs takes several forms. The key activity, especially in a community that sees addiction as primarily a crime problem, is the attempted arrest of addicts for possession of drugs or for crimes committed to pay for drugs. Addict arrests per policeman, a reasonable measure of productivity of the police effort, declines as the effort increases, because intensive police activity causes addicts to be more careful and therefore more difficult to apprehend. With a large police effort in action, each officer also has fewer arrest opportunities than with a smaller level of effort. Together, the level of effort directed against addict criminals and the per-man productivity of this effort determine the arrest rate. However, the actual imprisonment rate of

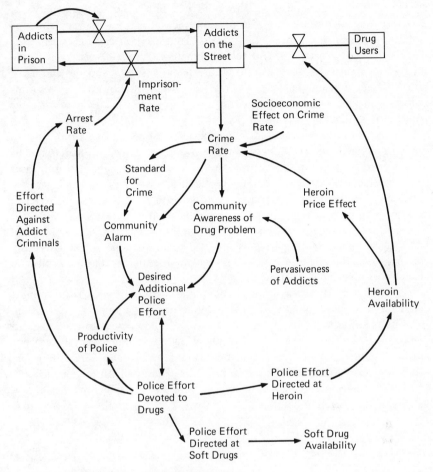

Figure 2-5. Police Response

addicts is far less than the arrests due to problems of establishing guilt, the filing of many cases, and the frequent use of probation instead of prison for addict criminals. Imprisoned addicts flow from the street to prison, and later usually go back to the street after serving out their prison terms or after receiving parole.

This use of police indicates another negative—or control-oriented—feedback loop. The growth of addicts on the street increases the crime rate, increases community factors leading to more police effort directed against addict criminals, increases the addict arrest and imprisonment rates, thereby decreasing the street addict population.

A second use of police is against the heroin supply and the supply channels. This police effort has two effects. By reducing the actual availability of heroin and by reducing the attractiveness of pushing, this effort helps retard the growth of the addict population. However, reduction of heroin availability also drives up the price of the drug, as previously discussed, forcing the addicts to commit more crime to support their habits. Thus every increase in heroin price has a significant "marked-up" effect on community crime. A part of the total drug-related police effort is also often directed at soft-drug supplies and users, under present laws and practices. As previously explained, however, the resulting reduction in soft-drug availability may actually lead to an increase in the community's addict potential.

The forces responsible for changes in community attitude toward the drug problem and the effects of this attitude are shown in Figure 2.6. The way the community's residents perceive the nature of the narcotics problem is what we identify as the "community definition of the problem". At one extreme, a community might believe that addiction is solely a criminal problem that needs to be, and can be, dealt with by sufficient police effort. At the other extreme, a community might believe that the problem has a significant social and medical dimension, requiring treatment programs to cope with it. Obviously community attitudes range widely between these extremes and are subject to change over time and circumstances.

Lack of sophistication about the heroin problem causes most communities to have initial attitudes bordering on the "criminality" definition. But this initial community definition is affected by exposure to media and to community education programs. Attitude change does not usually take place, however, until the community residents realize several things. First, the police solution favored by the community's initial definition of the problem must fail to stem the increase in crime caused by a growing addict population. Frustration with the police solution alone tends to initiate a search for alternative methods

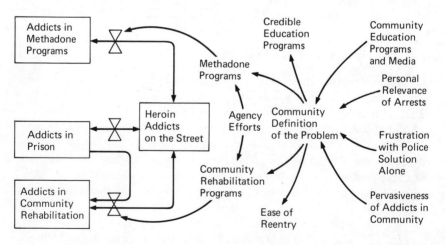

Figure 2-6. Community Attitude

of coping with addiction. As the number of arrests increases in response to growing addiction and crime, some of the youths arrested are more likely to be familiar to residents. When narcotics arrests become more personally relevant, members of the community cease blaming the problem on other people. Recognition that youths from "good families" are involved in narcotics forces people to discard an exclusively criminal view of addiction and to accept some of its social and medical aspects. The pervasiveness of addiction in itself also tends to persuade residents that the problem cannot be coped with by police methods alone.

As these realizations develop, media and community education begin having an impact on community attitudes. Eventually, if attitude change continues, the community accepts addiction more as a social and medical problem with criminal manifestations rather than one of a solely criminal nature.

Definition of the addiction problem as one with a significant medical and social nature has several effects. One of these is the implementation of therapeutic community rehabilitation programs and methadone programs in the community. If residents feel that addiction is solely a criminal problem, attempts to establish treatment programs in the community are vigorously opposed out of fear that the programs will merely concentrate dangerous sociopaths in the area, with little benefit for the community itself. Only after the community develops a medical definition of the problem and drops its stereotype of the addict is it willing to permit implementation of some programs advocated by social agencies. Even when the community has a favorable attitude toward treatment, it may still make reentry to "straight" society difficult by treating the ex-addict as a criminal and not trusting him with jobs or other rewarding social contact. An ex-addict facing this bleak prospect could easily find returning to addiction to be his most desirable alternative. In order for reentry to be facilitated, the community must see the addict as a person who was formerly sick, but who has now been cured.

A final effect of a favorable community attitude is that it enables credible education programs to be established. An education program in a community with a criminal definition of the problem is likely to be scare-oriented and therefore more likely to alienate youth than to dissuade them from addiction. A medical and social definition of the problem is assumed to be requisite for community acceptance and sponsorship of education programs that deal honestly with drugs, merely presenting the facts with a minimum of value judgments attached. If drug education programs are to be effective at all, they need to satisfy this condition of credibility, since most youths know too much about drugs to be fooled by scare techniques.

Part II

The Heroin System in Detail

INTRODUCTION

In developing our model we gathered information from a variety of sources in order to: (1) identify precisely the major variables of the heroin system and their interconnections; and (2) specify those relationships quantitatively.

Part II communicates that information base as it relates to the three major stages of the heroin system. Chapter 3 concerns itself with the process by which new people are added to the population of addicts. The initial punitive response of a community is dealt with in Chapter 4. Chapter 5 describes the origin and impact of alternative sociomedical approaches to the problem.

In each chapter the discussions produce conclusions about important assumptions that we have included in our system dynamics model. Throughout the chapters we refer the reader interested in complete technical elaboration to the relevant equations of the Appendix.

As in any complex real-life problem, the information base is incomplete and often controversial. The illicit nature of heroin further complicates our task.

A matter seemingly as straightforward as determining the total addict population of the United States or of any city turns out to be a difficult and uncertain task. For example, at the national level, as of December 31, 1968, the U.S. Bureau of Narcotics and Dangerous Drugs (BNDD) reported a total of 64,011 addicts in the country, an increase of 3 percent over the year before. In the same year New York state alone reported 60,000 addicts. Another estimate for that point in time was given as 100,000 to 200,000.[1] A year later, based on 1969 data, the BNDD estimated that there were 315,000 addicts in the United States. Two years after that, in 1972, the BNDD reported 560,000 known addicts. Senator Charles Percy of Illinois used information from the Treasury

Department's Office of Planning and Program Evaluation to derive an estimate of 700,000 addicts in the United States in early 1972.[2]

Similar disagreements are evident in estimating the addict population in a city. In 1968, the Narcotics Register reported 50,000 addicts in New York City. The register grew 42 percent from 1969 to 1970.[3] Estimates of the city's addict population made by government and health officials generally fall between 100,000 and 200,000, with 125,000 accepted as a best estimate. Some feel that the number is higher, but The RAND Corporation and the Hudson Institute assert that the Narcotics Register is more accurate than it is usually thought to be, and present 85,000 and 70,000 respectively as their estimates as of 1972. One study projected that the addict population would reach 210,000 by 1975.[4] A more recent report estimated that the cumulative number of narcotics abusers in New York City between 1964 and 1970 was 316,918. This estimate includes some people habituated to Demerol and certain other drugs (but not barbiturates and amphetamines) and does not account for people having left the addict pool. It is based on a reported total of 151,219, and adjusted for under-reporting.

These discrepancies stem from a number of factors: (1) under-reporting is characteristic of an illegal practice; (2) registry data report only cases that come to the attention of certain agencies; (3) the quality of reporting techniques varies, usually improving over time; (4) panic responses tend to inflate estimates; and (5) estimates may be distorted through political motives.

Since some of the factors we are considering are many times more illusive than the matter of estimating the addict population, our task is not easy. Nevertheless it is important to proceed even if in partial ignorance. Because the reality is so fuzzy, it is that much more urgent to be precise in our thinking about it.

All ignorance will not disappear soon or suddenly. We have made the best estimates possible given our information base. In some instances our estimates may be very far from the truth. The important question is how far wrong can we be in our particular assumptions and still be right in our general conclusions and policy suggestions? Sensitivity analyses of our model that are reported in Part III attempt to answer this question.

REFERENCES

1. *A Federal Source Book: Answers to Most Frequently Asked Questions about Drug Abuse* (Washington, D.C.: National Clearinghouse for Drug Abuse Information), p. 22.
2. "Percy: Heroin Addicts May Number 700,000", *Christian Science Monitor,* March 6, 1972.
3. David Burnham, "City's Drug Users Placed at 300,000", *New York Times,* May 1, 1972, p. 1.

4. Alan C. Leslie, *A Benefit/Cost Analysis of New York City's Heroin Addiction Problems and Programs* (New York: Health Services Administration, Office of Program Analysis, March 1971), p. 3. See also John Surmeier, "Development of an Issue Paper on Narcotic Addiction in New York City" (New York: RAND Corporation, unpublished document, February 1969); and Max Singer and Jane Newitt, *Policy Concerning Drug Abuse in New York State* (Croton-on-Hudson, N.Y.: Hudson Institute, 1970).

Chapter Three

Becoming Addicted

In specifying how people become involved, with drugs in general and with heroin in particular, Figure 3.1, abstracted from Figure 2.1, shows the underlying pattern of flow into the addiction system.

Despite significant differences between heroin and other drugs, in a structural sense the forces that control the rate of flow into the drug-user category are similar to the forces that affect entry into the category called "heroin addicts on the street". For this reason we will look first at the appeal factors, then at the deterrent factors, calling attention to the different ways that the various appeals and deterrents apply to the flows into the two population groups.

The two factors contributing to the appeal of drug use are drug-associated culture and poverty and ethnic status. Drug-associated culture is a complex phenomenon that involves both the use of drugs and the cultural

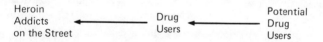

Figure 3-1. Path into Drug Use and Addiction

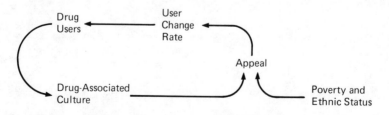

Figure 3-2. Factors Affecting the Appeal of Drug Use

trappings that arise around drug use making it more attractive. These trappings may be tangible, as with style of dress, or may include intangibles such as a feeling that "everyone is into drugs". As more people use drugs, both the likelihood of people being initiated by their friends and the feeling that everyone is into drugs become greater.

Poverty and ethnic status have a clear effect on drug use, though differences between drug use in urban ghettoes and wealthy suburbs may be narrowing. Youths in an impoverished environment are more likely to use drugs if only because of the lack of alternative recreational opportunities. Drugs also provide an escape from slum life. The type of drug used also varies from community to community on a socioeconomic basis. Heroin use and addiction are clearly more prevalent in lower-income areas.

Under the most extreme conditions, about 80 percent of the youth population is assumed to be susceptible to drug use. Yet the practical limit of such susceptibility to the totality of appeals is no more than one-third to one-half of that number. (This estimate is derived from Equations 2 through 7 in the Appendix.)

As with drug use, the rate at which people become addicts is dependent on the level of drug-associated culture in the community and the community's poverty and ethnic status. With a higher level of drug-associated culture, drug-taking is more widely accepted and even heroin use seems less deviant. Poverty and ethnic status are much more important influences on people becoming addicts than on those becoming drug users. While youths from middle and upper income backgrounds may use drugs on an occasional basis, they have a much wider range of opportunities for education, careers and recreation than slum youth, and are much less likely to turn toward the life-style of the addict. Increases in addiction found in well-to-do suburban areas have been far surpassed by the spread of addiction in the inner city.

Psychopathology has two aspects. One is the set of individual characteristics that drive a person to addiction. The other is the attractiveness of addiction deriving from the public clamor against it. This reaction identifies addiction as an excellent outlet for the disturbed youth's antisocial tendencies.

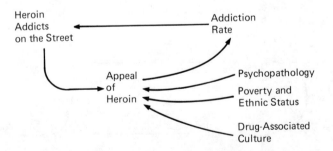

Figure 3-3. Factors Affecting the Appeal of Addiction

Because being an addict involves a total commitment to a deviant life-style, some level of psychopathology or some emotional problems is probable. On the other hand, drug use, involving no real commitment to a life-style, is less likely to involve the presence of severe emotional problems.

The number of addicts in a community also affects the rate at which drug users become addicts. A larger number of addicts are able to introduce more people to heroin and increase the addict population at a faster rate.

Under the most extreme conditions about 50 percent of the youth population is assumed to be susceptible to heroin addiction. Twenty percent represents the practical limit of such susceptibility to the totality of appeals. (This estimate is derived from Equations 35 through 51 in the Appendix.)

3.1 DRUG-ASSOCIATED CULTURE

The level of drug-associated culture in a community has two components. One is derived from forces present in the broader culture that make drug-taking seem acceptable. These forces include both the styles of the youth culture and aspects of adult culture such as the notion that no discomfort need be tolerated if there is a pill available for its alleviation. The other component resides in the local interactions among youths in peer groupings. Attitudes about drugs as well as the drugs themselves and information on taking and enjoying them are passed from one youth to another in these groups. Both components work together to cause the spread of drug use and addiction. Their interaction forms a vicious cycle or positive feedback loop, as shown in Figure 3.4.

The number of drug users in a community affects that community's susceptibility to drug-related forces from society at large. This relationship is embodied in our system model as shown in Figure 3.5. A small number of drug users in a community have little effect in encouraging their friends to use drugs, due to the absence of a supportive climate. As the number of users grows, their influence grows disproportionately as more people talk about drugs and begin to experiment with them. Drugs begin to appear less deviant, and young people are

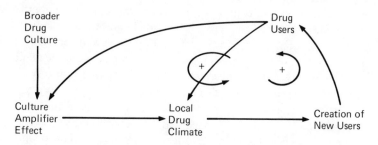

Figure 3-4. Growth of User Population through Drug-Associated Culture

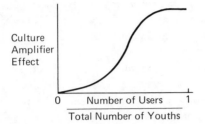

Figure 3-5.   Effect of the Number of Users on Community Susceptibility to Broader Drug Culture

then more likely to be influenced by their friends. The rapidity with which drug use has spread through some communities suggests that the indirect influence of a large current user population may make an uninitiated youth three to four times more likely to begin to use drugs at his friends' urging. No matter how strong this effect, at some magnitude it saturates. Some fraction of the youthful population will resist even the strongest societal cultural pressures to try drugs. (This phenomenon is modeled in Equation 12 of the Appendix.)

Local drug climate, which is largely stimulated by soft drugs, also has an effect on heroin use. This is not to say that the user of soft drugs directly causes addiction. Prevalent drug use and the cultural attitudes that come with it create a climate in which experimentation with many different kinds of drugs is fashionable, and trying heroin does not seem so deviant. This effect also seems to be small when drug-associated culture is of little consequence, but rises rapidly as the culture begins to have a significant impact on a community. Again, this effect has its limits. Most young people in a community avoid the use of heroin no matter how strong the pressures.

The number of addicts in a community also affects the growth of its addict population. Addicts introduce their friends to heroin as a favor. Addicts are also motivated to encourage heroin use among their peers because a broader addict base helps to assure a more stable flow of heroin into the community. As each addict comes in contact with nonaddicts, he has the potential for creating several new addicts. This growth potential, however, is limited by the large fraction of young people in the community who avoid contact with addicts and are resistant to social pressures. The relationship between the number of addicts in a community and the rate at which the addict population grows can be seen in the graph of Figure 3.6 (see also Equation 38 of the Appendix).

The formulations so far described in this section are derived from various published and unpublished materials concerning the broader culture and peer-group phenomena. The broader culture gives young people cues about drug-taking. A federal government sourcebook on drug abuse[1] presents several facets of culture's impact:

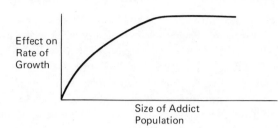

Figure 3-6. Effect of Addict Population on Its Rate of Growth

1. The widespread belief that "medicines" can magically solve problems;
2. Easy access to drugs of various sorts in an affluent society;
3. A search for sharpened perception and increased creativity, which some persons believe that they can obtain from mind-altering drugs;
4. The use of drugs, especially marijuana, in a social context, with a role similar to that of alcohol;
5. The tendency of persons with psychological problems to seek easy solutions with chemicals.

Various authorities have pointed out that the emphasis of the mass media, from television to rock records, is so oriented toward drugs that the resultant mass culture (or "youth culture") is itself drug associated. One expert felt that it would be nearly impossible for anyone growing up or living in this society not to be exposed to drug-oriented values.[2] Two drug educators indicated several trends contributing to increases in drug use.[3] Movement toward greater independence, search for new identities and more relevant values, and development of a peer culture all create a potential for a greater involvement with drugs. A trend toward immediate gratification is also a part of this. Further, as they point out, "an important first step is to realize that we all use drugs." Essentially, changes have occurred in standards of acceptability and the problem itself begins with the social acceptance of drugs.

Alienating forces are another class of impact that society has on youth. For the slum youth, these forces are overwhelming. A classic study in the field, *The Road to H,* stresses the influence on youths becoming addicts of the complex of conditions found in slums (poverty, low educational attainment, disrupted family life, families headed by females, overcrowded housing, etc.).[4] The delinquent orientation prevalent among slum youth is an additional contributor toward involvement with addiction. Young people living in such areas become thoroughly alienated and drift toward heroin as a relief from these oppressive conditions. Society's failure to cope adequately with poverty and urban decay lays the groundwork for continuing addiction problems.

Other alienating forces also drive youths toward drug use and heroin addiction. One writer describes society's negative impact as a lack of "constructive alternatives so that each individual may pursue socially useful roles which are not self-directed and artificially pleasure-oriented."[5] Without these alternatives, youths find drugs an acceptable solution to the problem of having to choose among an array of equally unsatisfying roles. The federal sourcebook identifies "the numbers of young people who are dissatisifed or disillusioned or who have lost faith in the prevailing social system" and "a lack of alternatives which appear meaningful to the 'counter culture' " as two factors partly responsible for the recent period of growth of drug use.[6] Dissatisfaction with society as it is now structured and a perceived lack of constructive alternatives lead many youths to participate in a drug culture that offers pleasure and a sense of belonging.

While the larger society provides a backdrop for drug use and addiction, peer-group interaction is the medium through which they spread. Peer groups make drugs available to their members both for experimentation and sustained use. Group members experienced in the use of a particular drug teach uninitiated members to appreciate the drug's effects. Norms and values held by the group affect an individual's decision to use or avoid a certain drug. Norms may be specifically related to drugs (for example, requiring drug-taking for group membership) or may generally place importance on factors that create a climate conducive to drug experimentation and use. A middle-class peer group may encourage marijuana use, but reject individuals who become "strung out" on heroin. Peer groups in the slums may require heroin use, without addiction, as the test of manhood.

"Peer pressure—which leads an individual, especially a young one, to conform to current styles in dress, behavior, entertainment and drugs" is a major factor responsible for increasing drug use in recent years.[7] A study of high school youths in a Boston suburb found that the "social environment" is a central factor in teenage drug abuse. Half of the multiple drug users in the sample reported that they had initiated someone else to the use of drugs. In addition, nearly all marijuana users had several friends who smoked marijuana, while most nonusers had few if any friends who used the drug. Marijuana users were also much more likely than nonusers to have friends who had used other drugs.[8]

Deviant subcultures provide the means for individuals to learn the essentials of carrying out a deviant practice. Whether it is learning to appreciate the effects of marijuana or to use a needle to inject heroin, the novice needs more experienced friends to teach him the necessary techniques. Maintaining a supply of drugs for continuing experimentation and use is also an important function of a peer-group network. Most importantly, a peer-group network tends to invest much intellectual effort in developing a rationale for its particular form of deviance. The novice who might otherwise be dissuaded from becoming a deviant by moral sanctions uses this rationale to justify his participation in the deviant activity. In the case of drug use, ideological support from the subculture is of key importance in helping the novice to overcome his aversion to or fear of drugs.[9]

A similar process operates in the case of heroin. Apparently heroin, too, is ordinarily introduced to people by friends and acquaintances. The New York City Addiction Services Administration surveyed 1166 members of its patient population and found that 52 percent were introduced to drugs by friends of the same age, 33 percent by older friends, 3 percent by relatives, and only 3 percent by a pusher. In 88 percent of the cases, the person making the introduction was an addict himself. The same study revealed that stated reasons for drug experimentation were: curiosity derived from a friend's influence, 60 percent; thrill-seeking, 24 percent; psychological problems, 7 percent; curiosity engendered by films or printed materials, 5 percent; and medical problems, 1 percent. Another study, of 100 addict prisoners at New York City's Riker's Island, found that 75 percent were introduced to drugs (and heroin in particular) by street friends, and only 16 percent by pushers.[10]

Friendships are so important in spreading heroin addiction that this spread may take on many of the characteristics of an epidemic. For example, around 1970 many New York neighborhoods experienced a rapid increase in the number of addicts once their addict population reached some critical size.[11] Similar epidemic-like experiences have been cited in: Crawley, England; Grosse Point, Michigan; and Chicago.[12] Peer-group interactions, rather than microbes, are the medium through which this epidemic spreads. This epidemic-like spread of addiction has prompted some to advocate quarantine measures. A Hudson Institute study argued that addiction ought to be managed by strong public-health measures designed to get addicts off the streets as rapidly as possible. To do this, they proposed work camps and other forms of incarceration for older addicts and special schools for younger ones. Some voluntary programs were proposed for well-motivated addicts with careful monitoring to ensure compliance. Suspected addicts would be screened and mere evidence of recent heroin use would be sufficient to have a person committed to this set of programs.[13] Though this approach to controlling addiction may seem extreme, it indicates the importance with which some policy researchers view the spread of heroin through peer groupings.

Not only do peer-group interactions facilitate the initiation of new people into drug use and addiction, they are also required for the ongoing distribution of illicit drugs. One account of soft-drug distribution stresses the importance of social interaction in the marketplace. Current attempts to separate buyers and sellers with differential legal penalties are seen as unrealistic. A majority of drug users sometimes engage in selling. The network of friendships through which drugs are distributed renders buyers and sellers indistinguishable.[14] Enforcement pressure directed at heroin makes small-group interaction essential for distribution. One picture of the heroin distribution industry emphasizes the need for small distributional units at all levels of the industry, especially in dealing with the ultimate consumer. This arrangement has several advantages in view of the climate of enforcement against sellers. In small groups, information about drug prices and the location of "drops" is quickly and efficiently exchanged. Adjustments in behavior are made rapidly without elaborate planning or negotiation. Information leaks are less likely and spread less widely when they do occur. Sales to a small group of loyal customers help to reduce the probability of the dealer's arrest as well as allow him monopoly powers over his customers. The fact that expansion to a larger scale of operations makes dealers more vulnerable to arrest as well as bringing them competition causes most dealers to view interaction with small groups as the optimum means for doing business.[15]

3.2 POVERTY AND ETHNIC STATUS

While the factors described in the previous section are present in all communities, poorer urban neighborhoods have had serious addiction problems for many years and continue to suffer most. Poorer communities are much less likely to offer vocational opportunities and recreational diversions as a meaningful alternative to drug use and addiction. Youths in such communities are extremely vulnerable to the appeal of drugs. The futility and despair of the urban ghetto creates a compelling need to escape, something that makes the properties of both heroin and soft drugs quite attractive. For the black or Spanish-speaking youth with his additional handicaps of racial prejudice, heavy drug use and addiction seem like a desirable accommodation to an otherwise bleak situation.

Our discussions with people working in drug treatment and prevention and the literature of drug problems indicate that the propensity of youths to become involved in both drug use and addiction is inversely proportional to the socioeconomic status of their community. Differences between poorer and wealthier communities are much greater for heroin addiction than they are for occasional drug use. Occasional soft-drug use is widespread in upper-income communities. The middle- or upper-income youth can use drugs on the sly without turning his back on the better opportunities his environment affords him. He is likely to avoid heroin, however, because of the potential of addiction and its commitment to an alien life-style. Individuals from poor communities have much less to lose in the way of opportunities and may see the addict life-style in a less unfavorable light.

An idea of the relative effect of the relationships between poverty and ethnic status (actually socioeconomic status) and drug use and addiction is given in Figure 3.7. The effect on the potential user population varies less over the full range of socioeconomic status than does the effect on the potential addict population. Though more drugs are used in poorer communities, substantial usage does occur in wealthier ones (see Equation 6 in the Appendix). The effect on the potential addict population varies significantly over the full range, with poorer communities having a much greater addiction potential than their wealthier counterparts. The higher-income community has a much lower potential because of the unattractiveness of the addict life-style (see Equation 36).

The effect of peer group interaction on individual drug-taking behavior is very much a function of the environment in which the interaction takes place. Slum areas present a special set of forces that mold the interactions. One view of the effect of slum culture focuses on the coveted status of the "stand-up cat". This view is presented by a former street worker who later did research in addiction and emphasizes the role of the slum's social code in encouraging experimentation with heroin. One becomes a stand-up cat by becoming involved in behavior that is exciting, tough, daring and dangerous. Using heroin without becoming "strung-out" (i.e., addicted) may be a prerequisite or enabler of the stand-up cat status. When heroin use is perceived in such a manner by the youths in a particular neighborhood, heroin is apt to spread rapidly as many of them seek to attain or maintain the stand-up cat status. Unfortunately, once involvement with heroin has begun, these youths are likely to forget about being stand-up cats and sink more deeply into addiction. The standards for becoming a stand-up cat and the prestige placed on this status provide essential ideological supports to heroin use. Though becoming strung-out or addicted clearly is not part of this mystique, it may sometimes be the unfortunate result of experimentation.[16]

The slum environment does not, of course, always produce forces conducive to addiction. Chein's research indicates that fighting gangs, long considered the scourge of urban slums, had a preventative effect against addiction during the fifties. Though gang members used drugs, including heroin, a set of norms kept them from becoming addicted. Heroin prevented them from being effective at fighting, an essential capability for street gangs. According to Chein the loners on the fringes of gang activities (not subject to gang norms)

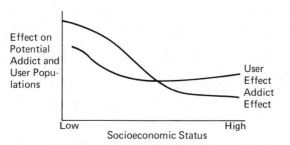

Figure 3-7. Effect of Socioeconomic Status on Potential Addict and User Populations

were the ones most likely to become addicted. Those deeply involved in the gangs shunned addiction and were not likely to get strung-out as long as they remained with the gang.[17] More recently, Black Panther and Black Muslim organizations have worked to prevent addiction by organizing groups of youths and instilling them with antidrug norms. Informants close to the drug scene in 1974 report a resurgence of fighting gangs simultaneous with a deemphasis on heroin as a drug of abuse.[18]

Most accounts of initiation into addiction deal with addiction as an adjustment to social and emotional pressures facing young people. Chein relates drug use to a delinquent orientation conducive to use, unhappiness, a sense of futility, mistrust, negativism, defiance and a manipulative and "devil-may-care" attitude on the way to get something out of life."[19] This orientation is, in itself, an adjustment to the dreary lives and bleak futures faced by slum youths. Where heroin and other drugs are available and their use is supported by peer-group norms, the delinquent orientation is a powerful force to encourage drug use as a way out of the grim realities of slum life.

3.3 PERSONALITY FACTORS AND PSYCHOPATHOLOGY

Personality has some bearing on a young person's becoming an addict. While no one becomes an addict in a vacuum, many individuals are exposed to pervasive appeal factors without becoming habituated or addicted. Why do some avoid heavy involvement with drugs, while others fall victim? According to Chein, those boys who live in high drug-use areas and do not become involved are generally "actively resistant to sociocultural pressures in those directions". They tend to be more active, participate more in sports, have more realistic expectations, and stay in school longer. They are more likely to have more stable and intimate friends, and come from more cohesive families than heroin users (although not more likely to come from such families than delinquents who are not users). Their families are less likely to have members with police records, and are more likely to be regular churchgoers. They are also more likely to have a masculine ideal to emulate, whether it be a father (more likely) or a teacher, minister or other surrogate. Those who become users are more likely to have friends with police records and to have the general activities, interests, and attitudes of nonusing delinquents. "The evidence indicates that all addicts suffer from deep-rooted, major personality disorders." These include an inability to make lasting friendships, difficulty in assuming a masculine role, a frequent sense of futility, expectation of failure, general depression, feelings of frustration and anxiety, and an inability to cope with such feelings. "To such individuals, heroin is functional; . . . the drug does not contribute rich positive pleasures; it merely offers relief from misery."[20]

Many of the earlier studies of individual factors in addiction attempted to find an "addictive personality". However, these studies focused on

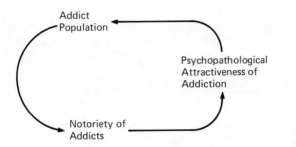

Figure 3-8. Psychopathological Attractiveness of Addiction

populations made up entirely of addicts, and only a few of them used nonaddict control groups. Once researchers knew they were working with addicts, they looked for certain classes of psychopathology and inevitably found what they were after. Studies were unable to distinguish between disorders causing and caused by addiction. The socially deprived background of most addicts produces a high rate of personality defects that show up in addicts, but may not be necessary preconditions for addiction. "Personality disorder, no more than any other single factor could, does not cause addiction. For most identified addicts it is part of the constellation of misery which pervades the socio-economic deprivation in the big cities."[21]

Despite our concurrence with the viewpoint that personality factors have been overestimated, the heroin system does seem to include one dynamically relevant component that is represented in our model. This component involves the young person's response to the community's view of addiction as deviance. The more serious the problem becomes, the more strongly the community is likely to pay attention to its addicts. The drug user or addict identity may be attractive to the youth who has had little opportunity to distinguish himself. These factors form a vicious cycle, which is shown in Figure 3.8. As the addict population grows, there is increased public outrage, more attention given to addicts, greater pathological attractiveness of addiction, and a higher rate of growth for the population. This effect makes only a small contribution to the rate of growth compared to the other forces, such as the total size of the addict population (see Equation 43).

3.4 DETERRENTS TO DRUG AND HEROIN USE

In addition to the availability of drugs and their appeal, as discussed already, the heroin system contains several forces that we have classified as deterrents. Two factors—fear of arrest and drug education—have been identified as possible deterrents to drug use. In addition to these two forces, heroin use can be discouraged by the fear that heroin addiction is an irreversible condition and by the availability of alternate, less dangerous drugs. The factors deterring heroin use are shown in Figure 3.9.

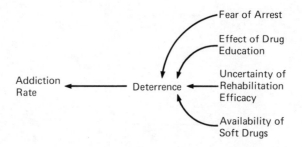

Figure 3-9.   Factors Affecting Deterrence to Heroin Addiction

A primary deterrent is the illegality of drug possession and the seriousness of being caught with heroin in particular. The increased prevalence of drug abuse, however, has caused many people to realize that police action alone cannot stop the problem. In response some states have reduced penalties for soft-drug possession and have become more lenient toward people found merely in possession of hard drugs. More local police effort is aimed at those who sell drugs rather than at those who use them. This is a fortunate turn of events as far as the humane treatment of drug abusers is concerned, but does weaken the effect of illegality as a deterrent, since laws can influence behavior only when they are enforced and have meaningful penalties. The large numbers of users and addicts also make it difficult for the police to pose a credible threat to any one individual. Recent court decisions on the admissibility of evidence found in searches have also reduced the perception that police efforts are to be feared. Laws and their enforcement remain a deterrent for many young people, but are not a strong enough force to deter many others. The legal deterrent is discussed further in the next chapter, which deals with the community's punitive response.

The deterrence of heroin's illegality is largely attributable to the visible impact of enforcement efforts. As suggested in Figure 3.10, as the addict arrest rate increases, the fear of arrest also rises. This phenomenon is likely to lessen the attractiveness of heroin by 30 percent at the maximum[22] (see Equation 50 in the Appendix).

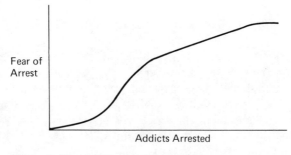

Figure 3-10.   Addict Arrests as a Deterrent

Until recently it has been felt that education about the dangers of drugs will prevent people from using them. There is some evidence for this. Chein found a strong inverse relationship between knowledge about the effects of heroin and heroin use. In one study it was found that prior to taking it, only 17 percent of the heroin users in a sample had learned anything about heroin that might have deterred them. Seventy-nine percent of a control group of delinquent nonusers had learned about heroin's dangers to life and health before they reached the critical age for onset of addiction.[23]   Other researchers found that delinquent nonaddicts had received more negative information about opiates during their critical period of exposure—they had seen overdoses or watched a cold-turkey withdrawal.[24] Though education and exposure to information may be an important means of preventing drug abuse, education must be done in a credible manner to be effective. The Task Force Report on Narcotics and Drug Abuse cautions that information giving must not be equated with information acceptance. Information given in a frightening or noncredible manner is likely to be rejected.[25]

A recent study shows that even credible education may have its limitations as a deterrent. It was found that knowledge about drugs per se did not play a significant role in teenagers' resistance to becoming involved with drugs. The study suggested that education methods should shift to group dynamics techniques that focus on the problem of users and potential users rather than on the properties of the drugs.[26] Apparently, even credible education may no longer be an effective deterrent to drug use because it only warns young people of the potential dangers in drugs without dealing with some of the more basic forces that cause them to become involved in drug use. Furthermore, after a two-year study of the nation's drug problems, the National Commission on Marijuana and Drug Abuse concluded, "No drug education program in this country or elsewhere has proven sufficiently successful to warrant our recommending it."[27]

This evidence, as well as our discussions with drug educators, caused us to assume in our system model a very limited or (possibly) negative effectiveness for noncredible education and only a limited effect for education that is highly credible. We also assume that education, within its limits, can be much more effective in dissuading young people from addiction than from occasional soft-drug use. The prevalence of soft-drug use alone makes it difficult to convince young people that such activities can be harmful. At best, even with highly credible education, we estimate that no more than 5 or 6 percent of the individuals who might otherwise try soft drugs will refrain from doing so (see Equations 20 and 21).

For education aimed at addiction, highly credible education may dissuade as many as 20 percent of the people who might otherwise become addicts from doing so (see Equations 40 and 41). Education that is not credible may actually encourage drug use, especially if it conveys information that its recipients know is not factual.

Another possible deterrent, fear of lifelong addiction, is becoming a less significant threat as rehabilitation programs become more common, and begin to demonstrate some degree of success. The potential addict who might previously have been deterred by the image of lifelong enslavement to heroin may not be as hesitant to experiment with heroin. Some program administrators are concerned that the use of ex-addicts by rehabilitation programs in positions with relatively high salaries makes being an addict seem even more attractive. How else could a slum youth land such a high-paying job?[28] The breakdown in the fear deterrent may cause some youths who might not have otherwise become addicts to do so (see Equation 44). Even positive programs can thus have their negative aspects.

The final deterrent cited in Figure 3.9, soft drug availability, recognizes that some drug users may be prone to switching drugs under conditions of drug scarcity. If marijuana or hashish is not available, some may be tempted to try heroin or other addictive substances, as seemed evident during the 1969 Operation Intercept. Alternatively, readily available and much less expensive good-quality marijuana or hashish may suffice to satisfy a number of heroin-prone drug abusers. Thus, availability of alternatives to heroin may affect the addiction rate by perhaps plus or minus 10 percent (see Equation 42).

REFERENCES

1. *A Federal Source Book: Answers to Most Frequently Asked Questions about Drug Abuse* (Washington, D.C.: National Clearinghouse for Drug Abuse Information), p. 2.

2. Interview with Dr. Richard Brotman, Director, New York Medical College, Department of Substance Use, January 13, 1970.

3. Dana L. Farnsworth and Paul A. Walters, "Some Principles of Drug Education Programs", presented at the Regional Conference on Drug Education sponsored by Boston Coordinating Council on Drug Abuse, July 28, 1970.

4. K. Chein, D. L. Gerard, R. S. Lee and E. Rosenfeld, *The Road to H* (New York: Basic Books, 1964).

5. Seymour Rudner, "Drug Abuse and Social Policy—A Theoretical Approach" (Nassau County Drug Abuse and Addiction Commission), p. 79.

6. *Federal Source Book,* p. 2.

7. Ibid.

8. "Brookline, Mass. Study Links Marijuana, Dangerous Drugs", *Christian Science Monitor,* March 6, 1972, p. 10.

9. Howard S. Becker, *Outsiders: Studies in the Sociology of Deviance* (New York: Free Press, 1963).

10. Alan C. Leslie, *A Benefit/Cost Analysis of New York City's Heroin Addiction Problems and Programs* (City of New York, Health Services Administration, Office of Program Analysis, March 1971), p. 7.

11. Ibid.
12. Leon G. Hunt, *Heroin Epidemics: A Quantitative Study of Current Empirical Data* (Washington, D.C.: The Drug Abuse Council, May 1973).
13. Max Singer and Jane Newitt, *Policy Concerning Drug Abuse in New York State* (Croton-on-Hudson, N.Y.: Hudson Institute, 1970), pp. 10–27.
14. Erich Goode, "The Marijuana Market", *Columbia Forum* (Winter 1969), pp. 4–8.
15. Mark Moore, *Economics of Heroin Distribution* (Vol. III of *Policy Concerning Drug Abuse in New York State*) (Croton-on-Hudson, N.Y.: Hudson Institute, 1970), pp. 28–29.
16. Harvey W. Feldman, "Ideological Supports to Becoming and Remaining a Heroin Addict", *Journal of Health and Social Behavior* (June 1968): 131–139.
17. Chein et al., *Road to H.*
18. Personal communication from John Langrod, March 1974.
19. Chein et al., *Road to H.*
20. Ibid.
21. *Task Force Report on Narcotics and Drug Abuse* (Washington, D.C.: President's Commission on Law Enforcement and the Administration of Justice), pp. 51–52.
22. Patrick V. Murphy, "Enforcement Not Sole Answer to Drug Problem", *N. Y. Law Journal,* December 6, 1971, p. 40.
23. Chein et al., *Road to H,* as cited in *Task Force Report*, p. 50.
24. George H. Stevenson, *Drug Addiction in British Columbia* (Vancouver, British Columbia: University of British Columbia, 1956), as cited in *Task Force Report,* p. 50.
25. *Task Force Report,* p. 50.
26. "Brookline, Mass. Study".
27. Report of the National Commission on Marijuana and Drug Abuse, *Marijuana: A Signal of Misunderstanding* (N.Y.: Signet, 1972).
28. Interview with Dr. David Laskowitz, Director of Drug Abuse Services, Lincoln Hospital Mental Health Services, December 3, 1969.

Chapter Four

The Punitive Response

Punishment is the community's initial response to heroin addiction. Because it is associated with crime committed by addicts to support their habits, addiction is thought of as a crime problem and dealt with in a punitive manner. This orientation prevents or delays the development of rehabilitation programs, since they are deemed inappropriate for a crime problem and threaten to concentrate many addict-criminals in the community. The result may be a revolving door of addicts being shunted in and out of prison with few programs to reduce or control the number of addicts. Thus the punitive response may contribute to the problem's persistence.

This chapter deals with this first phase of the community's response to heroin addiction. It explores the effects the addict has on his community and the punitive response these effects elicit. Various forms of a punitive response are discussed, including police action and criminal prosecution (against both addicts and sources of supply) and civil commitment. The benefits and limitations of these forms are analyzed. Finally, we explore the forces that lead to a broadening of the community's definition of the narcotics problem to include a sociomedical component. This change is necessary before advocacy of treatment programs can begin to be effective.

4.1 THE IMPACT OF ADDICTION ON THE COMMUNITY

The community's costs of addict crime can be measured in both fear and dollars. The principal dollar cost is a loss of property from households and businesses.

Additional dollars are spent to pay for police, courts and prisons. Further, the addicts' removal from the job market deprives the local economy, while increasing the welfare tax burden.

Once an addict population is established, it attracts an increased and more stable heroin supply, thus enabling further spread of addiction. Individual families perceive this spread and fear that their own children may become involved. Addict arrests and deaths sharpen this response, sometimes to the point of panic. The alarmed community responds with both fight and flight.

4.1.1   **Crime.**   Opinions diverge greatly concerning the magnitude of addict crime. The reasons include our inability to determine the number of addicts in an area (underreporting due to the penalties for being an addict, overreporting due to panic reactions) and our difficulty in determining the total amount of crime (underreporting, especially in poor communities, and problems in detecting such addict crimes as shoplifting). The uncertainties surrounding the estimation of the addicted population were treated in the introduction to Part II. Crime rates are characteristically underestimated, by a factor of two to five in various U.S. cities, according to a 1974 report.[1]

Even if we knew the number of addicts and the total amount of crime, the problem of estimating the amount of addict crime would remain unsolved. No one accurately knows what percentages of the addict population support their habits by property crime, consensual crime (such as prostitution and selling drugs), and legitimate means (jobs, welfare, family funds). Guesses about the size of an average addict's habit (in dollars per day) vary greatly. The assumed fencing ratio—the ratio of the value of goods stolen to the amount of cash received by addicts from dealers in stolen goods—also varies. The mix of crimes (burglary, robbery, etc.) committed by addicts is also different in the assumption of estimators.

The wide divergencies in the following four estimates of addict crime made over several years are therefore not surprising:

1.   A conservative estimate of crimes per addict was reported in a Hudson Institute study. The study carefully divided the addict population in New York City into groups relating to addict type and method of raising money. Such groups included "joy poppers", "small habit dependents", "large habit hustlers", "large habit dealers", and "women". Habit size (in $5 bags/day) for each group and fraction of the addict population represented by the groups were estimated and used to calculate an average habit of $28 per day in 1970 prices. Combined with assumptions about the means the various groups used to raise money, and their estimate of New York City's 1970 addict population of 70,000, the Hudson Institute's staff computed the annual cost of addict property crime as approximately $500 million.[2]

2.   According to an Arthur D. Little study, only 28 percent of the nation's addicts committed property crimes to support their habits, while 42 percent committed consensual crimes such as prostitution and pushing, and 30 percent raised funds through legitimate means. The study also estimated that a 1967 addict required $5,000 per year for heroin and at least another $2,000 per

year to cover his other basic needs. Applying an assumed fencing ratio of five, the average property crime addict had to steal $35,000 worth of property per year.[3] Taking the Hudson Institute's conservative estimate of 70,000 addicts in New York City, these estimates and assumptions yield a total of 70,000 addicts times .28 times $35,000 per addict-year = $686 million per year. One-hundred thousand addicts would yield a comparable crime total of about $1 billion per year.

3. The Narcotics Task Force of the President's Commission on Law Enforcement and the Administration of Justice estimated a habit size of $15 per addict per day based on a 1965 study of heroin users arrested by the New York City Police Department. The Task Force further implied a fencing ratio of a little more than 3-to-1 in computing a daily property crime requirement for each addict of $50. Though the Task Force report acknowledged that many addicts do not resort to property crime, it offered no guess of the value of that fraction.[4]

4. Howard Samuels, a former member of the Mayor's Narcotics Coordinating Council in New York City, estimated in a 1970 position paper that 60 percent of all addicts commit property crimes, while the other 40 percent engage in various consensual crimes. Using this and other estimates, he arrived at a total of $2.5 billion per year in property taken by the addicts in New York state.[5] This total was based on a very low estimate of the addict population.

In addition to the factors included in these estimates it is necessary to consider several other factors. Crime rates are vastly different in very poor and middle-class communities. A study done by the New York City Criminal Justice Coordinating Council reported that burglary in certain sections of Harlem was twenty-five times greater than in the middle-class community we studied. An even greater variation existed in robbery rates.[6] For the portion of crime committed by addicts alone, this degree of variation is due partly to differences in numbers of addicts, partly to the fraction that commit property crime, and partly to the number of crimes that an addict must commit to get a given amount of money. Still another determinant is the type of crime committed and the value of property taken in each type. Using statistics from the FBI's 1968 Uniform Crime Reports, we estimate the value of an average property crime to be $190 by computing the average values of the three major types of property crime (burglary, robbery, and larceny under $50) weighted by the fractions of the total property crime incidence in the New York metropolitan area represented by those crimes.[7]

For our system model it is necessary to reconcile these estimates in order to arrive at a relationship between an addict population of any size and the number of property crime incidents it produces in a community. Differences in crime for communities with different socioeconomic levels are caused by differences in the fractions of addicts relying on property crime and in the number of crimes an addict must commit. If there is less wealth in a community, more crimes are required to support a given habit size. Our model accepts 30 percent as the fraction of addicts committing property crimes when the community is poor. However, when the community is more affluent, with greater availability of funds from allowances, possessions to be sold and unnoticed thefts from parents, this fraction goes down to 10 percent or less (see Equations 83 and 84 in the Appendix). To get the number of crimes committed by each property crime addict we assume an average $28/day habit, since this is the most carefully reasoned estimate, and that a fencing ratio of five-to-one prevails. We further assume that each crime nets goods worth $190 in an upper- or middle-income community, and decreases to $95 when the area is very poor. This set of assumptions implies that the property crime addict commits twelve crimes per month in the lower income community or six crimes per month in wealthier neighborhoods (see Equation 82). Frequency of individual property crimes is in our view a more accurate measure of the impact of addict crimes on a community than the dollar value of those crimes. Each additional addict crime is a contributor to the community's sense of alarm and outrage.

The price of heroin also importantly affects the addict property crime rate. Higher prices require more crime to support a given habit size. At the extreme, however, addicts get by with less than their accustomed amount and suffer some discomfort. Short-term price changes come about as enforcement efforts or other events, such as dock strikes, temporarily decrease the availability of narcotics in an area. Numerous heroin panics and their attendant crime waves have been reported. We estimate that an extreme low-supply, high-price situation produces as much as a threefold increase in the crime rate (see Equation 81). Figure 4.1 summarizes these phenomena.

4.1.2 **Economic Costs.** In addition to addict thefts, as analyzed above, three other categories of cost exist: enforcement, productivity losses and welfare. The cost of enforcement includes the arrest, trial and imprisonment of addicts who commit consensual or property crimes. Leslie estimates added enforcement cost of $1640 per addict per year. He bases this estimate on the assumption that addicts account for one-third of all the crime committed in New York City and that they would commit half of the crimes they do commit if they were not addicts.[8] Of this cost, $900 is attributable to additional police requirements, $90 for courts, and $650 for the cost of incarcerating convicted addicts. The Arthur D. Little study deals only with arrests for narcotics, and estimates that these alone cost $46 million in 1966, of which $34.4 million went toward the arrests themselves, $1.6 million to trials, and $9.9 million covered costs of incarceration.[9] Instead of relying upon similar attributed costs, our system model directly represents and accounts for the number of policemen-equivalents assigned to narcotics as well as the expense of maintaining addicts in prison. Police costs include both an overhead and a direct cost per officer that

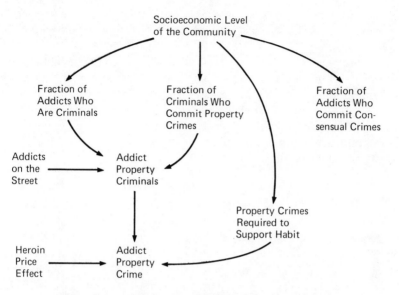

Figure 4-1. Factors Affecting Addict Property Crime

totals, for example, $77,500 per month when there are 50 police officer-equivalents assigned to this function. Prison costs $250 per imprisoned addict per month (see Equations 302–304).

Productivity and welfare costs are not represented in our systems model, because they are unlikely to motivate community response to addiction. Nevertheless, these costs are real and substantial. The New York City Health Services Administration estimates an average net annual gain to New York City's economy of $3260 for each addict rehabilitated to the point of being able to work. This estimate is derived by dividing the addicts treated by the NYC Addiction Services Agency into occupational groups and multiplying the number in each group by its median wage, adjusted to reflect the relatively lower employability of the addicts.[10] This estimate is probably high because of the increased prevalence of addiction among school-age youths who make no net addition to the economy. Yet the Arthur D. Little study, using a different set of numbers, arrived at the even higher annual productivity loss of $4400 per addict.[11]

4.1.3 **Spread of Addiction.** Families in communities with growing addiction especially fear the danger of contagion to their children. When the addict population in an area is small, there is only enough heroin for the addicts living there and little surplus heroin for initiating new users. As the population grows, wholesaling and distributing heroin within that area become profitable. According to a description of the heroin distribution system attempted by the

Hudson Institute staff, several hundred addicts are required to support a "connection", a wholesale dealer who maintains inventories of several days to several weeks worth of heroin for the population he "serves".[12] Once one or more connections or even higher level wholesalers become established in a community, heroin supply becomes less of a hand-to-mouth operation. Heroin then becomes more available for casual users and experimenters.

The fear that their children may be among the experimenters has a significant impact on the attitudes of local parents, as we found in interviews with residents of the Bronx community we studied. Their alarm leads them to demand a strongly punitive response.

4.1.4 **Addict Deaths.** Death attributable to narcotics was reported as the leading cause of death in the 15 to 35 age group in New York City in recent years. According to statistics released by the City Medical Examiner, 1006 New Yorkers died of drug-related causes in 1969, and 1002 in 1970.[13] Of the 1969 total, about one-fourth were said to be teenagers.[14] Another account puts the average age of known drug death victims at 22 years.[15] In Washington, D.C. opiate overdose deaths were reported to total 62, 82 and 71 for 1970–72, respectively, and to "occur primarily in young, black, inner-city males". Also relevant is the evidence that 55 percent of Washington's heroin addicts first used heroin between the ages of 16–20.[16] Addict deaths are not separately represented in the system model, since the 1 to 2 percent who die are a small number relative to the total number who leave the population each year. Nevertheless, growing numbers of drug deaths cause people to become concerned about the problem and increase their fear that addiction may involve their own children.

4.1.5 **Panic.** Panic is the result of all the other impacts of addiction that have been discussed. It can cripple rational efforts to solve the problem. Our interviews in the Bronx revealed high levels of panic characterized by unrealistic estimates of the local addict population. The most alarmed respondents estimated that as many as 75 percent of the community's teenagers were heroin users. Many people were more interested in attempting to export the problem than in coping with it in the community. People in other communities voiced the same sentiments. This panic has, perhaps, been the most importance force that has moved communities to combat the addiction problems in their midst (see Equations 85, 93 and 145). It has also induced exodus to other communities that appear less troubled by drugs. Naturally this migration contributes over long time periods to a major change in a community's population and character. (For a fuller discussion of this, see Section 6.7.)

The impact of addict crime on the community is an important basis for the punitive response. A lack of any proven alternatives to punishment, especially during the first phase of response, also creates a tendency toward police-oriented solutions. During the middle to late 1960s, there was very little experience with treatment programs except the Federal Narcotics Hospitals whose recidivism rates were over 90 percent. This made treatment seem like an inferior alternative. Locking addicts up appeared to be the only thing that kept them off the streets and might even deter new people from becoming addicts.

4.2 GROWTH OF POLICE ACTIVITY

In the system model additional police are assigned to arresting addicts and controlling drug supply based on the number of property crimes being committed by addicts (see Equations 90 to 92). In fact, in many large cities police are assigned by a complicated formula that considers the number of residents, the numbers of shoppers, workers and theatergoers that might pass through an area, and the relative danger to policemen as well as the number of reported crimes.[17] However, we felt that a simpler assumption based on the number of crimes was sufficient for our analysis and was most relevant to addiction. Estimates of arrest productivity and the eventual disposition of arrests are also relevant to the decision of how many policemen are required for an area. Evidence also indicates that estimates of required manpower arrived at by police departments are subject to political and budgetary constraints in determining some actual number of officers to be added. At one point, the New York City Police Department (with a 30,000-man force) claimed that it needed an additional 7000 men to do its job effectively, but could not hire them because of a lack of funds.[18] Resources that are added to the police effort are allocated between the apprehension of addict criminals (including arrests for possession) and the reduction of drug availability.

These allocations of police manpower are a function of a community's definition of the addiction problem. A community that views the addict as a victim might encourage the allocation of more police effort to reducing supply; while a community that views the addict solely as a criminal would encourage more intensive police action against addicts themselves (see Equations 16–19 and 70, 71, 104, and 105).

4.3 IMPACT OF POLICE

Figure 4.2 portrays the principal effects of police activity. This figure is abstracted from Figure 2.5 and is augmented by the inclusion of three indirect but important effects omitted from the earlier diagram.

Police effort directly affects both the number of addicts on the street and the availability of heroin. Individual addicts are arrested for the crimes they commit, including the sale of narcotics, as well as for possession of drugs. Addiction itself is not a crime, a fact that was established in the 1962 decision in *Robinson vs. California.*[19] This decision made it clear that addiction is, instead, an illness.

The addict is more vulnerable to arrest than the average nonaddicted

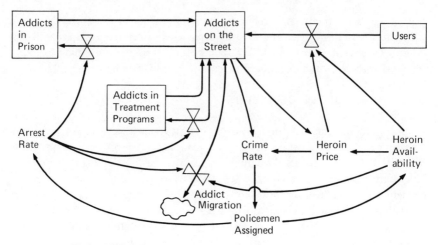

Figure 4-2. Effects of Police Response

criminal. Because he is often more desperate, he is more likely to commit his crimes in a careless manner that leaves him open to arrest. Because addicts are considered untrustworthy, they are unlikely to be members of organized crime groups that could afford them some protection against arrest. Once arrested, the addict is also less likely to have the funds for bail or an attorney and therefore is more likely to end up in prison than is the nonaddict. Dealers in narcotics, at least those above the level of the addict pusher, are extremely difficult to arrest and even harder to convict. Elaborate organizational structures shield these higher-level people from detection. Even if they are caught, it is usually impossible to prove their involvement in the drug traffic. Enforcement efforts against local drug supplies that do succeed require many months of time-consuming and expensive police work. In fact the primary police impact on heroin supply is via the decreased attractiveness of pushing that can follow strong police harassment.

The available evidence indicates that police effort can be effective in removing some addicts from the street and in reducing drug availability. But simple arithmetic shows that these effects are limited and that police effort alone cannot bring the addiction problem under control at a tolerable level.

There are several reasons why police effort can have only a limited effect. Only a small fraction of the addict criminals are arrested for the crimes they commit. One study, done by New York State's Narcotic Addiction Control Commission with a representative sample of addicts, showed that less than 1 percent of the crimes committed by these addicts were cleared by arrest. Moreover, the study found that only a small fraction of the crimes committed were actually recorded in crime statistics.[20] On the national level, the FBI reports that only 16.1 percent of the property-crime offenses known to the police are cleared by arrest.[21] It should be remembered that this was for reported offenses and that the clearance percentage for all offenses would be much smaller. Some advocates of a strong police response to addiction claim that what is really needed to solve the addiction problem are more police officers and advanced technology to improve their efficiency. This premise, however, does not hold up in light of another study done in New York City. The study showed that, despite wide variations in the proportion of policemen assigned to work in various areas of the city, arrests for robbery and burglary in relation to reports of those crimes were roughly equal for all areas.[22] While arrests of addicts do have some impact on the problem, we are forced to assume that the marginal impact of additional police officers decreases as more officers are added. Additional officers may produce some arrests, but productivity per officer will drop as more are added (see Equations 102 and 103).

Another limitation is that only a small fraction of those arrested end up in prison. FBI statistics show that only 4.4 percent of all known offenses result in convictions with an additional 0.6 percent resulting in convictions on lesser charges.[23] Again, these figures were based on known offenses and the percentage for all offenses would be considerably smaller. We assume, for purposes of our analysis, that 25 percent (i.e., ~4.4/16.1) of the arrests made result in convictions (see Equation 179).

Finally, supply reduction activities are also limited in effect. Though some spectacular drug busts have been made and millions of dollars worth of narcotics confiscated, only a small fraction of the drug supply is affected. Former New York City Police Commissioner Leary admitted in 1970 that his department was "not making any indentation at all" in its fight against narcotics. He spoke of some "fabulous successes" including one raid that netted $120 million in heroin, but said that the drug trade was still flouishing.[24] One journalist writing at the time concluded that the department's war on heroin was a "failure, a monumental waste of manpower and money" that had had "no appreciable effect on the flow of drugs in New York City."[25] Drug raids have been able to capture only a small fraction of the nation's heroin supply. In the late 1960s, for example, federal enforcement agencies concluded that only 10 percent of an estimate annual heroin flow of 1500 kilograms was seized by all enforcement agencies in the United States combined.[26] Another report puts the annual traffic in marijuana in 1968 across the Mexican border at 1200 tons, while only about 35 tons were detected.[27] It is even more difficult to detect heroin, which is less bulky and easier to hide. A factor that further reduces the impact of police on drug supplies is the difficulty in obtaining convictions. One survey conducted in New York City showed that the fraction of people arrested for possessing a pound or more of heroin (presumably for sale) who ended up in prison ranged from 32.2 percent in the Bronx, 15.7 percent in Manhattan, 14.3 percent in Queens, to only 4.4 percent in Brooklyn.[28] Given the initial difficulty in even making an arrest, these low conviction figures show how hard it is to put a dealer out of business for any length of time. Because of these limitations we assume in our model that, at a maximum, only 20 to 30 percent of the narcotics supply in a community can be eliminated, even with an intensive and skillful police effort. Unfortunately, even these reductions are temporary, creating panics that last until new supply-lines are established (see Equation 69).

Even more important than this direct effect, visible police activity creates three sets of indirect consequences, which are also shown in Figure 4.2. First, police activity affects the local price-purity of heroin, which in turn tends to increase the quantity of property crimes. For example, the purity of street heroin was seen as declining by a factor of two to three in New York City over a several-year period[29] and by a comparable amount in Washington, D.C. over an even shorter period of time.[30] Second, the appeal of various treatment programs is enhanced, as addicts give greater weight to the risk of arrest. Third, more police activity tends to increase the net flow of heroin addicts into adjacent geographic regions. The available evidence suggests that all of these effects are short-lived, unless police activity is sustained at an effective level for long time periods.

The flow of addicts into various treatment modalities may be increased as much as 100 percent as a result of a very high level of police harassment (see Equation 187 and 188). A similar degree of impact is assumed upon addict migration out of the community to neighboring areas (see Equations 73 and 74).

In the systems model, heroin price is formulated in terms of the typical daily cost of an addict's habit rather than dollars per milligram. Changes in availability relative to the addict market are the basic influences upon price change, and are difficult to characterize statically (see Equations 54 and 55).

4.4   CIVIL COMMITMENT

Civil commitment represents an evolutionary step between a punitive response and one that is rehabilitative. Civil commitment refers to programs to which addicts are committed involuntarily or those they enter "voluntarily" as an alternative to a prison sentence. This category also includes voluntary commitment by noncriminal addicts.

Earliest civil commitment programs provided for the commitment of addicts to mental hospitals in the same way mentally ill people are committed. This form of commitment was not used very frequently and failed when it was used because the hospitals were not equipped to deal with addicts, found them disruptive and discharged them with no attempt at treatment.[31] A more recent form of civil commitment is the sentencing of addicts who have been convicted of or pleaded guilty to crimes, or the "voluntary" entry of addicts charged with crimes (in lieu of prosecution) to compulsory treatment programs. Commitment gets the addict into a treatment-oriented program much more quickly than if he had to first serve a prison term. It also allows him to avoid the stigma of an additional conviction. However, if the addict is innocent or would only be sentenced to a short term, commitment to a compulsory program of several years' duration is unfair and raises civil liberties questions.[32] Because these programs are involuntary, or at best an alternative to something worse, addicts entering them lack the motivation so necessary to successful treatment.

Experience in California reflects this shortcoming. The California program consists of an in-patient segment ranging from a minimum of six months up to seven years for those convicted of more serious offenses, followed by a three-year supervised outpatient program. Addicts abstaining for the full three years are discharged from the program. Of a group of 1200 committed to the program, only 56 (5 percent) successfully completed the program by abstaining for the full three-year period. Even when one only considers those who completed the inpatient segment, fewer than 20 percent completed the program. This result may owe more to the supervised after-care than to the institutional segment.[33]

Voluntary commitment programs have also been largely unsuccessful, but for a different set of reasons. Addicts are not required to stay for the full duration of the programs and often leave before they receive a meaningful amount of treatment. In fact, many people enter these programs to reduce the size of their habits to a manageable level, not to become rehabilitated.[34] The Federal Narcotics Hospital at Lexington, Kentucky had a recommended stay of five months, but found that many of its patients were leaving against medical advice after shorter stays. One follow-up study of 1900 New York City residents discharged from Lexington between 1952 and 1955 indicates that 90 percent became readdicted; most within six months of their discharge.[35] The shock to the ex-addicts of abruptly reentering their home communities after being at Lexington for several months probably contributed to this high recidivism rate. One approach that offers some promise employs compulsory supervision after discharge from voluntary programs.[36] Alternatively, programs that have voluntary admissions but compulsory lengths of stay might deter the less motivated addict, but keep those who do enter long enough to provide a meaningful level of treatment.

In considering how civil commitment programs fit into the community addiction system, we conclude that the involuntary and quasivoluntary programs have high enough recidivism rates and offer little enough promise of rehabilitation that they play essentially the same role as prisons. Voluntary programs also have high recidivism rates, but at least offer the motivated addict a place to withdraw from heroin and pull himself together away from the pressures of the street. Such programs usually take addicts far away from their home communities, but they have a special role in providing a form of rehabilitation in a community whose attitudes have not shifted sufficiently to permit community-based programs. Based on the most optimistic assessment of existing programs, we estimate that, at an absolute maximum, 40 percent of a street addict population could be drawn into such programs and only 30 percent of those people would remain abstinent for an appreciable length of time after completing the program (see Equations 181, 199, 200, and 194, 208). These high values could be reached only under extreme conditions, which have not existed in the recent past.

4.5 FAILURE OF THE PUNITIVE RESPONSE AND REDEFINITION OF THE PROBLEM

Communities have historically relied heavily on the punitive response, but their experience has shown punishment to be insufficient. Typically the number of addicts and the amount of crime they commit both rise, even in the presence of stringent police measures. Until recently rehabilitation programs were few. Ex-addicts released to the streets had little success in remaining abstinent. Many people simply demanded more police. Rehabilitation programs were seen as a form of coddling addicts or, at best, not worth spending money on because of their dubious efficacy.

Recently, however, changes in attitudes toward addiction have occurred as evidenced by the many new programs that have appeared. Not limited to rehabilitation programs, these include hotlines, drop-in centers, educational programs, and others that deal with soft-drug dependency as well as addiction. Support of marijuana legalization has also become much more respectable. More startling is the call by public figures, including some enforcement officials, for experimentation with heroin maintenance programs. Why have such changes taken place?

The people we interviewed in the Bronx in 1969 and the impressions we got of other urban communities from the press revealed a consistent view of the addiction problem. Addiction was seen as a great threat, both in terms of crime and of the dangers to their own young people. It was a problem that originated with "those other people", never the problem of the interviewee's own reference group. Addiction was something the police ought to be dealing with, and doing a more effective job. Rehabilitation programs merely concentrated the community's own addicts and attracted others into the community.

These impressions were substantiated by a survey done by the New York State Narcotics Addiction Control Commission in the late 1960s, which showed that these various beliefs were interrelated. People who most frequently viewed drug use as a problem in their community or who knew drug abusers were more willing to accept in-community rehabilitation programs. They typically lived in slum neighborhoods. Middle- and working-class people saw drug use as a less prevalent problem within their own neighborhoods and consequently favored programs only outside of their communities. Wealthier people saw drug use in their community as least prevalent and were willing to accept in-community treatment, presumably because they expected almost all of that treatment to go on elsewhere. In general, the survey found an amorphous, but clearly negative attitude toward drug use marked by widespread ignorance.[37]

As the addiction problem grew rapidly in the late sixties and early seventies, attitudes began to change. An emphasis on police efforts dictated by the addict-as-criminal view led to frustration when police efforts failed to have their expected effects, especially when people found that adding still more police resources failed to have much impact. Frustration grew, and people begin to seek other programs. While addiction was a relatively limited problem, and one confined primarily to the urban ghetto, the middle class was exempt from the problem. As the problem grew, more young people from middle-class communities became involved and came to the attention of the authorities, usually by arrest. Affluent young people, even some from our "distinguished" families, were arrested. The middle class could no longer keep the problem at a distance.

This awakening created an impetus to incorporate the sociomedical component into the definition of the problem. The pervasiveness of addiction also contributed, highlighting the fact that legal sanctions were simply not working. Finally, the media, in bringing information to people that contradicted their stereotypes of addicts, also helped to change definitions of the addiction problem. The stories about addicts who were successfully rehabilitated and did not return to crime or of youths from middle-class families who became addicts forced a changed view of addiction. Frustration with police efforts, greater personal relevance of addiction, greater pervasiveness of addiction, and the effect of information from the news media, working in combination, changed the nature of the response to addiction from purely punitive to encompass the sociomedical element (see Figure 2.6 as well as Equations 108–118). (This formulation, while the responsibility of the authors, receives considerable support in the social psychological literature on attitudes and attitude change; see, for example, Katz[38] and Festinger[39].)

This shift in definition enables the development of alternative programmatic efforts.

REFERENCES

1. Donald A. Santarelli, Administrator, Law Enforcement Assistance Administration, as quoted in *Christian Science Monitor,* April 16, 1974.

2. Max Singer and Jane Newitt, *Policy Concerning Drug Abuse in New York State* (Croton-on-Hudson, N.Y.: Hudson Institute, 1970), Volume I: *The Basic Study,* p. 9.

3. Arthur D. Little, Inc., *Program Memorandum on Narcotic Drug Abuse* (for the National Institute of Mental Health), June 1, 1967.

4. President's Commission on Law Enforcement and the Administration of

Justice, *Task Force Report: Narcotics and Drug Abuse* (1967), p. 10.

5. Howard Samuels, *Narcotics: A Position Paper* (1970), p. 10, as quoted in Singer and Newitt, op. cit.

6. David Burnham, "A Wide Disparity Found in Crime Throughout City", *New York Times,* February 14, 1972, p. 1.

7. Federal Bureau of Investigation, *Crime in the United States* (Uniform Crime Reports), 1969, pp. 13–25.

8. Alan C. Leslie, *Benefit/Cost Analysis of New York City's Heroin Addiction Problems and Programs* (City of New York, Health Services Administration, Office of Program Analysis, 1971), pp. 9–11.

9. Arthur D. Little, op. cit.

10. Leslie, op. cit., pp. 4–6.

11. Arthur D. Little, op. cit.

12. Mark Moore, *Policy Concerning Drug Abuse in New York State* (Croton-on-Hudson, N.Y.: Hudson Institute, 1970), Volume III: *Economics of Heroin Distribution.*

13. "Who Knows What About Drugs", *New York Times* (editorial), March 11, 1971, p. 38.

14. Richard Severo, "Children's Use of Heroin Held Rising", *New York Times,* October 23, 1969.

15. "President Deals Smashing Blow to International Drug Traffickers", *First Monday,* August 2, 1971, p. 7.

16. Robert L. DuPont and Mark H. Greene, "The Dynamics of a Heroin Addiction Epidemic". *Science* 181 (August 24, 1973), pp. 717–718.

17. David Burnham, "Police Efficiency Constant All Over City, Study Finds", *New York Times,* Feb. 15, 1972, p. 1.

18. Carl J. Pelleck, "We're Losing War on Drugs–Leary", *New York Post,* April 17, 1970, p. 2.

19. President's Commission on Law Enforcement, op. cit., p. 10.

20. James A. Inciardi and Carl D. Chambers, "Self-Reported Criminal Behavior of Narcotic Addicts", paper presented at the 33rd Annual Meeting of the *Committee on the Problems of Drug Dependence,* Feb. 16–17, 1971.

21. Federal Bureau of Investigation, op. cit., p. 98.

22. *New York Times,* Feb. 15, 1972, op. cit.

23. Federal Bureau of Investigation, op. cit., p. 103.

24. *New York Post,* April 17, 1970, op. cit.

25. David Burnham, "Police Shift Tactics to Curb Heroin Sale", *New York Times,* April 21, 1971.

26. President's Commission on Law Enforcement, op. cit., p. 6.

27. "Pop Drugs: The High as a Way of Life", *Time,* Sept. 26, 1969, p. 68.

28. David Burnham, "Report Estimates City's Drug Abusers", *New York Times,* May 1, 1972, p. 1.

29. M. A. Farber, " 'Victory' over Drugs", *New York Times,* March 26, 1974.

30. DuPont and Greene, op. cit., pp. 719–720.

31. Dennis S. Aronowitz, "Civil Commitment of Narcotic Addicts and Sentencing for Narcotic Drug Offenses", Appendix D of *Task Force Report,* p. 149.
32. President's Commission on Law Enforcement, op. cit., p. 17.
33. Aronowitz, op. cit., pp. 150–151.
34. Aronowitz, op. cit., p. 157.
35. U.S. Department of Health, Education and Welfare, *Narcotic Drug Addiction,* Mental Health Monograph No. 2 (1963), referred to in Aronowitz, op. cit., p. 151.
36. George Vaillant, "A Twelve Year Follow-Up of New York Narcotic Addicts: IV. Some Characteristics and Determinants of Abstinence", *Am. J. of Psychiatry* 573 (1966).
37. Daniel Glaser and Mary Snow, *Public Knowledge and Attitudes on Drug Abuse in New York State,* Research Monograph of the New York State Narcotics Addiction Control Commission, Sept. 1969, pp. 60–63.
38. Daniel Katz, "The Functional Approach to the Study of Attitudes", *Public Opinion Quarterly,* 1960, pp. 163–204.
39. Leon Festinger, *A Theory of Cognitive Dissonance* (Palo Alto, California: Stanford University Press, 1957), pp. 1–31.

Chapter Five

Alternatives for Coping

Once a supportive community attitude emerges, the strategy of forcing the addict to refrain from heroin may be complemented by education, treatment or the use of substitute drugs.

The "force" strategy described in Chapter 4 is based on the belief that the problems of heroin addiction can be forced into oblivion. This type of strategy is quickly adopted by individuals and groups in response to new threats.

The "educate" strategy assumes that if potential addicts understood the hazardous consequences of heroin addiction, they would avoid becoming addicted. Education may be aimed at the addict prospects themselves, usually youths, or at their families and the larger community around them. Education may be strictly informational, or it may create sensitivity to alternate means of satisfying the various needs that attract some to drugs.

A strategy of "helping", as the term is used here, is neither prevention nor dissuasion oriented. It arises with the recognition that addiction is already present for some people and that these people need help—it's too late for prevention to work for them. Help can be provided in a variety of places and forms. Addicts can be sent out of the community for treatment, counseling, and reconstruction of their lives, or they can be helped locally. The help may be rendered by professional psychiatrists, psychologists and social workers in private practice or in formal institutions, or by motivated ex-addicts or other peers or adults in therapeutic community settings or in self-help programs. The objective of these types of rehabilitative approaches is to help an addict into a drug-free existence, aided in getting there via a drug-free program.

The "substitute" strategy often reflects a further degree of resignation with respect to the likelihood of restoring the addict fully to community life. Now the underlying assumption is that the addict needs some kind of chemical support in order to continue functioning. If the person is to be moved from the status of "street addict", reliant upon heroin, this strategy assumes the need for a substitute drug. Methadone is most frequently the drug employed for this purpose. Limited British experience and active U.S proposals have sought the substitute of administered heroin maintenance programs for street heroin activities.

Clearly, communities attempt combinations of several or all of the above strategies. Force, for example, may be maintained, even when other strategies are also being undertaken. Substitute programs may be initiated in hope of gradual replacement by help strategies. This chapter discusses the strengths and weaknesses of the major types of preventive and rehabilitative programs that have been proposed or that are already in operation.

5.1   EDUCATIONAL PROGRAMS

Most drug education programs aim at prevention, either by dissuading the potential addict from drug abuse or by shifting community attitudes in a more favorable direction. The most important question about preventive programs is "What works?" Too few programs have been able to demonstrate success. A major problem in discovering what works is a lack of adequate evaluation methodologies. Because the set of factors underlying drug use is so complex, it is difficult to discern the effect of a preventive program. Until this can be done, the role of education in curbing drug abuse is a matter of faith.

The traditional scare-oriented theme has come under increasing criticism. One authority points out that scare tactics fail with young people because they or their friends have had either pleasant or neutral experiences with drugs and find the information dispensed by the program to be less than credible. He points out that a frequent failing of such programs is their employment of police officers or other adult authority figures who are not knowledgeable about drugs and who fail to distinguish between marijuana and more dangerous drugs.[1]

Even factual drug education programs have their shortcomings. One study observed that youths who use drugs already knew more about the effects of those drugs than their nonusing peers. It found that "knowledge about drugs did not play a significant role in teenagers' resistance to becoming involved with drugs."[2] Some fear that facts about the pleasurable effects of drugs may create an additional drug-favoring influence.[3] Another view is that continued exposure to factual information about drugs may markedly alter attitudes toward drugs and make them more acceptable rather than prevent their use.[4] One major problem with these programs is that they often do not have their facts straight. The National Council on Drug Abuse and Information estimated in 1970 that perhaps more than 60 percent of the literature in circulation among school children contains at least some unsound information about drugs.[5] Programs of uncertain efficacy also create a problem. As Helen Nowles commented to a Senate committee considering new education programs, "Unexamined and unevaluated information and education are certainly no answer; and it is safe to say that in some instances, they may be as harmful in the long run as no programs at all."[6]

Much importance has been assigned to the role of peer-group interaction in spreading drug abuse; such interaction may also afford a potential for discouraging abuse. Peer groups facilitate discussion of the problems that lead adolescents to drug use. Peers currently dealing with the same problems might be more helpful in dealing with an adolescent's problems than an adult authority figure. Such peer-group efforts are alleged to impart even the facts about drugs better than programs with a lecture format. One source suggests that the curricula for these programs be prepared by students themselves rather than depending on materials from adult experts.[7]

A prevalent notion is that prevention depends upon the provision of alternate means of satisfying the needs that encourage drug use.[8] "Basically, individuals do not stop using drugs until they discover 'something better', and maximize opportunities for experiencing satisfying nonchemical alternatives."[9]

Based on the available evidence, several points can be made about the potential role of education and other preventive programs in the addiction system:

1. These programs at best have a limited effect on drug abuse and addiction. Because soft-drug use is spread in a cultural context rather than as a result of ignorance or emotional maladjustment, only a negligible impact on the use of these drugs can be expected. The use of the more dangerous "soft" drugs (such as barbiturates) would be modestly discouraged (see Equation 21–23). Exposure to the dreary side of the junkie's life and to the health dangers associated with taking heroin have a greater, though still limited, effect in preventing the initiation of new addicts (see Equations 40 and 41). Peer-group and "alternative" approaches may prove successful, but such effect has not yet been demonstrated, even on a small scale (see also Section 3.4).

2. Credibility is an essential characteristic of any preventive program. Facts must be correct and presented in an objective, value-free manner. Credibility of these programs is a function of the community's definition of the drug problem. A sociomedical definition is likely to spawn highly credible programs, while a criminal definition will encourage programs that are scare-oriented (see Equations 142–144).

3. The impact of preventive programs, within their restricted and narrow range of effectiveness, is limited by the level of resources committed to them relative to the potential user and potential addict populations. Within those limits, a higher level of funding will result in greater impact.

Another class of education program is aimed at parents and community leaders. Its thrust is not only toward presentation of factual information as it relates to the children of their concern, but at changing the community's definition of the drug problem. The process of redefinition, visualized in Figure 2.6 and discussed in Section 4.5, occurs in part as the result of national social forces. However, these social forces may be facilitated by a community education program designed for that purpose. These "media effects" are covered in Section 4.5 above.

5.2   TREATMENT PROGRAMS

Methadone maintenance and drug-free therapeutic communities are now the predominant means of treating heroin addiction. Detoxification is also in widespread use. Small-scale experimental work is underway with several narcotic antagonists. In addition, heroin maintenance is advocated by some outspoken community leaders.

5.2.1   **Methadone Maintenance.**   Methadone is an addictive synthetic narcotic that, when administered orally, has been found to eliminate some addicts' craving for heroin and to block the euphoric effects of injected heroin. As of April 1972, there were 434 methadone maintenance programs in the nation with a growing patient population estimated at 65,000. At an annual cost of about $1300 per patient, expenditures for methadone maintenance programs total approximately $85 million per year. Some methadone maintenance programs have reported sharp decreases in criminality and concomitant rises in employment.[10]

Methadone maintenance was first introduced in the mid-1960s by Dole and Nyswander in a pioneer program at the Beth Israel Hospital in New York. The Beth Israel program produced impressive results compared to previous efforts. In the three years prior to September 1969, 2205 addicts had been admitted to Beth Israel's program. As of that date 82 percent were still in the program and heroin free. Only 2 percent of those patients in the third year of the program were arrested; 92 percent had jobs or were in school. Only 8 percent were on welfare as opposed to 51 percent of those in their first six months in the program.[11] This program and its successors have had considerable success with the addicts they have treated. The Narcotics Treatment Administration of Washington, D.C. reported a 74 percent retention rate in its high dose methadone program, with a 17 percent arrest rate.[12] Such results far surpass those of drug-free programs. Perhaps the most significant impact, over and above improving the lives of the addicts themselves, may be in terms of crime. Robert DuPont credits methadone maintenance as a significant factor in the decline in crime in Washington.[13] Moreover, an addict in a medically run program is not likely to suffer an overdose or to contract hepatitis from dirty needles. Those on methadone maintenance are more able to hold jobs and to remain off welfare. Figure 5.1 shows the flow of addicts that come in contact with methadone maintenance programs. Entry into methadone programs is a function of several factors, displayed in Figure 5.2

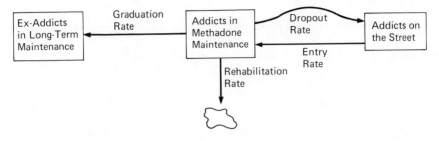

Figure 5-1. Flows through Methadone Maintenance Programs

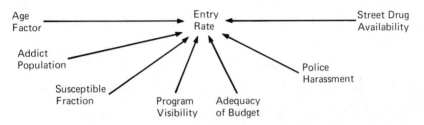

Figure 5-2. Factors Affecting Methadone Maintenance Entry Rate

Methadone treatment is not equally useful to all patients. A study of Beth Israel's records showed that between February 1965 and February 1968 a total of 1233 addicts were seen. Of these, only 42 percent were actually accepted into the program, and 59 percent of those not accepted were rejected by the staff; the others either failed to appear or to complete screening.[14]

The patients in this original study were doubtless a select group, more motivated than the typical addict. After substantial numbers of these more motivated addicts have been drawn into programs, the remaining addicts are more difficult for programs to attract. In our system model the fraction of the addict population susceptible to methadone maintenance ranges from 60 percent to nearly zero, depending upon the balance between addicts enrolled and addicts still on the street. Figure 5.3 displays this relationship (see also Equations 213 and 214).

Age also influences entry into methadone maintenance. Young addicts are apparently less attracted to this modality. Moreover, questions have been raised about the desirability of methadone maintenance for younger addicts. Greater numbers of younger, less motivated addicts, those seeking a "quick cure" or a temporary substitute for scarce heroin, have been observed in methadone programs with a concomitant increase in dropout rate.[15]

Figure 5.4 displays the relationship between the average age of the addict population and the fraction of the population otherwise eligible who are likely to enter the program (see Equations 217–221).

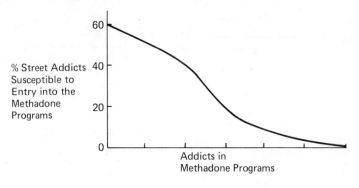

Figure 5-3. Susceptibility to Methadone Treatment

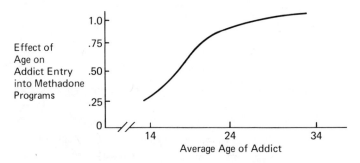

Figure 5-4. Age Effect on Entry to Methadone Programs

A program is relatively more attractive to potential patients if it can afford supportive services, a high staff-to-patient ratio, outreach and various amenities. (These factors that relate to size of budget are taken into account in Equation 215.)

Street heroin availability and police harassment affect the rate of entry into methadone maintenance. Avoidance of incarceration is a significant motivating force for addicts entering these programs. A high arrest rate will provide this sort of motivation (see Equation 222). Heroin availability on the street is another factor that affects the entry of addicts into methadone programs. Low availability makes life difficult for addicts and moves them toward finding a way out. A large amount of heroin in the community makes life easier and removes some of the incentive for entry (see Equation 223).

Finally, program visibility influences entry into methadone programs. As a larger proportion of the addicts in the community enroll, the program's visibility grows, encouraging others to enter. As the percentage of addicts in methadone programs increases from 5 percent to 30 percent of the local addict population, the visibility effect embodied in our system model is capable of increasing by about 50 percent the rate at which addicts are attracted to methadone maintenance (see Equations 224 and 184).

Once in the program, patients either remain, drop out or become rehabilitated (no longer require methadone). These fractions are determined by a variety of circumstances. Most of these circumstances have been accounted for in the preceding discussion of entry. For example, age only minimally affects the drop-out rate since the age factor has already severely restricted the age range of patients in the program.

Our system model explicitly represents only the effects of budget adequacy and susceptibility of the patient to treatment. In our system model the patients in a highly selective program will be susceptible to treatment in almost all cases. The patients in less selective programs may be only 50 percent or even less susceptible to treatment (see Equation 228).

Budget adequacy has a significant impact upon program success. Well funded programs suffer as little as 35 percent dropout rate. Impoverished programs have difficulty in rehabilitating many patients, as indicated in Figure 5.5.

When a patient has been in a methadone program for a period of three years, he is unlikely to return to heroin. In our system model he graduates to an ex-addict maintenance status in which he continues to receive methadone, but to differ in no material way from other nonaddicts (see Equations 232 and 233).

While the requirement that addicts in methadone treatment be maintained over a long period of time is a particular disadvantage of methadone maintenance, it is nevertheless superior to the life of a junkie. Several attempts to withdraw people from methadone after a short period of maintenance have met with failure. The Narcotics Treatment Administration in Washington reports that their methadone-withdrawal program had a dropout rate of 86 percent and an arrest rate of 40 percent as opposed to a dropout rate of 26 percent and an

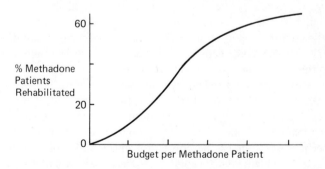

Figure 5-5. Budget Effect on Methadone Rehabilitation

arrest rate of 17 percent for its high-dose methadone maintenance program.[16] Of 350 patients withdrawn from the Beth Israel program for voluntary or disciplinary reasons, nearly all became readdicted to heroin or asked to return to the program.[17]

Growth of methadone maintenance programs adds significantly to the total quantity of narcotics flowing through the community. Some portion of this flow is diverted to the illicit market. While security measures can limit leakage, they cannot eliminate it. Given adequate staff to supervise distribution in our system model, leakage is held to 6 percent of the methadone supplied by the program. Under severe budgetary limitations affecting program security, we estimate that as much as 20 percent of the methadone might find its way into the illicit drug market (see Equation 234).

As early as 1971 methadone-dispensing clinics run by the city of Boston were cited as contributing to black-market supplies of methadone.[18] That program spent only about half the national average per patient,[19] offered few supporting services, and lacked sufficient personnel to prevent diversion of methadone to illegal channels. As another example, a private clinic run by a physician in New York City also dispensed methadone with few supporting services. This clinic made little attempt to positively identify its patients or even to ascertain that they were addicts.[20] Similar experiences have been cited in Washington, D.C.[21,22] Such a situation creates a great potential for diversion of methadone to the black market. Though the highly motivated addict may benefit from easy access to methadone, many others will use such a lax arrangement to supplement their heroin needs in times of scarcity. Liberal take-home policies for dispensing methadone have contributed to the problem. The apparently limitless ingenuity of addicts was demonstrated when several patients concealed syphons in their sleeves to suck methadone into hidden containers. Others furtively spit methadone into plastic bags for sale on the street. In New Orleans, a "spit-bag" of methadone reportedly sold for $5 in 1972.[23]

One serious consequence of diversion is a growing death rate due to methadone overdose. In the first two months of 1972, New York City and Washington, D.C., which have the two largest methadone maintenance populations in the country, reported more deaths due to methadone overdoses than in all of 1971. In New York there were fourteen deaths during those two months, and only thirteen during all of 1971. In Washington there were nine deaths in two months of 1972 compared to eight in the year 1971.[24] In the first half of 1973, deaths attributable to methadone exceeded those that involved heroin.[25] While they are not immediately relevant to our system, other objections to methadone maintenance have been voiced. Some black community leaders see it as a superficial solution to the crime problem, which omits concern for the well-being of troubled young people.[26] Robert DuPont noted opposition to methadone among blacks who felt that its use would fasten addiction on the large numbers of black youths. Other critics charge that the use of methadone treatment allows the underlying causes of addiction such as poverty and lack of education to be ignored.[27] Some medical critics even point to evidence that methadone can cause brain damage.[28]

5.2.2 **Therapeutic Community Approaches.** Therapeutic communities are founded on the assumption that pathological personality problems cause addiction. Such programs seek to rehabilitate addicts by changing the behaviors and attitudes that lead to and accompany being an addict. Most of these programs are residential, requiring addicts in the process of rehabilitation to live in a house for a period of several months to several years. Though the quantity of professional input varies from one program to another, they are usually run by ex-addicts who serve as role models for those in rehabilitation. These programs emphasize personal choice and responsibility for decision-making. The aim is to overcome the addict's self-defeating conviction that he is a passive victim with little or no control over his fate. Socially approved adaptive behavior is rewarded. Disapproval and other punishments are meted out to those who persist in addiction-associated behavior patterns.

Residents work their way up through a continuum of responsibility. They first perform menial tasks around the house and then move up to more responsible jobs as they demonstrate readiness. A basic premise is that the addict is typically underdeveloped in his ability to relate to others. A sense of community and interdependency with other residents is taught. "Straight" or "square" behavior is stressed and residents are reprimanded for behavior that resembles the way an addict acts. The underlying idea here is that deviant behavior is learned in social settings and that socially desirable behavior can similarly be taught by providing role models and a reward structure. Addicts who succeed in this process of behavior change become role models and advisers for newly admitted addicts. Once a resident has completed the program, he usually leaves the house, but continues to come back for frequent meetings and other activities that support his reentry process.[29]

Because of their smaller scale, higher costs, poorer retention rates, and poorly documented success rates, therapeutic community programs are at a severe disadvantage in the highly competitive struggle for funds.[30] Several treatment centers were closed in New York City, reportedly for reasons that included: (1) not enough youths coming to these facilities for treatment; (2) not enough emphasis on treatment and a lack of individual assessment to come up with a therapy plan for each resident; (3) poor or nonexistent patient records; (4) inability to account for financial expenditures; and (5) no follow-up to ensure sufficient guidance during the reentry process.[31] Programs often form around dynamic ex-addicts, professionals or other leaders, and as a consequence are not amenable to large-scale expansion.[32] Evaluation is also a problem. Synanon House, a prototype therapeutic community, has not permitted evaluation, making it ineligible for outside funding. This program charges high admission fees to support itself. Daytop Village, on the other hand, permits assessment of its program and facility and evaluation of alumni and dropouts.[33] Evaluation is difficult in any event because the programs have unique styles of operation.

      Extensions and modifications of the traditional therapeutic community format are in operation. They are being used as transitional elements in multi-modality programs that also employ methadone maintenance.[34] Members live in these communities for a period of time before returning to their homes on methadone maintenance. Day programs are emerging as a variation on the therapeutic community approach.[35] Such programs as Reality House and Exodus House in New York provide daytime group therapy and workshops for developing vocational skills and good work habits. Encounter, Inc., and Samaritan Halfway Society, also in New York, offer group encounter therapy in the evenings and night residence for their enrollees. They have much higher retention rates than day programs and may be more economical to run than full-time residential programs. The flow of addicts through these programs is shown in Figure 5.6. The rates at which addicts enter the programs from the street and prison are affected by several factors. These are arrayed in Figure 5.7.

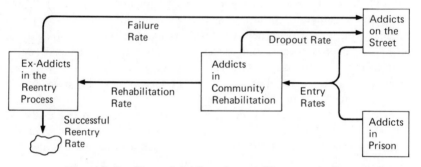

Figure 5-6. Flow of Addicts through Therapeutic Community Rehabilitation

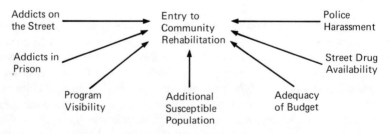

Figure 5-7. Factors Affecting Community Rehabilitation Entry Rate

Only a limited fraction of the addict population will respond to treatment in a therapeutic community. An older addict set in his ways is unlikely to be an appropriate candidate for a program that seeks to change his behavior. A young impressionable addict is a better choice. Most programs screen candidates to make certain that they are sufficiently motivated, because of the interdependency among residents. A greater proportion of the most promising candidates for therapeutic communities enter these programs first. After substantial numbers of the more motivated addicts have been drawn into programs, the remaining addicts are more difficult for programs to attract. In our system model the fraction of the addict population susceptible to therapeutic community programs ranges from 40 percent to nearly zero, depending upon the balance between addicts enrolled and addicts still on the street. Figure 5.8 displays this relationship (see Equations 181 and 182).

The attractiveness of therapeutic communities to new residents is closely tied to budget. A high staff-to-resident ratio is required. The total cost of operating a program is $5000 to $7000 per year for each resident, according to one source.[36] Another source puts the cost of a two-and-a-half year stay in a Phoenix House in New York at $17,225.[37]

Figure 5.9 displays the impact of budget adequacy upon program attractiveness as it operates in our system model (see Equation 186).

The other factors that influence entry into therapeutic communities shown in Figure 5.7 have already been discussed in terms of their influence upon methadone maintenance programs (see the discussion of Figure 5.2). While the specific numerical values that apply to therapeutic communities differ in some instances, most notably in the impact of heroin availability, the causal structures are identical to those described in the discussion of entry into methadone programs. (Equations 177, 180–189 and 197–200 treat all of the factors that influence entry into therapeutic communities.)

The success of any individual program depends upon a number of considerations including its policies, its operating procedures and other factors, which in turn depend upon the personal qualities of those involved in it. The qualities required for successful rehabilitation are not uniformly distributed

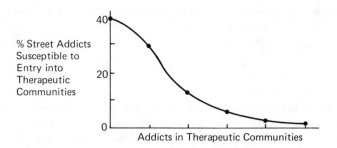

Figure 5-8. Susceptibility to Therapeutic Community Treatment

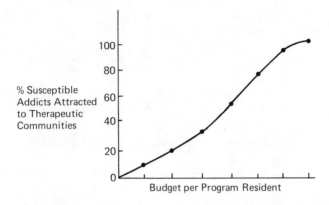

Figure 5-9.   Budget Adequacy Effect on Therapeutic Community Admissions

among all programs. In the aggregate, program success as measured both by dropout rate and by rehabilitation rate are primarily a function of the motivation of the residents and the adequacy of the budget. A large fraction of entrants drop out no matter how adequate the services because they find life in the therapeutic community too harsh and demanding or because they crave heroin and other features of addict life. One study estimated that 40 percent of the residents in a program complete the prescribed stay.[38] Other accounts, however, report much lower success rates with very few actual graduates.[39]

After a period of successful operation, a program will tend to have depleted the pool of promising prospects. Its success will decline as it attempts to provide assistance to the more resistant portion of the addict population that remains (see Equation 195).

Figure 5.10 shows the extent of success that can be affected by adequacy of budget in our system model (see Equation 194).

Those who do complete a therapeutic community must struggle to regain an acceptable role and status in the larger community. Several factors combine to determine the outcome of that struggle. Heroin availability plays a role. The income level of the community also affects the fraction that successfully adapts. A poor community is likely to offer fewer opportunities for employment and education. Most important, the community's definition of the heroin problem facilitates or inhibits the process of reentry.[40] A definition that is heavily sociomedical is more like to bring with it an assumption that rehabilitation is possible. A community with a favorable view of the ex-addict extends vocational, residential and social opportunities to him. Finally, the provision of follow-up services for ex-addicts in reentry can also make a difference. Visits to the residence for recent graduates are sometimes provided. Frequent visits with a counselor are reported to be an effective form of

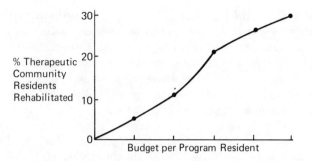

% Therapeutic
Community
Residents
Rehabilitated

Budget per Program Resident

Figure 5-10. Budget Effect on Community Rehabilitation

follow-up.[41] Vocational training is also assumed to be important to reentry (see Equations 235–249 for treatment of the reentry process).

5.2.3 **Detoxification.** Detoxification programs assist an addict in overcoming physical dependence on heroin. This may be accomplished by providing some sort of drug to ease the discomfort of withdrawal symptoms or by providing a narcotic, usually methadone, in decreasing doses over a period of time. For the sake of completeness our system model includes a detoxification component. However, its importance is not great compared to other modalities.

The earliest rehabilitation programs employed this approach on an inpatient basis. Such programs have long-term success rates of only 5 to 10 percent, though one source expresses a belief that the rate could be raised to 10 or 20 percent, albeit with careful screening.[42]

Even if a sufficient long-term success rate cannot be reached, detoxification serves a useful purpose in allowing the addict to escape the pressures of the daily hustle and to reduce his habit size to a level he can support. Such a program reduces the addict's need to commit crime. Ambulatory detoxification may be justifiable, even assuming a long-term success rate of only 0.5 percent, if it temporarily reduces crime and induces addicts to enter other forms of rehabilitation.[43] (See Equations 274–286.)

5.2.4 **Opiate Antagonists.** While methadone is the favored substitute drug, research continues on several narcotic antagonists, especially cyclazocine and naloxone. The antagonists block the action of heroin on the central nervous system; they are not addictive and produce no euphoria. The antagonists may offer promise for highly motivated addicts who feel they need the drug only for security to help avoid re-addiction. Antagonists have also been proposed as useful for treating newly addicted youths who may give up heroin if their highs are blocked.[44] Several programs are actively using antagonists (they are still classified as experimental drugs) including King County Addictive Diseases Hospital and Metropolitan Hospital in New York and the Connecticut

Mental Health Center in New Haven.[45] The first two require inpatient stays while the addict is withdrawn from heroin with decreasing doses of methadone, then built up to an appropriate cyclazocine dosage. Out-patient status follows, with daily visits for the administration of the drug and occasional urine testing for signs of heroin use. The New Haven program operates as a day-patient program, with heavy emphasis on therapy and adjustment counseling and dispenses naloxone at the beginning and end of the day.

As with other forms of treatment, the use of antagonists encompasses a number of problems. Some basic problems deal with the drugs themselves. Both have an extremely short duration in the body and require at least daily doses to remain effective. Current efforts are directed at developing long duration forms of the antagonists or a method of implanting capsules containing the drug for slow release over a longer period of time. Cyclazocine also has certain undesirable side effects. New drugs are being developed with longer lasting effects than naloxone, less severe side effects than cyclazocine, and greater effectiveness than naloxone.[46]

The dominant characteristics of the antagonist programs are a low attractiveness to addicts and a low retention rate. Antagonists can be helpful only to a small segment of the addict population.

Given their limited applicability, antagonists play only a minor role in the system model. See Equations 287 to 301 for their complete description.

5.2.5   Heroin Maintenance.

Some of those who see shortcomings in current treatment approaches advocate governmental distribution of heroin as the only way to control its undesirable social consequences. These critics reason that a significant proportion of addicts are resistant to all current treatment modalities, including methadone. Free heroin supplied by a maintenance program might attract and retain even the most reluctant addict. Crime would decline since addicts would not have to steal or hustle to support a habit at street prices. Health hazards would be reduced by provision of clean needles to prevent hepatitis and precisely measured doses to avoid overdose. Another argument offered in favor of heroin maintenance is that it would, by providing unbeatable competition, drive the illegal heroin industry out of business, thereby ending the problem forever.

Apart from the purely emotional responses, there are some serious logical and factual flaws in the strategy of heroin maintenance. One problem stems from the transient behavior of the illicit heroin market. Even though the illegal market for heroin in this country might dry up after several years of competition with governmental distribution, the transient effect of heroin maintenance would be to depress the street price and make heroin more readily available. By the time the illicit market was eliminated, many more people would have become addicts than if heroin were kept less accessible by high prices. The British experience discussed below suggests that the illegal heroin market may never really be eliminated. When we begin with as well developed an illegal supply system as exists in the United States, the task becomes even more difficult. Under pressure of governmental competition, the illegal supply system might even resort to a deliberate marketing effort in order to compete.

The pharmacology of heroin also presents pitfalls for a heroin maintenance effort. Heroin's effect is of short duration. Addicts must receive injections every four to six hours to prevent withdrawal symptoms. The dosage required to prevent those symptoms varies for each individual and grows over time for most addicts. These characteristics present two dilemmas for the heroin maintenance program. Having to come to a clinic several times a day for their heroin would make it difficult for maintained addicts to hold jobs or have normal family lives. Giving addicts heroin to take away with them may result in diversion in the illegal market. Giving out small doses may result in discomfort for many addicts who would seek supplementation from street supplies. Giving out large doses may result in significant leakage, which would increase availability to new heroin users at low prices.

Another problem, anticipated by Finney, former director of the New York City Addiction Services Administration, is resentment by minority groups.[47] This sort of resentment has already been displayed in controversies about methadone. Treatment with addictive drugs is seen as sacrificing minority group youth to protect the white majority from the crime that accompanies addiction.

Real world experience with free heroin distribution is scanty. Many Americans mistakenly think of the "British System" as one in which free distribution of heroin is the principal means of coping with the addiction problem. In Great Britain prior to 1968, any physician could prescribe heroin at his own discretion.

But during the early 1960s the number of addicts passing in and out of heroin maintenance began rising sharply as the drug culture reached England. Much of this increase was thought to have been aided and abetted by careless overprescribing of heroin by physicians. The Dangerous Drug Act of 1968 sought to control this by restricting heroin distribution to specially designated clinics and by requiring physicians to register all addict patients within seven days of discovering their condition. With the enactment came a trend away from heroin toward methadone maintenance.[48] Of 1446 addicts registered at the end of 1969, 1011 were receiving methadone and 204 were receiving heroin (often in combination with other drugs).[49] An illegal market in imported heroin has emerged that is patronized by maintained addicts seeking to supplement their dosages as well as by new addicts who have not yet been registered. Maintained addicts themselves also supply the market with methadone and heroin that they have received but do not need. Some sell methadone to get money for heroin.[50] In addition to an illicit market in heroin, the use of other drugs has also increased. While arrests associated with heroin declined slightly in 1969 and

1970, arrests related to cannabis and LSD increased from 6185 to 9897 and 161 to 746, respectively.[51] Injection of dissolved barbiturates is also on the increase, an especially serious problem since this practice causes the collapse of blood vessels and the onset of gangrene infections. A final problem indication is that a substantial portion of the addict population is not enrolled in any of the maintenance programs on a steady basis. Though 1430 addicts were receiving prescribed maintenance drugs at the end of 1970, a total of 2661 had come in contact with programs during the course of that year. Various estimates put the total British addict population as high as 3000.[52]

Great Britain and the United States and their heroin problems are not identical. The comparative sizes of the addict populations, 3000–4000 there as against 300,000–600,000 here, is the most striking difference.[53] The system in England never had to contend with a large illegal drug distribution system and in fact now has a modest problem with illegal distribution despite the clinic system. A third difference, asserted by one authority, lies in the psychological makeup of the British addict versus his American counterpart.[54] The greater homogeneity of the English population and the small nonwhite minority are other characteristics of the environment there that make comparisons difficult. Unfortunately, most comparisons made for purposes of advocacy have been made in a vacuum that ignores these important differences and focuses only on apparent British program results.

Some proponents argue that small-scale experiments can do little harm, can be terminated if they don't work out, and have a significant potential for success. A program proposed by the Vera Institute in New York would start with a small number of addicts who had dropped out of methadone programs.[55] Addicts in the program would receive a comprehensive set of supportive services. Expenditures per patient would be unusually high, both to pay for the supportive services and the personnel to supervise the frequent administration of the drug. The experiment would start with thirty addicts and gradually add an additional hundred. Its duration would be four years, with addicts being switched from heroin to methadone after one year. They would be compared with a similar group of methadone program dropouts who were enrolled in a special methadone program. Evaluation of the two groups would be done at the end of the four years. Though such an experiment might show the comparative advantages of heroin maintenance for hard-core addicts, one critic fears that success with hard-core addicts might be used to promote the use of heroin maintenance on a much larger scale. This would be especially misleading if the high funding level per addict had more to do with the experiment's success than heroin maintenance itself.

In a structural sense heroin maintenance programs would function in essentially the same manner as methadone, as is shown in Figure 5.1. However, the mere fact of heroin's greater attractiveness to the addict indicates some important potential differences between heroin and methadone maintenance programs. Though actual evidence is limited, it can be assumed that heroin maintenance will appeal to and retain a larger fraction of the addict population than would methadone maintenance. Some people would enter the program looking for a source of free heroin with no intention of achieving rehabilitation. Figure 5.11 compares the presumed relative attractiveness of heroin and methadone maintenance. The fraction of the remaining addict population susceptible to the two types of maintenance programs is plotted as a function of the size of the addict population already in those programs (see Equations 213 and 252 for methadone and heroin, respectively).

Heroin maintenance programs would be attractive even if budgets were low and supporting services were scant. The relationship between adequacy of budget and program admissions are plotted in Figure 5.12 for heroin and methadone maintenance (see Equations 215 and 254 for methadone and heroin, respectively).

Unless it were proscribed legally and enforced effectively, heroin maintenance would tend to enroll somewhat greater numbers of young addicts. This is true both because a number of methadone maintenance programs

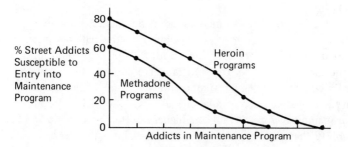

Figure 5-11. Comparison of Susceptibility Functions

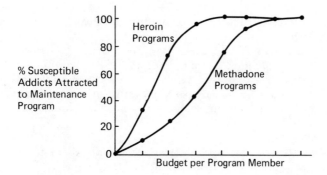

Figure 5-12. Comparison of Adequacy of Budget Effects

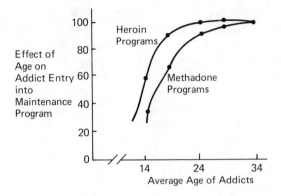

Figure 5-13. Comparison of Age Effects

intentionally exclude younger addicts, and because some younger addicts find methadone maintenance unacceptable. Following this reasoning the effects on program admissions of the average age of the addict population are as shown in Figure 5.13 (see Equations 217 and 257 for methadone and heroin, respectively).

Dropout from methadone maintenance programs was described earlier as a function both of susceptibility of the patients in the programs to treatment and of budget adequacy. Both factors also would influence dropout from heroin maintenance. Dropout rates are likely to be higher for both forms of maintenance as a larger fraction of the total addict population becomes involved. Lower resource availability also leads to higher dropout rates. Again, heroin maintenance is tolerant of a higher fraction involved and a lower resource availability than methadone maintenance (see Equations 227–228 and 261–262 for methadone and heroin, respectively).

REFERENCES

1. Seymour Halleck, "The Great Drug Education Hoax", *The Progessive,* July 1970.
2. "Brookline, Mass. Study Links Marijuana, Dangerous Drugs", *Christian Science Monitor,* March 6, 1972, p. 10.
3. Dana Farnsworth and Paul A. Walters, Jr., "Some Principles of Drug Education Programs", paper presented at the Regional Conference on Drug Education, sponsored by Boston Coordinating Council on Drug Abuse, July 28, 1970.
4. Halleck, op. cit.
5. *Teaching Topics,* Educational Division, Institute of Life Insurance, in cooperation with Health Insurance Institute, N.Y., Vol. 20, No. 1, Winter 1970–71, p. 3.

6. Ibid.
7. Farnsworth and Walters, op. cit.
8. Joseph Pilati, "Peer Influence Seen Key to Effective Drug Education", *Boston Globe,* February 6, 1972, p. 33.
9. Allan Y. Cohen, "The Journey Beyond Trips: Alternatives to Drugs", in *Heroin in Perspective,* D. Smith and G. Gay, editors (Englewood Cliffs, N. J.: Prentice-Hall, 1972), p. 189.
10. James M. Markham, "Antinarcotics Programs Held Fiercely Competitive", *New York Times,* April 10, 1972, p. 25.
11. Jay Levin, "The Addicts: Which Way Out? (Article V.: Day Care and Methadone", *New York Post,* April 17, 1970, p. 41.
12. William C. Selover, "Nixon Turnoff for Addicts", *Christian Science Monitor,* December 28, 1971, p. 1.
13. Robert L. DuPont and Mark H. Greene, "The Dynamics of a Heroin Addiction Epidemic", *Science* 181 (August 24, 1973).
14. M. Perkins and H. Block, "Survey of a Methadone Treatment Program", *American Journal of Psychiatry* 126, May 1970.
15. Jay Levin, op. cit.
16. Richard Severo, "Ethics of Methadone Use Questioned", *New York Times,* April 18, 1971, p. 1.
17. "Methadone Plan in South Hailed", *New York Times,* May 7, 1972.
18. Richard C. Selover, op. cit.
19. Alan C. Leslie, *Benefit/Cost Analysis of New York City's Heroin Addiction Problems and Programs* (City of New York, Health Services Administration, Office of Program Analysis, 1971), p. A-14.
20. Personal interview with Dr. C. Rosenberg, former director of Boston City Hospital Drug Clinic.
21. DuPont and Greene, op. cit., p. 721.
22. James H. McMearn, in Smith and Gay, op. cit., p. 122.
23. James M. Markham, "Methadone Found Rising as Killer", *New York Times,* March 14, 1972, p. 48.
24. Richard C. Selover, op. cit.
25. M. A. Farber, "Victory Over Drugs", *New York Times,* March 26, 1974.
26. Dana Adams Schmidt, "Doctor Links Methadone Treatment to a Decline in Crime in the Capitol", *New York Times,* March 13, 1972, p. 18.
27. Dana Adams Schmidt, "Use of Methadone Scored at Parley", *New York Times,* May 14, 1972.
28. Ibid.
29. For a good comparative discussion of drug-free vs. maintenance programs, see David Laskowitz, "Treatment Models for Opiate Abusers", unpublished paper, presented at the New York Society of Clinical Psychologists, New York City, September 1969.
30. *New York Times,* Book Review Section, review of Glasscote's book, May 21, 1972, p. 33.
31. James M. Markham, "Quarantining of Drug Addicts Urged to Halt Epidemic", *New York Times,* May 8, 1972.

32. James M. Markham, "Antinarcotics Programs", op. cit.
33. Laskowitz, op. cit.
34. Ibid.
35. Jay Levin, op. cit.
36. Conversation with Malcolm Johnson.
37. Leslie, op. cit., p. A-17.
38. Ibid.
39. *New York Times,* May 21, 1972, op. cit.
40. Ray Marsh, "The Cycle of Abstinence and Relapse among Heroin Addicts", in Howard Becker, *The Other Side: Perspectives on Deviance* (New York: Free Press, 1964).
41. George Vaillant, "A Twelve-Year Follow-Up of New York Narcotics Addicts: Some Characteristics and Determinants of Abstinence", *American Journal of Psychiatry,* (1966), p. 573.
42. Leslie, op. cit., p. A-25.
43. Ibid.
44. "Narcotic Antagonists: New Methods to Treat Heroin Addiction", *Science* 173 (August 6, 1971): 503–506.
45. Ibid.
46. Ibid.
47. "Heroin-Experiment Proposal is Opposed by the Head of the City's Addiction Services", *New York Times,* June 2, 1971, p. 29.
48. Alvin Schuster, "British Emphasis on Methadone Stirs Illicit Sales of Heroin", *New York Times,* July 9, 1972, p. 2.
49. Dan Rosen, "In Britain, the Government is a Pusher", *Boston Globe,* February 6, 1972, p. 4-A.
50. Alvin Schuster, op. cit.
51. Robert Nelson, "British Goal: Best Method to Curb Drugs", *Christian Science Monitor,* 1972.
52. Alvin Schuster, op. cit.
53. James M. Markham, "A Try at Heroin Clinics Wins Increasing Support", *New York Times,* February 27, 1972, p. 59.
54. Letter by Dr. Donald B. Louria to the *New York Times,* April 14, 1972.
55. James M. Markham, "What's All This Talk of Heroin Maintenance?", *New York Times Magazine,* July 2, 1972.

Part III

Policy Experiments and Recommendations

Chapter Six

Alternative Heroin Futures

For each community the present represents but one set of points in a long history. The past, though often fuzzy due to lack of a reliable and comprehensive data base, can nevertheless be reconstructed into a reasonable portrayal of what has transpired. But what of the future? What set of heroin-related events, episodes or outcomes will occur in each community during the next decade or two?

This chapter reports an extensive series of exploratory forecasts of possible heroin futures. With the aid of our comprehensive computer model of the addiction process at the community level, we have probed the scenarios that are most likely to occur in response to the various approaches contemplated for dealing with the problems of heroin addiction. The resulting anticipated futures are not more reliable than the underlying assumptions that the computer has used in its calculations. But those assumptions are in fact the most accurate that we have been able to assemble from the literature and from our interviews and consultations with various area experts. The policy implications that stem from our analyses are highlighted in Chapter 7.

First, in Section 6.1 we review in greater depth the pessimistic scenario originally presented as Figure 1.8 in Chapter 1. A more realistic base run is then generated and described. In the base run used as a benchmark for other analyses, our system model is programmed to respond in a limited manner to the growth of the heroin problem.

The next series of scenarios in 6.2 considers variations of police strategies and a range of assumptions about the speed, strength and effectiveness of police activity. Section 6.3 explores the potential of education programs. Rehabilitation is considered in Section 6.4.

The policy of providing a substitute drug, either methadone or legally supplied heroin, is explored in Section 6.5. Various combined programs are evaluated in the scenarios of Section 6.6, and finally, in Section 6.7 a series of scenarios is considered in which the nature of the community may change in response to its perception of the heroin problem.

6.1   THE "BASE CASE": MODERATE POLICE RESPONSE

Let us begin by recalling the pessimistic scenario presented in Figure 1.8 of the first chapter. That run assumes that in response to the development of heroin addiction a community might do nothing. What would result?

To generate a community's future under this assumption,* the computer model that has been described was started up with an initial addict group in the year 1965 of 150 in a community with a population of 180,000 and a youth population (vulnerable to drug use) of 51,000. About 20 percent of these youths at the outset of the simulation are occasional users of drugs.

As the computer run begins, the number of addicts on the street (plotted by the computer in Figure 1.8 using the letter A) is rising at a steady rate. With no program response by the community, not even police directed at addict criminals, the positive feedback loops that enlarge the addiction problem are dominant in the community. Addict and drug-user populations expand due to concurrent and ever-increasing growth of drug culture, exposure to addicts, and increasing availability of heroin. The rapid unimpeded growth of the addict population makes selling drugs very attractive, bringing more drugs into the community and enabling even more rapid escalation of addiction. With the growth of the street addict population, the community experiences a concomitant development of addict crime necessitated by the addicts' need for income to support their drug habits.

By 1990, the end of the 25-year simulated future, street addicts have risen to 8300 and are still growing in numbers. Crime has risen to about 10,000 incidents per month and is still on the increase. But of course the community is spending nothing on police, prison or programs. Its costs are the economic and human burdens of addiction, theft and fear. These are the characteristics that have long described life in the urban ghetto. Without community resources under their control, many impoverished areas of large cities suffered these runaway addiction problems for years, until the larger city around them began to be hurt by the overflow problems from the ghettoes, and finally responded.

Let us now be more realistic. No community with resources at its command would long tolerate a runaway problem of addiction and crime without attempting some response. At the very least it would use police to try to combat the crime generated by addicts. And it might even do more.

In Chapter 4 we described the manner in which communities become aware of and initially respond to the problems of addiction. Force is

---

*The changes in the model to achieve this and other simulation runs described in this chapter are listed in the References at the end of the chapter.

characteristically used as addict-crime grows. This community response is embodied in our symptomatic or base run, against which we frequently will compare behavior produced under the influence of other remedial programs and policies. The base scenario is the development of a serious addiction problem over a period of twenty-five years with police effort alone being used to combat its growth. The major computer outputs are shown in Figure 6.1 (see the Appendix for complete model listing of this base case).

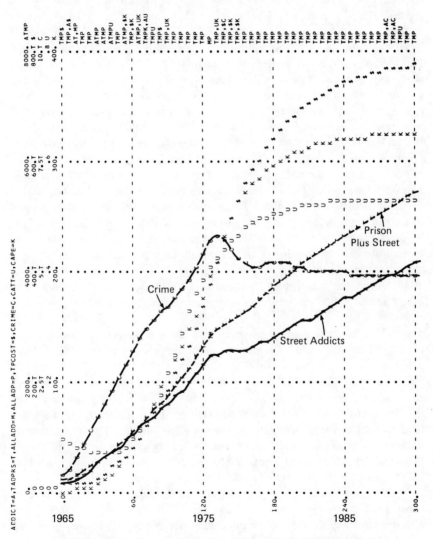

Figure 6-1. Heroin Addiction: "Base Case"—Moderate Police Response

As in the previous "do nothing" computer-generated future, the simulation begins in 1965 with·an initial addict group of 150 in a community with a population of 180,000, including a youth population of 51,000. As the run begins, the number of addicts on the street (the letter A in the graphic output) is rising at a steady rate. The number of total addicts on the street and in jail (T on the graph) is at about the same level as addicts on the street (A), because police effort is not yet great enough to arrest many addicts. The system structures of greatest importance during the first 100 months are the positive feedback loops that create the growth of addicts, and the increasing availability of heroin. During this period, the community definition of the problem (plotted as U) stays near its initial assumption that addiction is a solely criminal problem. Police have not yet responded sufficiently to produce frustration with that viewpoint. Nor have enough addicts been arrested who are personally known to a large segment of the community. The relatively low crime incidents (represented as C in the figure) reflects the small addict population and the moderate socioeconomic level of the area. Total monthly program costs ($ on the graph) remain low due to the small initial number of police, the only program element operating during this simulation run.

But as the addict population continues to grow, crime grows with it. The size of the police force recruited due to the addiction situation grows, too, as crime escalates and as the community becomes increasingly aware of and concerned with the addict-criminal problem. Note that these police are not the "narcotics squad" alone; usually relatively few of the police brought on by the community due to the drug problem are allocated exclusively to going after either drug supply, or pushers, or even after addicts for possession of drugs. Most of the new police are deployed to combat the increased robbery, breaking and entering, and other similar crime—the crimes typically committed by addict-criminals.

The increasing pervasiveness of addicts in the community leads to a heightened tendency to attribute the community's crimes to addicts. More police are allocated, increasingly pressured by the community to attempt to arrest addict-criminals. The rapid growth of police and their increasingly heavy arrest activity gradually produce some convictions. An addict prisoner population begins to build, drawing some addicts from the street. Not only does this tend to slacken the growth rate of street addict-criminals, but it also slightly slackens street demand for heroin, thereby easing price pressures on heroin. Fewer addicts and relaxed prices contribute to a turnaround in the growth of addict crime, leading to a period of decline of several years' duration.

But the lower price, and the large addict population, serve to encourage further entries into the addict pool. The increased police force is less effective relatively, increasing the number of arrests but not sufficiently to keep the street addict population from continuing steady growth. By directing attention more at addicts than at drug supply, the police action does lead to lower heroin prices. Thus the higher number of addicts only maintains but does not further increase the crime rate.

The increased arrest rate brings more addicts to prison, thereby only transferring a growing part of the addiction problem to jail (as reflected in the growing T curve). The large and growing police force and prison population lead to rapidly rising total program costs. They also produce a reaction in community attitude, generated by the growing frustration with the results of the police efforts and the increasing number of arrests perceived as relevant by the community.

Addicts on the street and total addicts both continue to grow near the end of the 25 year computer-generated future. This marks the ultimate inability of police effort alone to solve the problem. Here, the positive feedback loops producing the growth of the problem have gained dominance and overpower even strong police effort. Crime increases with the number of addicts and the community problem definition shifts more toward a sociomedical view as the residents become more frustrated with the failure of police effort. Program costs continue to rise as more police are hired and more addicts are imprisoned. In all, the narcotics problem has gotten out of control.

By 1990, the end of 25 years, the number of addicts on the street has reached 4160 with an additional 1280 in prison, and the total is still climbing. The crime rate persists at 4900 incidents per month. Program costs are running at $780,000 per month, of which more than 60 percent supports the direct and overhead costs of 325 policemen, the other 40 percent supporting the addict-prisoners.

This computer projection is the "base" case against which most alternative simulations will be evaluated. It represents a probably minimum reaction that can be expected from a community that encounters a growing incidence of addiction and its consequences.

6.2 FORCE STRATEGIES

When the community first becomes aware of its growing crime and addiction problems, its first response is police-oriented. Within this general framework, three alternative emphases are feasible:

1. Addicts (at least criminal addicts) can be forcefully repressed by arrest;
2. New addictions can be prevented by fear of legal consequences;
3. Overall addiction can be eliminated (or its growth prevented) by enforced reduction of heroin availability.

6.2.1 **Stronger Police Response.** We explore first the possibility that a community may elect to make a greater investment in police effort than was assumed in the base case. Some communities can be expected to follow this

course, which is after all only a logical extension of the basic strategy of attempting to force the problem out of existence. To examine the implications of a more vigorous police approach, a future was generated based on a police effort twice as great for any given degree of provocation as that which the base case would have provided.[2]

This approach leads to a community history that starts in the same manner as the base case.* But as the community begins to see a need for a punitive response to its increasing addiction-crime problem, it acts more forcefully. As a result police more actively attack the street addict population, attaining a higher arrest frequency at all levels of street population. The added police harassment makes drug-selling less attractive, somewhat lessening the drug supply, thereby leading to higher heroin prices and less easy entry of new prospects into addiction.

By the end of 25 years the street addict population is 2720, apparently saturating at about that figure. But this 35 percent reduction (from the base run's end-point) in street addicts is not matched by comparable reduction in other aspects of the problem. The prison-addict population is 2080, two-thirds greater than in the base case. The tradeoff that has been made of one-third less on the street for two-thirds more in prison, is not desirable. The total addict pool in 1990, including both addicts on the street and in prison, of 4800 is only 12 percent less than in the base case, hardly a dramatic change for so vigorous a police approach.

And while the street population is down 35 percent, its crime has been reduced by only 25 percent, to 3600 crimes/month. The added police efforts have had sufficient restraining effect on heroin supply to increase price somewhat, causing a higher rate of crimes per addict. Thus we have the disconcerting consequence that the by-product of increased police action partially offsets its initial impact on criminal head-count. In addition, the community's direct costs have almost doubled from the base case, running at the end of the simulated period at $1.38 million per month, about two-thirds of it going to support the huge force of 608 police devoted to heroin-related problems.

An inspection of Table 6.1 indicates that varying the degree of intensity of police programs produces a continuum of effects.[3] These results suggest that the strengthening of police programs is desirable in general.

However, in addition to the problems noted above, more intense police efforts generate other dysfunctional consequences. For example, the large

*It is worth noting that the scenarios we report are generated by modifying the structural components or policies of our base model before the run begins, not by simulating an active intervention at a specific time point in the model run. In the present case, therefore, we do not stop the run in a particular year and from that point onward double the allocation of police. Instead we assume from the outset of the run that the community is doubly supportive of this type of program. While runs using time-point interventions have been made, their results are not materially different in policy implications and are therefore not reported.

Table 6-1. Effects of Varying Police Program Intensity (End Conditions)

	Street Addicts	Addicts in Prison	Total Addicts	Crime Rate (000/mo.)	Program Costs ($000/mo.)
No police	8300	0	8300	10.0	0
Weak police program	6240	880	7120	7.7	540
Typical police program	4160	1280	5440	4.9	780
Strong police program	2720	2080	4800	3.6	1380

number of police involved in the strong program—1 for every 4.5 street addicts at the end of 25 years (compared with one per 12.5 addicts in the base case)—raises serious questions about other possible effects not explicitly treated in the system model. The quality of life in such a community would undoubtedly be diminished by the increased police presence. The consequences for civil liberties are also a matter for concern.

6.2.2 **Police and Soft Drugs.** Allocation of police effort to various enforcement tasks can be managed differently from what is assumed in our base model. Suggestions range from concentrating all police action against heroin addiction and leaving the soft-drug users alone (legalizing marijuana is often proposed), to concentrating all effort against suppliers (and leaving the addict alone), with many variants.

Let's look first at what would happen if none of the drug-related police effort were allocated against the soft-drug sector of users and suppliers. All police effort would thus be available to concentrate exclusively on heroin. The future we simulated provides little support for either advocates or critics of such a policy.[4] Almost as many addicts end up in the street—4080—by year 25 as in the base case. Almost as many addicts—1180—end up in prison. Crime is unchanged, direct costs are the same, police effort is the same as in the base case.

Why so little impact? First of all, the underlying base model of community response assumes that relatively little police effort is aimed against soft drugs. This is merely description of life as it already is in most communities, not a normative projection of what life might or should be. Eliminating a minimal effort should not be expected to have much effect.

Second, what of the dangers of explosion of the drug culture unchecked by police action? So long as marijuana and other nonaddictive drugs are still illegal, yet reasonably available, the network for their distribution has tended to stay in the hands of youth and the near amateur. Supply is adequate, yet the economic incentive for proliferation is not great. The illegality of marijuana, for example, despite normal enforcement, tends to control its use.

Continued threat of enforcement, and particularly the prohibition of mass distribution and marketing, seem sufficient to prevent explosive growth.

The benefits of withholding police effort from soft-drug control are threefold, though slight even in cumulative impact. First, somewhat more soft drugs are available, to provide an alternative for some potential addicts. Stated in proper perspective, we clearly avoid the condition of tightness of soft-drug supply that has in the past driven some drug users to try heroin. In general, police efforts have not succeeded in seriously restricting soft-drug availability. Second, the slightly lessened degree of police arrests of soft-drug users, under the reallocation studied, decreases the perceived harassment of youth. Alienation of young people is lower, producing less deviant behavior such as heroin experimentation. However, this entire effect is clearly only incidental in magnitude. Third, the complete attention of police toward addicts and pushers, rather than soft-drug users and suppliers, has the slight effect of added resources addressed to heroin.

To contrast the minimal effect that no police enforcement achieves, we computer-generated a community future that tests the extreme in which all police concentrate their efforts against soft drugs.[5] The results are about a 40 percent increase in street addicts from the base case—5680 vs. 4160—accompanied by an even greater increase in crime. Clearly this is not a desirable outcome.

6.2.3 Supply vs. Addicts.

How should police effort against heroin be allocated? Some have advocated that effort be concentrated against the addict-criminal: get him off the street, into prison; nip the problem at its source, the criminal deviant. Others have argued as strongly that police effort should be concentrated against heroin supply: nip the problem at its source, the supply of illegal drugs.

Both extremes have been examined with somewhat surprising results. When all police are allocated to pursuit of the addict-criminal, ignoring drug supply, hardly any change is detectable from the base case.[6] To be sure, at the end of 25 years a few less addicts are on the street and a few more in prison, the only outward change produced from total dedication of the police to arresting addicts. The other variable that we have been observing carefully, crime rate, is down only 10 percent from the base case.

Why are these results so similar to the base run? To some extent they reflect the dominance of the already present addict-orientation vs. supply-orientation of the police. This orientation is prevalent when a community is experiencing frustration with its police approach toward the drug problem. Not only does a community first redouble the extent of its police effort, but also it pressures the police to produce tangible results, i.e., addict arrests. Thus even in the normal base situation, police tend to devote most of their effort in pursuit of addict-criminals, not in trying to reduce heroin supply.

But there is another more subtle reason for so little change. The experienced reallocation of police effort sets up forces tending to cancel out any resultant overall changes. More police working against street addicts do have an impact—harassing and arresting addicts. But fewer police working against drug supply also have an impact—creating more attractive conditions for pushers and increasing heroin availability. In turn the increased heroin supply makes heroin use more attractive and more attainable, countering for the street addict the negative effect of increased direct police harassment. Thus the reallocation is more or less self-cancelling in outcome. In fact, the 10 percent crime reduction is not caused by police repression of crime or criminals. It is, rather, the opposite reason—the lessened effect on supply results in a slightly lower heroin price, thereby lowering the motivation for addict crime.

Let us now consider the contrary philosophy of police utilization, 100 percent allocation of police against heroin supply.[7] With all police working against supply, and none acting against addict-criminals, a surprisingly chaotic scenario is generated. Heroin availability is somewhat tightened up under increased police vigilance, but potential effectiveness is limited. And addicts are now not being arrested, with all police devoted to supply control. The result is a mushrooming of street addicts, with the indicated peak of 5680 street addicts significantly more than the base-run peak of 4160. But the crime increase is even more dramatic. More addicts ordinarily produce a greater number of crime incidents. Added to that direct effect, however, is the result of tightened supply, causing higher heroin prices and necessitating more crimes per addict to support heroin habits. The end outcome of 7300 crime/month is 50 percent greater than the comparative base case of 4900 incidents/month. In this situation the reallocation of police ends up worsening both sides of the community problem: more street addicts, and higher drug prices, too, causing even greater crime escalation.

The heroin system is sensitive to the allocation of police effort. Deleterious effects are encountered at either extreme of police against addicts or police against supply. A balancing act seems necessary to keep the addict population from escalating under no police harassment, while keeping drug supply in some medium position between overabundance (and low prices) and tight markets (with upward price and crime pressure).

Late in 1973 Nelson Rockefeller signed into law an aggressive force-oriented program he had championed for attacking heroin problems. At its heart is a combination of a strong police approach with severe penalties levied against convicted heroin pushers (mandatory life imprisonment). Our prior description of an anticipated future based upon a vigorous police program might be regarded as an initial assessment of key aspects of that law. But one of the law's important features is the assumption that pushing can be discouraged significantly by increasing pusher fear of the likelihood and consequences of arrest. To evaluate this policy, three additional computer scenarios were generated and contrasted with the strong police case presented earlier.[8] Table 6.2 indicates the not altogether favorable sets of outcomes that might be expected.

The top three sets of results listed show the consequences of merely varying the assumed strength of impact upon pushers of a Rockefeller-like policy. In all three cases some meaningful discouragement is assumed: the least powerful computer projection assumes that pushing can be made 15 percent less attractive by strong police harassment; the moderate analysis doubles that figure; and the strongest set of runs again doubles that assumption, permitting strong police action to lower the attractiveness of pushing by up to 60 percent. The results indicate proportional but small decreases in both the street and prison addict populations as the assumed impact is increased. Addict crime, however, which motivated the Rockefeller policy, is not reduced by making pushing less attractive. The reason is clear: though slightly fewer addicts are on the street, they are paying a higher price for heroin. The increased police harassment does meet its direct objective—it discourages pushing. But unfortunately this causes tighter supply, higher drug prices, and consequently greater need for each street addict to commit more property crime. Thus crime per addict increases, and overall crime rate remains essentially the same (in fact, grows slightly).

Another unfavorable implication of the Rockefeller policy stems from the addict's need to support his habit. Many, perhaps up to 20 percent, do so by selling heroin to other addicts. If the law succeeds in making pushing less attractive as a basis for habit support, thieving becomes more attractive. Left with fewer alternatives, more addicts are likely to rely upon property crime. The last anticipated future shown in Table 6.2 tests this probable shift in addict behavior and demonstrates the weakness of the overall policy. When the reasonable assumption is made that some addict pushers would become property

Table 6-2. Consequences of Strong Police Programs with Various Impact Assumptions

	Street Addicts	Addicts in Prison	Total Addicts	Crime Rate (000/mo.)	Program Costs ($000/mo.)
Lessened effect on pushing (15%)	2880	2160	5040	3.5	1380
Busic effect on pushing (30%)	2720	2080	4800	3.6	1380
Strengthened effect on pushing (60%)	2400	1920	4320	3.7	1340
Strengthened effect on pushing, but increased number of addict thieves	2000	2080	4080	4.5	1540

criminals instead, crime rate escalates markedly. Total program costs also increase due to the larger number of police called for by the increased crime. These cost features do not include the higher court costs that would be required.

Here we have another instance of the interdependencies in the addiction setting causing counterintuitive policy results. Lowering the number of addicts by lowering heroin availability by lowering attractiveness of pushing was the theory underlying the proposal. But less attractive pushing leading to higher drug prices leading to higher crime per addict confounds attainment of policy objectives. And a higher number of addict thieves, accompanying the lower number of addict pushers, defeats the policy. Possible additional effects of this policy on addict migration were not included in this analysis but are considered in Chapter 7.

6.3 EDUCATION STRATEGIES

A community turns toward education when two phenomena have occurred: (1) the community has realized the magnitude or at least the potential threat of its drug problem; and (2) the community has begun to experience frustration in resorting to a police approach alone for coping with drug use and addiction. Education follows enforcement because it is resisted by some in the community. Drug education programs are often seen as exposing youth to dangerous information. Thus drug education may be viewed as a threat rather than as a means for coping with a threat.

When education is adopted as a strategy, it can be manifested in

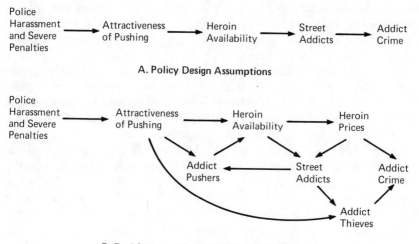

Figure 6-2. The Effect of Increasing Penalties for Heroin Sales

different forms, but is usually aimed at two principal classes of audiences: one approach directly targets those individuals who might be susceptible to heroin use, namely young people; the other addresses the community at large. In the first case the objective of any educational program is to discourage potential users from becoming actual users. The possible objectives of community education are more varied. While all community education programs attempt to increase community knowledge about drug use and abuse, a number of behavioral goals can be identified. For example, education might teach people to recognize the symptoms of drug abuse, to recognize different drugs, or to change some of their attitudes toward various chemical substances.

In our modeled conception of community education the assumed objective, as stated earlier, is to alter the community's definition of the nature of the heroin problem, to persuade people that the problem is not solely criminal in nature, but that it includes a significant sociomedical component.

6.3.1 **Dissuasive Education.** First consider the use of educational programs that attempt to dissuade potential heroin addicts from reaching that potential. When such an educational opportunity is provided in our modeled community, it brings about a reduction in the number of street addicts, and in the number of addicts in prison, which at the end of the run is about 20 percent less than in the base run.[9] Crime is also reduced proportionately. These improvements do not cause an increase in total cost because the cost of education is offset by savings in expenditures for police activity and in prison budgets.

A second simulation was made with a more generous assumption about program efficacy.[10] This was accomplished by assuming that a larger percentage of all young people are susceptible to persuasion. The results are even more impressive than in the run previously described, and total program costs are reduced to a level below the costs in the base run.

A further simulation was made to analyze the impact of credibility as previously described.[11] When maximum credibility is assumed, after 25 years the number of street addicts is reduced to 3040, and the total number of addicts to 4000, as against 4160 and 5440, respectively, in the base run. The effects are proportionately greater upon the prison population.

Unhappily, all of these runs are predicated upon the assumption that education has some measure of efficacy. Little empirical evidence supports this view, and one recent study found the reverse to be true. In that study children who were exposed to drug education were later found to be heavier drug users than an equivalent group from whom the program was withheld. In general, most recent assessments of drug education draw skeptical or negative conclusions.[12]

The cost of providing education that might be negatively effective is even greater than its direct and obvious effects, since the additional heroin addicts created will tend to increase the amount spent for other programs. In a simulation in which negative effectiveness was assumed, the final number of street addicts is 4280, only slightly higher than in the base run, but the number in prison is 1760, up from 1280 in the base run.[13] Crime is up 10 percent and total program budget is up almost 30 percent.

    6.3.2 **Community Education.** No visible difference is observable in simulated future outcomes between the base run and a run that includes a community education program.[14] The program is successful only in the sense that the community's definition of the problem shifts in the direction that the program intends. This shift in attitude, however, generates no further favorable consequences. The reason for this is that our formulation of community education limits its effects to facilitating other programmatic efforts and to easing the process of reentry from prison or program back to full participation in community life. In Section 6.6 we describe runs that present a more favorable picture of community education when it is coupled with other programmatic efforts.

    A potential side-effect of community education stems from the fact that while nonsusceptible persons (adults) are being addressed, children are listening. Giving greater publicity to drug abuse and to heroin and heroin addicts might strengthen the factors that generate heroin use.[15]

    We simulated this possibility by modifying the basic model to include a "publicity effect".[16] In the base model one of the principal structures in support of heroin use is a causal chain that links an increase in the number of addicts to an increase in young persons' awareness of heroin and knowledge about heroin and heroin-taking. Greater awareness and knowledge among persons who are attracted to heroin then increases their likelihood of involvement with it. In this simulation we made a 50 percent increase in the extent to which the presence of any number of addicts affects heroin attractiveness in the nonaddict youth population. This simulation results in a highly unfavorable scenario. The addict population after 25 years is increased about 35 percent over the base run, following a decline from a still higher peak. The prison population is increased a similar amount. Costs are running about 40 percent higher than in the base run, reflecting the increased prison population and the costs of policing a large street-addict population.

6.4 HELPING STRATEGIES

The use of force tends to alleviate but not eliminate the heroin problem. Education, if effective as a strategy, may also ameliorate the addiction growth rate. But even in combination, force and education do not halt the poppy's persistence. Force comes after the fact of existence of numerous addicts, and their numbers grow despite police efforts. Education tries to stem the tide of addict growth but newcomers are nevertheless added.

    A strategy of helping accepts the fact that addicts already exist as addicts, and that more will be added. As considered here, the objective of help is to aid the addict back toward a drug-free condition.

6.4.1 **Drug-Free Rehabilitation.** Regardless of the structure of a particular program, or the identity or profession of the person providing the assistance, any programmatic effort to assist the addict toward a drug-free state is considered here under the category of drug-free programs. The only distinction among such programs that is essential to our policy analysis is that of program location. A program sited within the addicts' community of residence is assumed to be different in certain important respects from one located elsewhere. In-community programs are assumed to be more attractive to prospective clients and to provide a more promising outcome during the reentry process.

On the other hand, out-of-community programs are assumed to offer one important advantage over in-community programs—they can be implemented without the hindrance of local community opposition. The experience of many program developers demonstrates clearly that it is far easier to rally community support in favor of a program somewhere else than a program right there. When we refer to an out-of-community program, we mean literally a program in a community outside of the one we have simulated, where the amount of organized resistance to implementation of the program is likely to be appreciably less than the amount expected in our community. Certain implications of this kind of reasoning are discussed in Chapter 7.

We have explored the consequences of our community's decision to add drug-free rehabilitation to its base police response within a range of effectiveness assumptions. Optimism was simulated by assuming the program could potentially attract up to 60 percent of the street-addict population. At the pessimistic extreme, only 20 percent of the addict population was assumed to be susceptible to attraction into drug-free rehabilitation programs. Realism was simulated by choosing figures midway between these extremes.[17]

The central conclusions of our simulations of drug-free programs is that such programs have a useful though modest contribution to make toward management of the heroin problem. For example, adding an in-community drug-free program to our base model yields a 10–20 percent reduction in the prison population (1040 in prison under a "realistic" rehabilitation assumption as against 1280 in the base case), which is matched by a similar decrease in the total number of addicts on the street—3680 versus 4160. A proportionately more favorable crime picture is achieved, because there are fewer addict-criminals during the course of this run. The direct dollar cost of these improvements is negligible, $860,000 per month against $780,000. But, overall, the reduction of total people involved in the addiction scene (on street, in prison, in program) is either nonexistent or negligible when drug-free programs are adopted. Even so, it is difficult to argue against the position that it is better to spend a dollar on helping than on policing, if the former investment is no less effective.

The performance of the model in contrasting in-community versus out-of-community programming reveals no striking differences.[18] In-community appears equal to or slightly superior on all performance measures. To a large extent the advantage of easy implementation for out-of-community programming compensates for the disadvantages of lessened attractiveness and lowered effectiveness. The contrasting end-point figures are shown in Table 6.3.

As Section 6.2 would lead us to expect, adding a much strengthened police response to either type of drug-free rehabilitation has a considerable augmenting effect.[19] Street addiction population falls by one-third and crime by one-fourth from the simulated case of rehabilitation with only normal police backup. Monthly costs do rise due to more police and prisoners from $860,000 to $1.4 million, but the benefits seem to justify the added cost.

In another simulation we removed all effects of community hindrance to rehabilitation program development with the initially surprising consequence that the results after 25 years are altered only trivially.[20] This differs markedly from the results of a computer run described in Section 6.3.1 on dissuasive education. In that run a more accepting attitude in the community, permitting maximally credible programs to be implemented rapidly, caused a discernible improvement in all drug-problem indicators. The explanation for this difference lies in the durations of relevant time delays in the system. Many months are required for a drug user to become a heroin addict, whereas dissuasive education, when effective, can work almost instantaneously. Any reductions in community hindrance, whose dynamics more nearly resemble those of the addiction process itself, naturally have a greater facilitating effect upon education. In other words, by the time a large number of addicts can be created in the model, community hindrance is already substantially overcome by natural processes. The implication here is that community education efforts are more important to undertake in a community that opts for a preventive rather than a rehabilitative approach to coping with its heroin problem.

Given that drug-free programs can be expected to contribute only modestly to total problem reduction, it is worth inquiring if the operation of

Table 6-3. Drug-Free Program Effectiveness: In-Community vs. Out-of-Community

	Street Addicts	Addicts in Prison	Addicts in Program	Crime Rate (000/mo.)	Program Costs ($000/mo.)
In-Community	3680	1040	640	4.4	860
Out-of-Community	3760	1200	400	4.5	880

such programs would have an inhibiting effect upon the successful operation of other types of programs with relatively greater promise of effectiveness. Specifically, given the rapid recent growth in use of methadone delivery systems, what are the consequences of a community decision to implement simultaneously programs of methadone maintenance and drug-free rehabilitation? As will be seen in Section 6.5.1 the total impact of such parallel programming is better than either program taken by itself, but not as favorable as the sum of the two individual programs taken separately. The greater attractiveness of methadone to many addicts causes some clients to select it who would have chosen a drug-free program were there no maintenance alternative.

6.5 SUBSTITUTE STRATEGIES

In the evolution of antidrug programming, force, education and help are chosen before a substitute is introduced. The antipathy to narcotics is so great that a community resists adopting substitute drugs. Yet the countervailing fear of addict crime leads eventually to trying and even preferring a substitute strategy, especially one in which methadone, an addictive narcotic, is substituted for street heroin.

6.5.1 **Methadone as a Substitute.** The reasons for the methadone substitution approach differ among communities. In some communities the primary motivation is providing a free heroin substitute so the addict will no longer need to commit crimes to support his habit. Other communities hope to use methadone to attract the addict into counseling and rehabilitation programs aimed at bringing him back into a constructive role in society. Mixtures of these motives are common.

In the anticipated futures generated using methadone programs in the simulated community, the primary assumptions are that those receiving methadone are not engaged in addict-crime while in the program. Some are rehabilitated without further drug support, while others are maintained in a long-term methadone-supported environment. These assumptions say little about the specific manner within which the local community methadone program is conducted.

To the base simulated situation we now add the possibility of a methadone program, to be developed by the community and implemented as it senses the need and as its overall attitude permits definition of the problem in a sociomedical manner.[21] This simulated case is shown in Figure 6.3 along with contrasting base curves. Note the key features of this methadone scenario. First the rate of growth of the street population is curtailed after month 120, once some addicts begin entering the methadone program. This leads overall to a marked decrease in street addicts (2320 at the end of 25 years in contrast with 4160 in the base case), and an even more noticeable change in the imprisoned

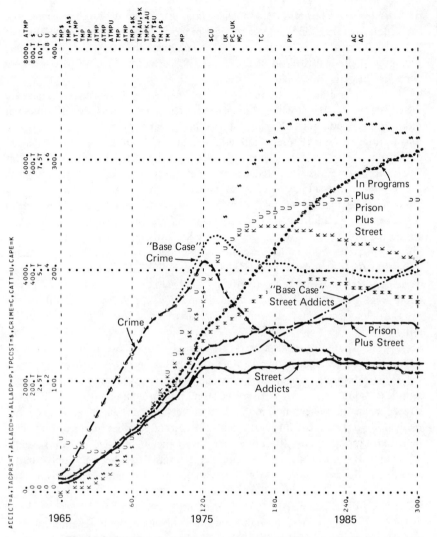

Figure 6-3. Heroin Addiction: Methadone Program Added to Moderate Police Response

addict population (640, rather than 1280). However, the enhanced drug supply creates 13 percent more total narcotic addicts, however disposed (6160 instead of 5440). Offsetting this, the methadone program has attracted into short-term and longer-term maintenance relationships 3200 addicts, many drawn from what would have been alternative dispositions in the street or in prison.

During this process crime decreases by a substantial amount, the 25 year-end figure of 2700 crimes/month being only about 55 percent of the base run's 4900 monthly crimes. Finally, in contrast with the base case, the methadone program ends up costing less money in direct program outlays, the $640,000/month being about 20 percent less than the base case. This is due primarily to the substitution of lower cost out-patient methadone care for more expensive in-patient prison.

The comparative benefits and costs of methadone maintenance are fewer addicts on the street, fewer in prison, less crime, lower dollar costs—but more total population induced into addiction and more ending up with a long-term commitment to an addicted life, albeit addicted to methadone instead of heroin. But if useful, is methadone by itself a sufficient response? This alternative future was simulated with dramatic results.[22] In the base case, using police but no methadone, 4160 street addicts resulted. In the present alternative attempt, using methadone but no police, 5360 street addicts are generated. In the base case, an additional 1280 addicts are in prison, making a total of 5440. In the methadone-only case, no addicts are in prison (no arrests are being made) but about 5000 more addicts are undergoing methadone treatment, producing more than 10,000 addicts in all. Crime is down about 10 percent from the base case, despite the 30 percent growth in street addicts, due to the heroin-price depressing effect of the enlarged methadone drug supply. But this slight benefit is insufficient compensation for the increased street and total addict populations.

When this alternative is contrasted to the "do nothing" case (see reference 1 at the end of the chapter) — no police, no programs—we again see the relative impacts of methadone. As an attractive substitute it does bring a significant number of addicts from the street into program control: 8300 on the street in the no-police, no-programs case, versus 5360 in the no-police but methadone instead situation. But it adds to the total number of persons involved in narcotic addition by attracting many into the methadone program itself— 4640 in this case. Thus supplementing the large street heroin supply that is available under the no-police situation with a supply of methadone adds to total drug availability. More youths are induced into heroin addiction, and from the street many of them are attracted into methadone programs.

If no police, in combination with methadone rehabilitation, is harmful, will strong police be helpful? The anticipated future for such a combination looks promising.[23] The introduction of a methadone program with normal police support has been estimated above as reducing the end-point street addict population to 2320 addicts. Strengthening the police support further reduces street addicts to 1600, now but 40 percent of the street addict population encountered in the base case. Some of those who are no longer on the street as addicts can be found as addicts in prison instead. The stronger police approach has caused a higher arrest rate of street addicts, contributing to the lesser street population and to the greater prison population of 1040 addicts at the simulation's end, up from 640 in the methadone situation with fewer police. The overall depressing effect on addition growth that is achieved by strengthened police shows up as well in methadone program enrollments. Whereas 3200 were entered in the prior methadone setting, only 2640 are enrolled in the stronger police scenario. An additional accompanying benefit is the lower crime rate of 2100 incidents/month, reflecting proportionately the lower number of street addicts. Other than the increased number of addict prisoners, the only other negative aspect of this situation is the directly related increased cost—$980 thousand per month—up 50 percent from $640,000 in the earlier methadone simulation.

These analyses of methadone include an assumption that some modest percentage of the methadone allotted to addict enrollees leaks into the community. This occurs primarily because addicts are often given several days' or a week's supply of methadone at each visit to the methadone center. Some addicts sell part of their methadone in the illegal drug market to raise money, sometimes to buy heroin instead. To test the sensitivity of our conclusions to this leakage assumption, two additional computer analyses were developed, testing methadone programs in which no leakage is assumed and those with larger amounts of leakage to the market.[24]

The end results shown in Table 6.4 indicate reasonable insensitivity of any of our conclusions relative to the assumption of methadone leakage. The largest variations of results are the 15 percent spread in street-addict population at the extremes and the 17 percent difference in methadone program enrollments. Prison, crime, and costs are all essentially unchanged despite the leakage differences. This is an important finding, since one of the main fears of communities is that methadone leakage leads to significant increased addiction and associated crime in their midst. The computer analyses show that going from no methadone leakage at all to large amounts of it produces hardly noticeable effects, a finding reassuring to proponents of methadone use.

No one knows how many heroin addicts are really susceptible to being attracted into methadone programs. Many addicts resist the needed open identification involved in a supervised drug-dispensing program. Regimentation limits voluntary participation of other addicts. Many community groups, and

Table 6-4. Sensitivity of Methadone Leakage

	Street Addicts	Addicts in Prison	Addicts on Metha-done	Total Addicts	Crime Rate (000/ mo.)	Program Costs ($000/mo.)
Methadone						
—no leakage	2160	720	2880	5760	2.8	630
—moderate leakage	2320	640	3200	6160	2.7	640
—large leakage	2480	640	3360	6480	2.6	650

rehabilitation workers as well, resist permitting young people to enter methadone programs, preferring drug-free environments for the young. These considerations led us to assume in the base model that 60 percent of the addicts at most might be susceptible to attraction into methadone, under the best of circumstances. But the available data are by no means conclusive; this estimate may be high or it may be low. Does it matter?

To answer this question two other possible heroin futures were generated on the computer, one based on assuming that only 40 percent of the addict population is susceptible to being enrolled in methadone clinics, the other assuming that almost all addicts, 90 percent, could under some conditions be attracted to methadone treatment.[25] The results show dramatic differences in the potential potency of a methadone program, but all the methadone scenarios are clearly preferable to the no-methadone alternative.

Figure 6.4 displays three sets of curves, developed from the data produced by the computer model simulations. If larger fractions of the addict population can be attracted under favorable conditions into methadone programs, significantly increased community benefits result. This shows up especially in the area of crime. With only 40 percent susceptibility, 2000 addicts are being treated with methadone at the end of the run, 2800 addicts are still on street heroin, and another 880 are in prison. Though this is a worse-case assumption, note that it is still significantly better than the base case of a police-only approach to addiction. In that base 4160 were on the street and 1280 more were in prison. Crime in the base case was running at 4900 incidents per month, nearly 50 percent more than the 3400 incident rate occurring under this "worst" set of methadone assumptions.

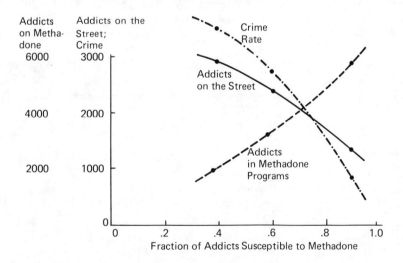

Figure 6-4. Sensitivity of Methadone Susceptibility

If methadone susceptibility is 60 percent, street addicts drop to 2320, prison addicts go to 640, and program enrollment increases to 3200. Crime falls importantly to 2700 incidents/month. But in the unlikely event that 90 percent of addicts are potential candidates for methadone maintenance, then disproportionate benefits accrue. Street addicts are reduced to 1280, prison population falls a bit more to 560, and methadone membership jumps to 5680. Crime now nearly vanishes to 800 incidents per month. The only undesired result is that the total narcotic-involved population does grow, from 5680 in the lowest susceptibility case (including street, prison and methadone program) to 7520 in the case of maximum feasible susceptibility.

This series of runs suggests two critical policy conclusions. Even under skeptical assumptions, methadone offers attractive benefits as a single program for assisting in coping with the heroin problem. Moreover, efforts to increase the scope of penetration of methadone programs into higher degrees of addict attractiveness are justified by the benefits. Even program costs support the desirability of increased utilization, going from $680,000 per month under low susceptibility to $780,000 under high susceptibility. The lessened prisoner support costs partially pay the bill for the larger number of methadone enrollees.

By the early 1970s many cities and towns had already tried various police-oriented strategies, some had experienced drug-free rehabilitative programs and some had also opened methadone centers. In one after another of these communities the battle raged among advocates of the alternative modalities. How much of each type of program should be run? To partly answer this question (more follows in Section 6.6), we have examined the impact of combined programs of police, drug-free rehabilitation, and methadone, and have placed special emphasis on studying the tradeoffs between the drug-free and substitute-drug approaches.

Overall, as indicated briefly in Section 6.4.1, the combination of drug-free and methadone-maintenance programs performs better than either program alone, but not as well as the sum of the two effects taken separately. As total program responsibility is shifted increasingly from drug-free dominance toward methadone dominance, street heroin addicts decline in meaningful numbers, and imprisoned addicts also decline somewhat. The total number of people involved with narcotics also declines slightly as program responsibility shifts toward methadone. This is clearly illustrated in Table 6.5, which shows the results of shifting the extent to which methadone supplements drug-free rehabilitation programs from two-thirds drug-free, one-third methadone all the way up to complete reliance upon methadone.[26]

However, the table also clearly indicates that more intensive methadone supplementation succeeds in part by drawing some people away from drug-free programs. As methadone becomes the tool of prime use, more—not fewer—people end up on narcotics, albeit a much larger fraction of them on societally controlled methadone. Some of those in methadone programs

Table 6-5. Methadone Supplementation of Drug-Free
Rehabilitation

Program Responsibility	Street Addicts	Addicts in Prison	Addicts on Methadone	Total Addicts on Narcotics	Addicts in Drug-Free Programs	Total Addicts
2/3 drug-free, 1/3 methadone	2610	718	2640	6030	270	6300
1/2 drug-free, 1/2 methadone	2420	710	2950	6080	200	6280
1/3 drug-free, 2/3 methadone	2340	670	3070	6080	140	6220
All methadone	2320	640	3200	6160	0	6160

adapt acceptably to community life, so the movement from drug-free programs is not entirely negative.

Furthermore, even the beneficial aspects of methadone move toward saturation as complete reliance upon it is reached. For all communities some equivalent saturation level must exist.

In all, the results suggest that methadone programs should be expected to have potent effects on a community's heroin addiction problems. In combination with some amount of drug-free rehabilitation programs, a somewhat larger potential population can be reached with added benefit. Of course, strong police programs further improve these results when combined with methadone plus drug-free programs.[27]

6.5.2 **Heroin Maintenance.** Advocates argue that heroin maintenance would cause a reduction in the amount of crimes committed to pay for illicit heroin. Yet few suggest that addicts be given all the heroin they desire. Rather the intention is to "maintain" dosage at some fixed optimal level. In fact the VERA proposal sees heroin maintenance as a temporary program status eventually to be replaced by methadone maintenance or by enrollment in a drug-free program. To the extent that an actual heroin maintenance program restricts the quantity of heroin provided to its enrollees, it would have a lessened, though not necessarily proportional, impact upon the number of property crimes committed.

Initially two runs were made to analyze the impact of a heroin maintenance program; one based upon the "realistic" assumption that 50 percent of those on heroin maintenance continue to supplement their supply by continued participation in the illicit heroin market, the other based upon the "optimistic" assumption that no enrollee in a heroin maintenance program commits property crimes.[28]

The results of simulation of the realistic heroin maintenance program were that crime rate drops to 2800 incidents/month, a decrease of more than 40 percent. In the optimistic case, as expected, crime is even more significantly affected. The crime rate at the end of the time period studied is 1800 incidents per month, a reduction of about 60 percent from the base run. Under both assumptions this reduction is not due simply to a reduction in the street-addict population, but by a marked drop in the illicit market price of heroin. (The ratio of crimes/addict was only about 0.5 per month against 1.2 in the base run.)

The positive effects on crime were not matched by improvement in the other facets of the addiction problem. The total population on heroin is about 9000, versus 5440 in the base run. In contrast to the base run there are 10 percent fewer street addicts and 25 percent fewer addicts in prison. Costs are running about double—$1.46 million per month, against $780,000 per month.

While the optimistic heroin maintenance simulation is an improvement over the more realistic run, it is arguable as to whether it represents an overall improvement over the base run and is by almost any criterion less desirable than the methadone maintenance runs reported above.

Is heroin maintenance more attractive when combined with other changes in model assumptions? In attempting to answer this question we have employed the optimistic rather than realistic version of heroin maintenance. Table 6.6 displays key end results of several of these scenarios.

Combining heroin maintenance with a stronger police response

Table 6-6. Analysis of Heroin Maintenance Scenarios

	Street Addicts	Addicts in Prison	Addicts on Heroin Maintenance	Total Addicts	Crime Rate (000/ mo.)	Program Costs ($000/ mo.)
(a) Base run	4160	1280	0	5,440	4.9	780
(b) Heroin Maintenance, Lessened Impact on Crime (realistic)	3870	1060	4070	9,000	2.8	1430
(c) Heroin Maintenance (optimistic)	3840	1040	4120	9,000	1.8	1460
(d) (c) plus Strong Police	3200	2000	3080	8,280	1.5	1680
(e) (c) plus No Community Resistance	1840	720	5280	7,840	0.8	1640
(f) (c) plus Slower Growth Heroin Maintenance	5680	1040	1040	7,760	2.8	920
(g) (c) plus Increased Heroin Leakage	3760	1040	5200	10,000	1.8	1480

produces only incremental improvements.[29] The crime rate is further reduced to about 30 percent of the base run. Total addicts are down to 8280 against 9000. About 1000 fewer are in programs, but about 1000 more are in prison. Costs are up about 15 percent over the base heroin maintenance case.

In another simulation we assumed that the community offers no resistance to efforts to implement a heroin maintenance program.[30] In other words, program capacity is able to grow in response to demand for program services without any constraint based upon the community's reluctance to spend money. This run was made not because the authors believed that communities are likely to be less resistant to heroin maintenance than to other programs (quite the contrary is probably true), but to explore the degree to which community resistance is an inhibiting factor. The results of this run are mainly beneficial. Community resistance does have an important effect. However, even wishing away the problem of community resistance does not solve the whole problem. Crime is down about 40 percent. Total addicts are about 20 percent lower than with heroin maintenance alone. However, 40 percent more total addicts exist than in the base run. Street addicts are greatly reduced (about half compared to heroin maintenance above), and about 30 percent fewer addicts are in prison. Spending is somewhat higher.

The case of heroin maintenance is further weakened when modifications of the model are introduced that are intended to more accurately reflect reality. When slower program growth is assumed, heroin maintenance is generally less effective than in its optimistic formulation.[31] After 25 years the total addict population of 7760 continues to grow. The street addict population is 40 percent greater than in the optimistic heroin maintenance run. The crime rate is roughly midway between the rate under the base run and the optimistic heroin maintenance case. It is clear that this run is dominated by an increase in heroin supply and a consequent reduction in the illicit street price of the drug. Only 0.5 crimes per month are being committed by the average addict, in contrast to 1.2 per month in the base run. Only modest leakage of heroin from programs to the illicit market was assumed in previous runs. When the assumption of greater leakage is made, the impact is principally upon the number of persons under maintenance (5280 versus 4120 in the optimistic heroin maintenance run).[32] Thus heroin-maintenance leakage reveals more of the same drawbacks that were observed in the initial analysis of heroin maintenance. Leakage adds more heroin to the market, just as heroin maintenance adds more heroin to the market. The greater availability attracts more people into addiction, and with heroin maintenance accessible, more eventually end up in the program.

6.6 MULTI-MODAL PROGRAMS

Despite occasional forays into multi-modality inquiries, most of this chapter has analyzed the single strategies of force, educate, help, or substitute. In this section we report the results of a large number of simulations of combined programs. In general the results indicate dramatic though by no means immediate reduction in addict-related crime. Fewer untreated and unimprisoned addicts eventually are at large to steal. Vigorous multi-modality action, however, tends to increase appreciably the total number of persons using narcotics.

In one multi-modality scenario we added drug-free rehabilitation, methadone and heroin maintenance, dissuasive education and community education to the normal police response included in the base case assumption.[33] In this run, as Figure 6.5 indicates, only 1350 street addicts remain after 25

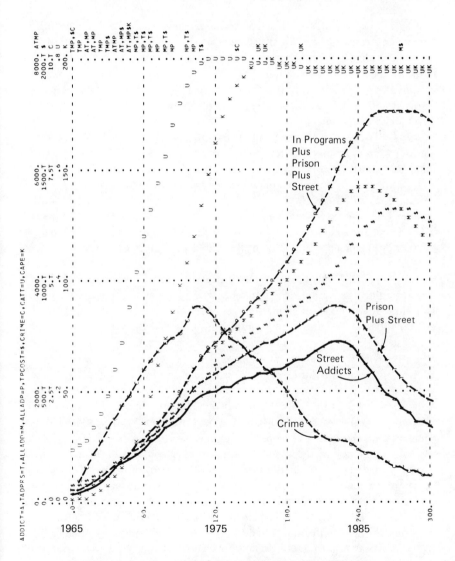

Figure 6-5. Heroin Addiction: Multi-Modality Response

years, about one-third of the base case's endpoint of 4160. The imprisoned population is proportionally reduced from 1280 to 480. An even more dramatic benefit is effected in addict-related crime, which is reduced by a factor of 8 to only 600 crimes per month versus 4900 per month in the base case. However, the grand total of persons involved with narcotics is 6860, as against the lesser number of 5440 in the base case. These overall improvements are achieved at approximately double the dollar cost. Monthly expenditures are running at about $780,000 at the end of the base run versus $1.27 million in this simulation.

Beyond this level of comprehensiveness, adding additional program components creates very small changes in the same general direction. For example, adding a narcotic antagonist program takes an additional 160 addicts out of the street population and 80 out of prison.[34] It is somewhat disappointing that these gains are not reflected in a lower total of persons involved with narcotics, which remains at 6880. All of the movement from the street and prison is into programs.

When still another modality, readily available detoxification, is added to the program mix, the results are similar.[35] Some 80 more addicts are removed from the street and 160 from prison. However, most of these persons add to the total population of those involved with narcotics, which is now increased to about 7200. Again, adding programs adds to costs. For this all-modalities run, $1.44 million is being spent each month at the end of the run. The crime picture continues to improve further, but only marginally so, to a rate of about 400 incidents per month at the end of the simulated period.

6.6.1 **Practicable Combinations.** Having established both the efficacy and the limits of comprehensive programming, what might less ambitious multi-modal combinations achieve? We examined a far more modest combination of programs in a simulation that added to the normal police response only drug-free rehabilitation, dissuasive education and community education.[36] This run shows an improvement over the base case, reducing street addicts by about one-third, with a similar reduction in prison addicts. Crime is also reduced by 25 percent. Some additional 320 addicts are brought into drug-free rehabilitation, but the total people involved in the street, prison and programs is decreased from the base by one-third, from 5440 to 4040. Monthly program costs rise by about 15 percent by the end of the run.

Should methadone be added to this combination? In the single-modality methadone simulations the answer seemed clear enough. But what occurs under multi-modal circumstances? This simulated future further supports the usefulness of methadone as part of an overall community strategy as indicated in Table 6.7.[37] More persons are involved in narcotics (in or out of treatment) when methadone is added to the other combined programs, but many are drawn into methadone from reductions in the street and prison

Table 6–7.   Incremental Effect of Methadone in Multi-Modal Program

Multi-Modal Programs	Street Addicts	Addicts in Prison	Addicts on Methadone	Addicts in Drug-Free Program	Total Involved	Crime Rate (000/month)	Program Costs ($000/month)
Base run	4160	1280	–	–	5440	4.9	780
Drug-free rehabilitation plus dissuasive and community education	2760	860	–	320	4040	3.8	890
The above plus methadone	2220	640	1350	270	4560	2.7	830

populations. Crime is decreased markedly and even total costs are down slightly, the cost of the methadone program being borne primarily by reduced prison and police expenses.

Should heroin maintenance have a role in a community's multi-modal strategy? Several simulations were required to answer this question. First, heroin maintenance was simply added to the prior scenario.[38] The results of this simulation are similar to the single-modality heroin maintenance runs discussed in Section 6.5.2. Street and prison addict populations decline, but this reduction is far surpassed by additions to the methadone and heroin programs. Total involved population escalates, especially those still steadily taking addictive narcotics. Addict crime nearly disappears, and costs jump. The key tradeoff question posed is the decrease in crime versus the increase in total persons involved with narcotics.

However, this scenario is unrealistically generous to heroin maintenance. It merely combined the single-modality assumptions, treating methadone and heroin maintenance programs independently. Actually, both substitute programs draw from one population of potential addict enrollees, to whom heroin is generally perceived as more attractive than methadone. To reflect realistically this interdependency, the underlying computer model was slightly modified, and another scenario was generated.[39] The results are displayed in the third line of Table 6.8.

When these interdependencies are taken into account, most of the benefits anticipated by the previous addition of a heroin maintenance program now disappear. Street and prison addict populations are now not substantially different from the combined program case without heroin maintenance (top line of Table 6.8). But the supply of narcotics augmented by the heroin program draws many more addicts into street experience and then into substitute program support. Crime remains importantly less than in the case in which heroin maintenance is lacking, but costs are still running higher. Compared with the first test of combined programs in which heroin was included (second line of Table 6.8), the benefits of adding heroin are now shown to be less and the liabilities more severe.

Further realism was introduced by assuming that half of those on heroin maintenance programs supplement their program drug supply with additional street-obtained heroin, with the results shown in the bottom line of Table 6.8.[40] The apparent benefits of heroin maintenance are further reduced, while the liabilities increase. Street addicts are about equal in number to those in the multi-modal case that had excluded a heroin program. Addicts in prison are only slightly fewer, but the total involved with narcotics is enormously greater. Crime is still down, but not by as much, and program costs are still up, relative to the nonheroin multi-modality scenario.

6.6.2 **Multi-Modal Programs Summary.** Several generalizations may be extracted from the total set of multi-modality runs. These runs tend to

Table 6-8.   Possible Impact of Heroin Maintenance on Combined Programs

Multi-Modal Program	Street Addicts	Addicts in Prison	Addicts on Methadone	Addicts in Heroin Program	Total Involved	Crime Rate (000/month)	Program Costs ($000/month)
Methadone plus drug-free rehabilitation plus dissuasive and community education	2220	640	1350	—	4560	2.7	830
Above plus heroin maintenance program	1350	480	2840	1930	6860	0.6	1270
Above with interdependencies between heroin and methadone maintenance	2110	550	1830	2230	7050	1.0	1270
Above with half of heroin maintained also engaged in street heroin	2210	530	1830	2260	7170	1.5	1260

be similar to one another and, in their gross characteristics, to the majority of single-program runs described earlier, in that all project an early rapid growth in the number of street addicts and in addict-related crime rates. However, in the multi-modality simulations, aided in large part by a program-created rapid shift in community problem definition, program capacity achieves significant levels quite early in the scenario. By about the fifth year (approximately 1970) in all such runs programs are drawing in considerable numbers of clients from the street addict status. Combined program growth that takes place past this point in time gives rise to several phenomena of interest.

First, the rate of growth of the street addict population slackens. This gives rise to the set of forces that eventually brings crime under control. Crime peaks around the tenth year (1975) and then recedes slightly in most futures. The causes of this eventual slackening in crime are the reduction in number of street addicts and a greatly reduced heroin street price.

At around the twentieth year the number of persons active in most of the programs peaks. The final five years are characterized by saturation or by a modest decline. The one exception to this generalization is in the number of persons in long-term narcotic maintenance. While the total number in all programs tends to level off, the proportion of that group in long-term maintenance continues to grow.

At the end of the 25-year period of multi-modality programming this is the general picture:

1. Addict-related crime is a mere fraction of its prior peak and is running as low as one-fifth its value during the 1974 peak period.
2. The population of street addicts has returned from its peak, which was two to three times higher than in the 1972 period. The final end-point simulated values are in the neighborhood of 30 percent worse than the situation in 1974, and the sum of street addicts plus prison population is as much as 80 percent worse.
3. A very large number of persons are involved with narcotics, the largest portion being in long-term maintenance. The grand total of addicts on the street, in prison, in active programs, and in maintenance of indefinite duration is at or near its peak value, which is about twice as great as in the 1974 period.
4. Depending upon the specific combination of modalities chosen, total program costs run at a rate between two to three times their 1974 values.

6.7 A CHANGING COMMUNITY

The causal structure developed in the initial chapters of this book, which formed the basis for the simulations just described, suffers from a significant structural omission. Our simulated community lacks the capacity to change in response to its residents' concern over the manifestations of the heroin problem. In some of the scenarios reported, the quality of community life deteriorates markedly. Yet our causal structure unrealistically allows no one to leave or enter, with the exception of the identified addicted subgroup.

This omission was really a simplifying assumption. Having analyzed the problem in a static community, we add to the model structure the potential for community change. Simulations based upon this augmented model reveal whether those more realistic, yet less verifiable assumptions, would cause us to make any substantially different inferences.

If the implications of these runs differ in substance from the static runs, it would be necessary to verify and to defend the specific community-change structure as fully as possible. If, on the other hand, the implications are substantially similar—with or without the assumption of a community change—potential confidence in our analysis would be strengthened. As the following discussion reveals, the latter conclusion seems to hold.

6.7.1 **The Structure of Community Change.** Figure 6.6 displays the structural forces that are capable of causing change in the socioeconomic condition of the simulated community.

Some fraction of the addicts in the community commit crime to support their habits. Awareness of crime and fear that it may affect them personally causes some portion of the community's residents to leave.* The fraction of the residents migrating is a function of the difference between the socioeconomic level compatible with the current crime incidence and the current socioeconomic level of the community. The concept of a compatible socio-economic level is based on the premise that it is worth more to an individual to be in a neighborhood that is relatively free of crime. As crime increases, people living in the community no longer find their old neighborhood as attractive as it used to be, and some decide to move to an area with less crime. But outsiders who have been living in areas with a higher crime incidence find the community of reference relatively crime-free and move in, filling the available housing. The new residents are of a lower socioeconomic level and therefore more vulnerable to many social problems, including addiction. This vulnerability leads in time to a larger addict population, which commits significantly more crime. Not only do more of the addicts commit crime to support their habits in a now poorer community, but more crime incidents are needed per addict to attain the same income. The increased crime then further drives down the compatible socioeconomic level. More migration occurs, aggravating the heroin problem and bringing about further community deterioration.

As migration takes place, community structure is weakened.

---

*People move for many reasons other than the incidence of addict-related crime. The present discussion refers only to the portion of out-migration attributable to this source.

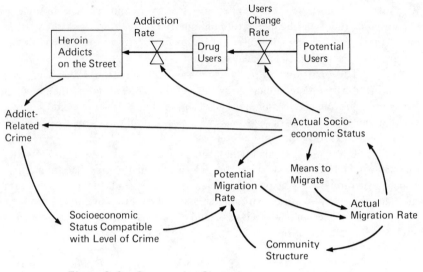

Figure 6-6. Community Change

Community structure is here defined as the sum total of ties people have to a particular community and is stronger among residents who have been living there for a long time. Strong community structure retards migration. When migration is rapid, the average length of stay in the community decreases and community structure declines because residents have less time to establish ties before moving out. Deterioration of community structure permits more rapid migration and further deterioration of structure.

6.7.2 **Simulating Community Change.** A series of simulations was made in which this potential for community change was added to the base model.[41] Broadly speaking, this structural change did not affect model behavior in an essential fashion. As Figure 6.7 indicates (in contrast with Figure 6.1), the two "base" simulations are nearly identical during the first ten years. Evidently the potential for change that was built into the model was not realized up to that time because the forces that promote change, principally addict crime, had not yet built up to sufficient strength.

Beginning at about 120 months, meaningful differences begin to be visible and then continue to grow throughout the remainder of the 300-month period. Crime escalates. The socioeconomic level of the community declines (shown as L in the computer graph). While the number of street addicts is less than in the base run, the grand total of addicts, including especially those in prison, is much higher. Despite the presence of fewer street addicts, the crime rate is up. More money is being spent, the greatest portion of the budget going for police and prisons.

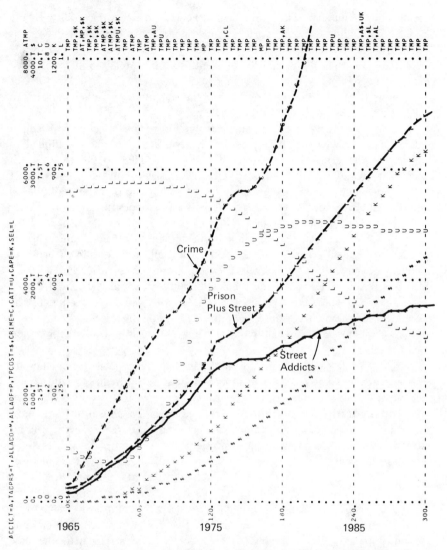

Figure 6-7. Heroin Addiction: Community Change—"Base Case"

These differences may be accounted for on the basis of the causal structures already discussed. As addict-related crime rises in the community-change case, out-migration begins to occur. Population replacement begins to cause a socioeconomic decline. As the problem becomes more visible in the community, residents who have the economic and ethnic means begin to leave the community for homes that they believe to be safer. They are replaced by persons who have left communities they perceived as less desirable than the simulated community. They bring with them a greater vulnerability to the problems of addiction and, perhaps more significantly, they are perceived as alien by older community residents. This may be marked if, as is usually the case, they are ethnically or racially different. Remaining older residents are then more likely to flee. As the rate of migration increases, this has the effect of weakening the bonds that historically held the community together and leads to an acceleration in the growth of the problem.

As this process gets underway the number of crimes committed per addict starts to increase, prompted by the two economic factors alluded to above. As the crime rate rises, more police are added to the force, at an increasing cost. The added police are effective in slackening the growth rate of the street-addict population, primarily by expanding the population of addicts imprisoned. Even so, the growth of the police force does not quite keep pace with the growing number of addicts.

In quantitative terms, adding the potential for community change produced these differences after 25 years. The grand total of addicts increases about 30 percent to a total of 6960. Their distribution is shifted heavily from street to prison. The original run predicted about three addicts on the street for each one in prison (4160 versus 1280). The corresponding ratio under the condition of community change is about 1:1, 3520 on the street against 3440 in prison. Crime rate and program costs have increased greatly to about triple their original values.

While the two runs are similar in their dynamic character, they do differ greatly in some details. The important question is whether the addition of the potential for community change causes us to reach different conclusions about the effectiveness of various coping policies. To answer this we must determine whether or not there are any important differences in the relative effectiveness of the main policy alternatives. Table 6.9 summarizes the results of a series of simulations of a changing community, and compares the outcomes with the results of comparable earlier simulations of a static community.

Strong police.[42] In the original static-community series a strengthened police capability achieved certain clear benefits. In comparative simulations of the community-change case, similar benefits were achieved. Crime rate and prison population are meaningfully reduced in comparison with the base community-change run. The relative impact of stronger police response is greater under community-change conditions. The causes of this are twofold. First, fewer street addicts are available to commit crime, and second, the presence of a stronger police capability reduces the degree of socioeconomic decline to an index value of 0.58 as against 0.37 in the base community-change simulation.

Drug-free rehabilitation.[43] As in the original series, slight but not decisive benefits were derived from this program. In the changing community the total number of addicts is reduced about 2 percent, which was poorer than in the original series in which rehabilitation resulted in about a 7 percent

Table 6-9. Comparative Impact of Policy Options in Static and Changing Communities

		Street Addicts	Addicts in Prison	Addicts on Methadone	Addicts in Heroin Program	Total Involved	Crime (000/ month)	Program Costs ($000/ month)	Socio-Economic Index
Base	—Static Community	4160	1280	—	—	5440	4.9	780	
	—Changing Community	3520	3440	—	—	6960	13.0	2200	0.37
Strong Police	—Static	2720	2080	—	—	4800	3.6	1380	
	—Changing	2720	2800	—	—	5520	6.0	1900	0.58
Drug-free Rehabilitation	—Static	3600	1120	—	—	5360	4.4	920	
	—Changing	3320	2740	—	—	6810	12.0	2110	0.39
Methadone	—Static	2320	640	3200	—	6160	2.7	640	
	—Changing	2400	960	3520	—	6880	4.2	870	0.58
Heroin Maintenance (optimistic assumptions)	—Static	3840	1040	—	4120	9000	1.8	1460	
	—Changing	3560	1400	—	5040	10000	3.6	2120	0.59
Multi-Modal (dissuasive educ., community educ., drug-free rehab., meth.)	—Static	2220	640	340	—	4500	2.7	830	
	—Changing	2060	700	400	—	4870	3.3	970	0.59

reduction in street addicts and an 8 percent reduction in the prison population. A barely detectable improvement in the crime and cost pictures occurs in the changing community. Similarly, this run was characterized by a high degree of socioeconomic decline, to a level of 0.39 compared to 0.37 in the community change base run.

Methadone maintenance.[44] Methadone maintenance, which was a desirable policy in previous runs, is relatively more effective under conditions of a changing community. While the total number of addicts is virtually unchanged from the base community-change run, their location is radically altered for the better—there are 2400 street addicts against 3520. The prison population is dramatically reduced from 3440 to only 960, nearly a fourfold improvement. Moreover, we can infer that the vast majority of those removed from prison are under methadone maintenance.

Other positive outcomes are a threefold crime reduction and a threefold cost saving. The money spent operating a large methadone distribution system was more than compensated by a reduction in police and in prison expenses. Socioeconomic decline was retarded, ending at 0.58 compared to 0.37 in the base case of community change. This factor, of course, contributed to the improved crime picture.

Heroin maintenance.[45] The poor original performance of heroin maintenance was matched or slightly exceeded in this run. The total involved with narcotics is up 50 percent over the community-change base case. While there is a reduction in the number of prisoners, that total number and many thousands more have become heroin-involved and have been inducted into heroin maintenance programs.

The benefits of heroin maintenance are also similar to the original series of runs. As stated above the prison population is down (to 1400 from 3400). Crime is greatly reduced to 3600 incidents per month compared to 13,000. Heroin maintenance adds no dollar cost to the base community change run. Socioeconomic decline is retarded to an endpoint level of 0.59.

Multi-modal programs. For purposes of completeness, several multiprogram runs were made, with results consistent with the single-program outcomes. Some incremental improvements are achieved by adding both dissuasive education and community education to drug-free rehabilitation.[46] For example, socioeconomic decline is held to 0.48 compared to 0.39 in the single-program run.

When still another program component—methadone maintenance—is added, impressive improvement is achieved.[47] Forty percent fewer addicts are on the street at the end of the simulation change than in the base community run. The prison population falls to a mere 700 compared to 3440. The grand totals of people involved with narcotics fall from 6970 to 4870, of whom 2110 are enrolled in methadone maintenance or drug-free programs.

Crime is reduced by a factor of four, which is even better than the results reported above for heroin maintenance. Program costs are less than half of the base changing-community run, because of savings on police and prison budgets.

In general this multiprogram methadone-maintenance dominated scenario performs relatively more favorably than the corresponding static community run. Insofar as the assumptions of this run are more realistic than previous runs—and the authors believe this—two conclusions are warranted. First, a strong multiprogram response, including methadone maintenance, is an effective programmatic approach. Second, it is most beneficial and most cost beneficial in communities with the greatest vulnerability to the heroin problem.

REFERENCES

1. To generate the "pessimistic scenario", the "base case" model listed in the Appendix was modified in the DYNAMO rerun mode by setting the value of the constant term AEC = 10000000. For further information on the use of the DYNAMO compiler-simulator language, see Alexander L. Pugh III, *DYNAMO II User's Manual* (Cambridge: M.I.T. Press, 1973).
2. The "stronger police" simulation was created by setting the constant term AEC = 2 in the DYNAMO rerun mode.
3. See Reference 1 above for "no police" conditions; see Reference 2 for "strong police program". The "base case" discussion in Section 6.1 describes the "typical police program". A "weak police program" was represented by setting AEC = 10.
4. By changing the table function for PASDTB, we simulated the case of no police acting against soft drugs. To do this we set PASDTB = 1,1,1,1,1,1.
5. We set PAAATB = 0,0,0,0,0,0.
6. PAAATB = 1,1,1,1,1,1.
7. See Reference 5.
8. The four lines in Table 6.2, respectively, were generated as follows: (1) AEC = 2 and EPATB = 1, 0.95, 0.925, 0.9, 0.875, 0.85; (2) AEC = 2; (3) AEC = 2 and EPATB = 1, 0.8, 0.7, 0.6, 0.5, 0.4; (4) AEC = 2, EPATB = 1, 0.8, 0.7, 0.6, 0.5, 0.4 and PROPTB = 0.5, 0.55, 0.6, 0.5, 0.45, 0.4.
9. EDUCAT = 1.
10. EDUCAT = 1 and PIEHTB = 0, 0.1, 0.24, 0.32, 0.36, 0.4.
11. EDUCAT = 1, TICP = 1 and AECTB = 1,1,1,1,1,1.
12. Report of the National Commission on Marijuana and Drug Abuse, *Marijuana: A Signal of Misunderstanding* (N. Y.: Signet, 1972), pp. 224–5.
13. EDUCAT = 1 and PIEHTB = 0, −0.05, −0.12, −0.16, −0.18, −0.20.
14. COMEDC = 1.
15. NCCDE reference in Chapter 5.
16. COMEDC = 1 and PAHDTB = 4.5, 3, 2.25, 1.5, 1.2, 0.9, 0.75.

17. "Realistic" assumptions embodied RHBPRG = 1, CMPR = 0.01, and CRR = 0.95; "pessimism" required adding to these changes CLFRAC = 0.2 and ECSTB = 0.01, 0.025, 0.05, 0.15, 0.20; "optimism" modified the "realistic" case by adding CLFRAC = 0.6 and ECSTB = 0.01, 0.10, 0.20, 0.40, 0.55.

18. OCRHBP = 1, CMPR = 0.01, CRR = 0.01, and ORR = 0.95; in-community was simulated using the "realistic" assumptions of Reference 17.

19. AEC = 2, CMPR = 0.1, CRR = 0.95, ORR = 0.01, RHBPRG = 1.

20. CMPR = 0.01, CRR = 0.95, ORR = 0.01, RHBPRG = 1, and AERTB = 1,1,1,1,1,1,1.

21. METHPR = 1, CMPR = 0.95, CRR = 0.01 and ORR = 0.01.

22. Reference 21 plus AEC = 10000000.

23. Reference 21 plus AEC = 2.

24. The "moderate leakage" case is Reference 21; "no leakage" required adding to those changes MTHLKT = 0,0,0,0,0,0,0,0; "large leakage" required Reference 21 plus MTHLKT = 0.4, 0.36, 0.3, 0.24, 0.18, 0.12, 0.08, 0.04.

25. "Moderate susceptibility" is embodied in the Reference 21 conditions; "lower susceptibility" required adding to those assumptions MLFRAC = 0.4 and EMSTB = 0.01, 0.05, 0.1, 0.2, 0.4, 0.4, 0.4; "higher susceptibility" was studied using the Reference 21 conditions plus MLFRAC = 0.9 and EMSTB = 0.01, 0.05, 0.15, 0.3, 0.55, 0.7, 0.8.

26. The "all methadone" case is Reference 21; two-thirds drug-free and one-third methadone requires METHPR = 1, RHBPRG = 1, OCRHBP = 1, CRR = 0.33, ORR = 0.33 and CMPR = 0.33; one-half and one-half is achieved by METHPR = 1, RHBPRG = 1, OCRHBP = 1, CRR = 0.245, ORR = 0.245 and CMPR = 0.50; the one-half drug-free and two-thirds methadone simulation was generated with METHPR = 1, RHBPRG = 1, OCRHBP = 1, CRR = 0.165, ORR = 0.165 and CMPR = 0.66.

27. To illustrate, add AEC = 2 to any of the cases described in Reference 26.

28. HERPRG = 1 and FHMC = 0.5 are used to create the "realistic" situation; HERPRG = 1 provides the "optimistic" run.

29. HERPRG = 1, AEC = 2.

30. HERPRG = 1, AEHPTB = 1,1,1,1,1,1.

31. HERPRG = 1, TIHP = 36.

32. HERPRG = 1, LEAKTB = 0.15, 0.3, 0.6, 0.9, 0.95, 1, 1.

33. RHBPRG = 1, OCRHBP = 1, METHPR = 1, CRR = 0.4, EDUCAT = 1, COMEDC = 1, HERPRG = 1.

34. Reference 33 plus SWA = 1.

35. Reference 34 plus SWD = 1.

36. RHBPRG = 1, OCRHBP = 1, CRR = 0.4, EDUCAT = 1, COMEDC = 1.

37. Reference 36 plus METHPR = 1.

38. Reference 37 plus HERPRG = 1; same as Reference 33.

39. Equations were changed in the basic model to the forms indicated below:

A MSUS.K = (MLFRAC*ADDADP.K-METHDN.K-MMP.K-HERMNT.K)/ ALLADP.K

A HSUS.K = (HLFRAC*ALLADP.K-HERMNT.K)/ALLADP.K

A AAP.K = (HA.K-URA.K*EHA.K-URNA*NADD.K)/URNA

A EHA.K = ADDICT.K-NADD.K+FMMC*METHDN.K+FHMC*HERMNT.K

    Parameters were set as in Reference 33.

40. Reference 39 plus FHMC = 0.5.

41. CSELTB = 0.8, 0.75, 0.70, 0.60, 0.50, 0.35, 0.25, 0.20, 0.20.

42. Reference 41 plus AEC = 2.

43. Reference 41 plus RHBPRG = 1, OCRHBP = 1, CRR = 0.4, ORR = 0.55.

44. Reference 41 plus CRR = 0.001, ORR = 0.001, CMPR = 0.95, METHPR = 1.

45. Reference 41 plus HERPRG = 1.

46. Reference 41 plus Reference 36.

47. Reference 46 plus METHPR = 1.

Chapter Seven

What to Do

Our analysis as presented in the preceding chapters points towards no single simple correction to the problems of the heroin system. Instead it has called attention to a number of causal feedback structures that account for the persistence of these problems. The following "dos" and "bewares" derive from our attempt to answer the question: What role might each of the presently available corrective measures play in achieving the goal of bringing the heroin system under control and managing it?

We have not attempted to be logically exhaustive in answering the question. Instead we have tried to be practical and sensible. The reader may want to know what the model advocates. If so, he will be only partly satisfied, since the model is incapable of creating policy. It is an analytic tool that forces its users to think clearly and comprehensively. In a sense, policy suggestions are merely the convictions of the authors. Our confidence in them is based upon our intensive participation in a series of conversations with the evolving model, which forced us continuously to reevaluate, refine and modify our views.

We do not pretend to speak the last words on this subject. It would be nearer the truth to say that these are among the first words spoken that have been subjected to careful and critical analysis.

7.1 DO

The points of advocacy are discussed in the order of their priority.

7.1.1 A Carefully Managed Police Response Is Essential. The community's natural tendency to alter police resources in response to changing crime rates is functional. The very pessimistic no-police scenario shown in Figure 1.8 is substantially improved by the addition of a moderate police response, as shown in Figure 6.1. While adding police does not solve the problem, it restrains

the growth of the addict population and substantially reduces addict-related crime. A more vigorous police response produces further improvements. However, an overly aggressive police response is hazardous. While an individual community may feel it to be in its best interest to pursue a more vigorous policy than its neighbors, from a societal point of view nothing is gained. Moreover, it is unlikely that any nonimpoverished neighboring community would long tolerate such a situation. In the long run one would expect a competitive escalation in law enforcement budgets in both communities. It is difficult to see benefit for either community in this scenario. In the long run the two communities would be subject to the identical set of system pressures; and for all practical purposes they could be considered a single larger entity, identical in all essentials to the community simulated here.

In the case of adjacent communities of greatly discrepant wealth—say a poor urban neighborhood located at the city line and an affluent suburb just over the line—a more likely scenario is that the addiction problem and its growth would be concentrated in the poor area. Indeed, the dynamics described account for the historical reality in which heroin is endemic to the ghetto. Policy formulation should assure that the phenomena of competitive escalation and exploitation of poor neighborhoods by affluent ones are avoided.

A similar competitive escalation of enforcement penalties can be seen at the state level. Passage of a strict enforcement law in New York in 1974 was followed immediately by demands for similar action in the neighboring states of New Jersey and Massachusetts, prompted by fears of addict in-migration. Lack of uniformity of narcotics enforcement laws contributes to the illusion that enforcement alone constitutes the solution.

We must manage not only the vigor of the police response, but its focus as well. Police efforts should be devoted to reducing both the supply of and the demand for heroin. In our simulations, exclusive concentration of police efforts on either of these two objectives worsens the problem, and at best fails to enhance the results of a balanced police response.

The balance need not extend to police action against marijuana and other, less dangerous drugs. Simulations which increased and decreased police efforts devoted to marijuana were similar to one another. We found no support for intensive enforcement of marijuana laws nor any evidence in support of legalization of marijuana. A case could be made in favor of the status quo in which the possession and sale of marijuana is illegal, but the laws are not strictly enforced. The status quo provides youth with a less harmful medium for the expression of deviance.

7.1.2 **Convince Ourselves that the Addict Is a Victim.** This policy is desirable not only because it is true, but because it helps. The readiness of a community to support any remedial efforts is influenced by its definition of the problem. If the addict is defined solely as a criminal, the community feels justified in forcing him to migrate to another community or in imprisoning him. If the addict is seen as a victim as well as a criminal, community willingness to pay for victim-oriented programs—programs aimed at helping the addict—is increased, as is the actual impact of the helping programs instituted.

In the ordinary course of events in our simulated community, a rising addiction rate and increasing crime are tolerated for a long period before substantial implementation of rehabilitation programs occurs. The community must go through a complex and lengthy natural process of education through frustration and failure in order to change its definition of the problem from a solely criminal one to one that includes a victim component.

When an explicit community education program, aimed at persuading the community of the social-medical nature of the problem is added, remedial action starts sooner and achieves greater effect.[1]

7.1.3 **Continue to Supply Methadone.** Methadone maintenance has one unequivocal advantage over other single-modality treatment approaches: it works. That is, it successfully achieves a limited objective for a significant number of persons.

The simulation displayed in Figure 6.3 indicates the contribution to problem management that can be reasonably expected from a methadone maintenance program. Methadone maintenance coupled with a normal police response results in a marked decrease in the number of street addicts and a comparable reduction in addict-related crimes. However, the maintenance program increases the supply of narcotics, which enables greater numbers to enter the addict pool with the result that over time additional numbers of persons become involved with narcotics. In our judgment the benefits of methadone maintenance in a wide variety of simulations greatly outweigh its negative consequences.

The geographic concentration of addicts and the methadone leakage that accompany operation of a methadone center lead to periodic community reactions against these programs. These pressures need to be resisted, and methadone capacity appropriate to the magnitude of the local addiction problem needs to be maintained.

7.1.4 **Coordinate Treatment and Enforcement Programs.** The combined effects of enforcement and methadone maintenance are greater than either approach by itself. These two types of effort may be mutually facilitating in a community or they may be in conflict. At a local level, instances of cooperation between enforcement officials and treatment personnel (cops and docs) are exceptional. Rivalry between them as to who "owns" the problem and how the problem is to be defined subvert opportunities for effective joint action. Too often the cops see the docs' efforts to rehabilitate as collusion with the "immoral" behavior of the addict-criminal. The docs are suspicious of the cops who are seen as insensitive to the human needs of the addict-victim. The crunch issue dividing them very often is the use to which information will be put.

Docs collect information in the service of treatment and rehabilitation. Cops collect it to aid in apprehension. These goals frequently conflict. When informed of the need to control local heroin availability during a period of rapid growth in methadone maintenance program capacity the typical doctor-administrator will acknowledge that such an effort is desirable, but is reluctant to initiate communication with the police because, as one program director said, "They'll put spies in my program."

The typical policeman is equally unable to initiate communication. He is keenly aware of the difference in frame of reference between him and the doctor and sees no promise in an effort either to affect the other's perception or to alter his own.

The split between the docs and the cops is reflected in and reinforced by the structure and policies of government at all levels. Even when Congress in 1972 sought to devote special effort to drug abuse, it divided responsibility between two Special Action Offices, one devoted to treatment, the other to enforcement. While this differentiation has many advantages, its cost is the difficulty in achieving successful integration of the supply and demand considerations our analysis reveals to be so central to the problem.

7.1.5 **Develop and Use Better Narcotic Antagonists, But Do Not Expect Miracles.** At the time of this writing, evidence suggests that better antagonist agents will soon be developed. In our view, however, the range of applications for any narcotic antagonist agent is limited. As a treatment for an existing case of narcotic dependency, antagonists suffer from the fact that they are not widely acceptable to drug-dependent people and are unlikely to become so.

An antagonist does not reduce the addict's craving for narcotics; it simply renders ingestion ineffective in producing the desired drug effect. Given the availability of alternate modalities, few addicts would accept an antagonist voluntarily. If a commitment to methadone maintenance had not been made, antagonist treatment might have been acceptable to a somewhat larger group. At this juncture a reversal of policy on methadone is not feasible since it would probably create more chaos and uncertainty than is justified.

Involuntary administration of an antagonist as treatment may be possible under certain conditions, such as an alternative to imprisonment. While this would be effective in some cases, in the usual situation it would not be clearly superior to existing alternatives such as methadone maintenance or drug-free rehabilitation. In general, antagonist treatment suffers by comparison to both methadone maintenance and drug-free rehabilitation, because it deprives the person of something without providing any compensation for the deprivation. Methadone maintenance compensates by helping to reduce the desire for heroin. Drug-free programs offer the addict an enhanced sense of his competence and self-esteem.

Powerful incentives exist for the addict to escape from coerced antagonist treatment. He will use his (often considerable) ingenuity to avoid taking the medicine and to discover methods for reducing its efficacy. If these efforts should fail, he may remain bitter, alienated and no less prone to criminal acts as a result of this "treatment".

Two other potential costs of coerced antagonist treatment are an increased death rate from heroin overdose, and an increase in abuse of other drugs. Several cases of overdose have been reported among addicts in experimental antagonist treatment. Apparently these patients took large doses of heroin in an effort to overcome the effects of the antagonists. The risk of subsituting other drugs for heroin is by no means peculiar to antagonist treatment, but the uncompensated deprivation of this modality would tend to increase this risk.

As a preventive agent, a narcotic antagonist, assuming that it had the right characteristics, would be a perfect pharmacological substance. A single dose of such a drug might provide life-long "immunity" to an entire population. Two very great problems remain unsolved. First, universal administration of such a drug would be desirable only if its nonspecific effects were completely innocuous. It would be difficult or impossible to demonstrate this satisfactorily in any short time frame. Second, the inevitable reluctance of many individuals and groups to undergo "innoculation" would be intense and supported by legal precedent. A perfect substance is not a perfect solution.

7.1.6 Make Detoxification Readily Available without Restrictive Conditions to Those Who Want It.

While detoxification is not difficult to achieve, its effects are generally not long-lasting. Some addicts periodically put themselves through a self-imposed detoxification process in order to reduce their drug tolerance to an economically feasible level. Often detoxification programs are used by addicts for the same purpose. In such instances the addict enters the program without motivation for rehabilitation and remains enrolled as long as its suits his covert purpose.

While this is a form of exploitation, as has been claimed by various critics, it seems nevertheless to have constructive consequences for the system we have described. Detoxification alone does not often lead to rehabilitation for the individual addict-victim. It does, however, reduce the amount of time he spends on heroin, the more so the greater the number of times he goes through the process. If we calculated the total number of drug-free or dose-reduced days for the aggregate population under this policy, it would probably be great enough to justify an expansion of detoxification capacity on economic grounds alone.

More important, detoxification may play a role during times of personal crisis in the careers of individual addicts. If, for example, a supply reduction policy were effective, driving up the local street price of heroin, detoxification availability might be successful in ameliorating the expected increase in crime. Whenever system pressures build, detoxification can provide the addict with an alternative to maximally destructive behavior.

7.1.7 **Do Not Supply Heroin.** Heroin maintenance has long been advocated strongly by a minority, impressed with the degree to which present legal restrictions tend to make certain facets of the problem worse. The important question is not whether a heroin maintenance program could work for some, but what would be the balance of costs and risks against benefits of implementing heroin maintenance on a broad scale. The potential benefits of heroin maintenance are unlikely to be greater than methadone maintenance, and the risks appear to be significantly greater.

The principal advantage of methadone as an agent for maintenance is that its pharmacological properties make it more convenient to adminster. It is a longer-lasting narcotic than is heroin. One daily oral dose suffices to eliminate drug craving in most addicts. Several doses of heroin are required to achieve the same effect. A heroin delivery system would require either that enrollees visit a dispensary several times a day, or that large quantities of heroin be entrusted to them. The first course is both cumbersome administratively and destructive of the patients' efforts to avoid a drug-dominated life. The second course risks the possibility that enhanced leakage of the drug will lead to an accelerated growth of the addict population.

A fundamental risk in simultaneously providing methadone and heroin on a large scale is that the greater attractiveness of heroin to many addicts would tend to have adverse effects on methadone enrollments. Many enrollees now apparently choose methadone maintenance as the least among several evils. The risks and pains of attempting to maintain oneself on street heroin become unduly burdensome. The addict then seeks out alternative means of coping with his problem. The present alternatives are methadone and to a lesser extent detoxification. Only after a methadone program demonstrates that it has positive advantages, and after the addict has personally confirmed the hypothesis that supplementary heroin doesn't have the desired effect, does he commit himself to changing his social and vocational orientation.

While it is possible for some addicts on heroin to work toward improved adjustment, it is certainly more difficult than with methadone. The apparent middle road between street heroin and legal methadone would be chosen by many addicts and, because of its greater potential for exploitation and manipulation, as well as its greater logistical difficulties, they would have been deprived of the opportunity of being in a program with greater probability of rehabilitation.

There is no question that there is a strong coercive element in this position. The addict prefers heroin; society prefers methadone. Yet the addict's preference for heroin is probably more cultural in origin than biochemical. Heroin is now the drug of choice, in part, because it is identified with a set of deviant attitudes and behaviors. The process of rehabilitation is more dependent upon the addict's decision to change his life-style and to conform to the dominant culture (give up street life, get a regular job) than to change his drug-related behavior. The fact that there exists both a socially approved drug (methadone) and a forbidden one (heroin) may well be a positive factor in the rehabilitation process.

The argument for heroin maintenance is not, in our view, at all compelling, and the risks of such a course are not imaginary ones. We wonder to what extent the argument stems from the unrealistic wish to be done with the problem at once. The simplistic conclusion that abundant heroin would eliminate crimes committed by addicts is unwarranted. Many addicts have conviction records that predate their addictions. We doubt that the most resistant addicts, for whom heroin maintenance is advocated most strongly, would stop committing crimes without altering their life-style in any appreciable measures. While our present laws have contributed to the growth of the heroin problem, the problem now has a momentum of its own, which we may be able to channel and direct within limits. We have long passed the stage where any simple action now available will fix the situation.

7.1.8   **Don't Expect Too Much from Drug-Free Therapeutic Community Programs.**   Drug-free programs are very helpful to small numbers of addicts, but cannot contribute very much to alleviating the overall heroin problem. To the extent a community is willing to support these programs, addicts seeking rehabilitation will be able to choose between a drug-free route and a substitute drug. We view this choice as desirable in itself. In particular, young addicts should be encouraged toward such an alternative whenever possible.

If adequate funds are available, both methadone and therapeutic community programs should be supported. If lack of funds forces a choice between modalities, methadone clearly is preferable in terms of cost/effectiveness.

7.1.9   **Dissuasive Education Should be Pursued Only with Great Care.**   Evidence in support of dissuasive education is scarce. Since such programs may add to the attractiveness of drugs, we question their value.

7.2   BEWARE

Any set of policies aimed at controlling the heroin system may create unintended and undesired consequences. The cautions listed below apply not only to the positions we have taken but to all policy and program recommendations. They derive from consideration of the important structural features of the heroin system.

7.2.1 **Price Effects.** As we have seen, the price-purity of street heroin may rise and fall as a result of various policies. A change in price tends to increase one or another facet of the heroin problem. Any revision in policy should be evaluated in relation to its probable effects on price. The same would apply to existing policies, which need to be monitored closely and revised as required by the dynamic nature of the system.

7.2.2 **Creating Incentives for Development of a Synthetic Opiate Supply.** If enforcement pressure against the import of heroin grows too intense, the narcotics industry may seek and discover alternate sources of raw materials. A synthetic opiate such as methadone, which could be produced domestically in a widely dispersed production system in large quantity at low price, would constitute an even greater challenge to enforcement efforts. A decisive law enforcement victory in the battle against heroin could lead to a loss of the war against narcotics.

7.2.3 **Creating Incentives for Casual Users to Qualify as Addicts.** This danger is endemic to any narcotic maintenance program. If you give drugs to "addicts," and punish "nonaddicts" for using drugs, the definition of addict becomes a matter of great substance. For example, a youngster whose exposure to heroin has been limited to weekend joy-popping, possessed of only garden-variety poor judgment, might bluff his way into a maintenance program in order to increase his access to narcotics. This risk is heightened if the program permits its enrollees to take supplies home for later use. Several days' methadone supply, even taken orally, and perhaps supplemented by an injection of heroin, might be a superior drug experience and a less expensive one than what he was accustomed to before qualifying as an addict. Following this regimen for any length of time would change the youngster's status from a borderline case to an unequivocal addict status.

7.2.4 **Leakage and Size of Dose Effects.** The amount of methadone that represents a maintenance dose is not free of controversy among experts. This is a significant problem; not because there is anything to be gained by insuring that patients do not derive any pleasure from the maintenance process, but because ambiguity about size of dose and procedural differences between programs provide the opportunity for manipulation and abuse. It is no favor to the patient, whose life-style has been oriented toward manipulation and deceit, to provide him the opportunity to continue to exercise these faculties while in a program, and in the process risk that drugs provided to him may have the effect of increasing the addiction growth rate.

This is one area where the goals of cops and docs appear to be in direct conflict. Program personnal often argue that treatment can only work if a certain degree of trust is eventually placed in the patient. Certainly, as one doc recently commented, "Addicts resent being treated like addicts." It is equally true that docs don't like to be seen as cops. What is needed is to determine objectively what the treatment requirements and leakage risks of a maintenance program really are and to standardize maintenance programs in such a way as to make the best of this trade-off.

7.2.5 **Creating Programs with the Potential for Unlimited Growth.** Those employed in treatment and enforcement depend for their survival upon the continued presence of an addict population. They have an incentive to create clients. While few individual docs or cops probably exploit this situation personally, treatment and enforcement institutions taken as a whole may well function in this way. The present reward system based upon the number of persons treated or apprehended may serve short-term purposes, but in the long run a way will have to be found to phase out existing programs. In principle, this is not difficult to achieve. We need to revise performance indicators. Instead of applauding the number of patients treated or ounces seized, we need to reward on the basis of declining prevalence and declining supply.

In practice this is difficult in the extreme. However, unless a means of accomplishing this is found, the long-run effect of our corrective policies might simply be to institutionalize the problem instead of solving it.

7.2.6 **Tendency for Changes in Public Opinion to Subvert Sustained Efforts.** As our analysis indicates, the time required to impact the problem fundamentally is long. Perhaps five to ten years of sustained effort may be required to achieve modest effects. Policy implementation requires public consent and political support. Both public opinion and political will shift and change over shorter time periods, corresponding to the cycle of U.S. elections.

The press and politicians use the narcotics issue to sell papers and win votes. Unless an informed public is capable of overcoming impatience and waiting longer than it would like, the danger is great that narcotics policies will continue to be adopted and abandoned too quickly to have real effect.

7.2.7 **Panic Response that Leads to Community Change.** Community concern about its narcotics problem is a requirement for implementation of any corrective efforts. However, beyond some optimum degree of concern is the real danger that a panic response, one that overstates the magnitude of the problem, will have negative consequences, triggering the cycle of migration and community change described in Section 6.7.

7.2.8 **Attempting Too Much.** The complex system that constitutes the narcotics problem is only partially understood at this point. As we have seen, it is characterized by a number of interacting causal feedback loops, which are capable of producing numerous counter-intuitive modes of behavior. The danger is that adoption of any extreme policy may unintentionally make the problem worse.

While inaction is not desirable because the problem is real, overreaction in any direction is perilous.

REFERENCES

1. Comparative examples of such simulated scenarios can be generated by changing the following parameters in reruns of the base model:
RHBPRG = 1, OCRHBP = 1, METHPR = 1
Also setting COMEDC = 1 adds the effect of a community education program to the above.

A Comprehensive System Dynamics Model of Heroin and the Community

The following pages present and discuss the simulation model under-lying our analyses and conclusions. The model is presented as a set of sectors involving drug use and addiction, community response to addiction, community change, incarceration, rehabilitation and reentry of addicts, and program costs. Each group of several equations is discussed in terms of its underlying assumptions and implications for model behavior.

EQUATION FORMATS

The model is represented in the DYNAMO simulation language. DYNAMO was developed at M.I.T. by Alexander L. Pugh III as a tool for carrying out what were then called Industrial Dynamics studies. (Application of the methodology to a broad set of social problems later led to the adoption of System Dynamics as the field's title.) DYNAMO has since been extended and improved by Pugh-Roberts Associates, Inc. It is useful to explain DYNAMO's equation formats at this point to help the reader understand the structure of the model and the nature of the assumptions embodied in it.

DYNAMO simulates the behavior of a system over time by com-puting changes that take place over each time interval and "updating" the status of the system to reflect those changes. The updated system becomes the basis for the set of changes to take place over the next time interval. In DYNA-MO's notation, .K refers to the current point in time, .J refers to the previous point in time (one time interval ago) and .L represents the next point in time (one time interval into the future).

Level equations describe the system's state at each point in time. There are two types of levels. One type represents measurable quantities such as addicts, police officers and dollars in a program's budget. Equations for these types of levels take the following form:

L   LEVEL.K = LEVEL.J + (DT) (RATEIN .JK - RATEOUT .JK)

This equation form indicates that a level at the current point in time (.K) is equal to its value at the previous point in time (.J) plus the net change that took place over the past time interval (.JK). Net change is the resultant of flows into and out of the level (there may be a number in each direction) multiplied by the appropriate time interval (DT) used in the simulation. Levels do not change instantaneously, but are subject to rates of change having this cumulative effect over time.

The second type of level equation represents an average of another quantity that serves as a descriptor of the system's state. One use of this type of level equation is to simulate the delay between the time a condition develops in a system and the time it is perceived by decisionmakers and others. Another use is to average a rate of change since rates of change cannot be observed at any one point in time and must be measured by the effect they have over time. This type of level equation has the following forms:

L   LEVEL.K = LEVEL.J + (DT) (1/TA) (QUANT.J - LEVEL.J)

or

L   LEVEL.K = LEVEL.J + (DT) (1/TA) (RATE.JK - LEVEL.J)

These forms indicate that a level of this type at the present point in time is equal to the level at the previous point in time adjusted by any change in its value that has taken place over the last time interval. That change is some fraction (1/TA) of the difference between the value of the quantity or rate of change being averaged and the previous value of the level multiplied by the time interval being used. This averaging process is referred to as exponential smoothing. It causes changes in these levels to occur gradually at a rate determined by the value of TA. In many of the model's equations, this averaging process is represented by the following equivalent shorthand:

LEVEL.K = SMOOTH(QUANT.K, TA)

or

LEVEL.K = SMOOTH(RATE.JK, TA)

Rate equations are based on the state of the system at the current point in time (.K) and indicate rates of change that will occur over the next time interval. These take the following form:

R RATE.KL = f(LEVEL.K, AUX.K)

As indicated, rates in the next time period are functions of level and/or auxiliary variable values at the current point in time.

  Auxiliary variables provide computational linkages between levels and rates of change. They take the following forms:

A AUX.K = f(LEVEL.K, AUX.K)

Auxiliaries are computed at the current point in time from level and other auxiliary values at the current point in time.

  Many of the auxiliary and rate equations in the model are straightforward algebraic expressions and require no explanation. One equation form that appears throughout the model does, however, require some explanation. It is the following:

A(or R) Y.K = TABHL(YTB, X.K, L, H, I)

This type of equation indicates a functional relationship between an independent (X) and dependent variable (Y). L, H, and I describe the low end (L), high end (H), and interval (I) between points in a set of values of the independent variable. YTB is an associated set of values of the dependent variable that correspond to each of the values of the X variable. Thus,

Y.K = TABHL (YTB, X.K, 0, 5, 1)
YTB = 3, 7, 9, 11, 13, 14

would represent the following functional relationship:

X	0	1	2	3	4	5
Y	3	7	9	11	13	14

DYNAMO interpolates when values of the independent variable fall between these discrete values to yield a pseudo-continuous functional relationship. Values of the independent variable falling below or above the L-H range are given the Y values at either end of YTB. Thus, in the example, an X value of 6.5 would be assigned a value of 14, the high-end value of YTB.

  DELAY3 and DLINF3 equation forms indicate the lagging of certain effects by an indicated period of time.

  The DYNAMO processor translates equations of these various types into computer instructions and causes system behavior to be simulated in the stepwise manner described earlier. Computations begin with a set of initial conditions (each level equation must have an initial condition associated with it) and produce rates of change during the first time interval being simulated. System states at the first point in time are then derived from these rates of change and become the basis for computing the next time interval's rates of change. Computations continue in this sequence for the duration of the simulation. DYNAMO's output routines print and plot the values of selected variables over that duration.

The heroin addiction model's equations follow.

User Sector

HEROIN ADDICTION AND THE COMMUNITY
    DEVELOPED BY EINSTEIN COLLEGE OF MEDICINE
        AND PUGH-ROBERTS ASSOCIATES, INC.

YOUPOP.K=PU.K+USERS.K+ALLADP.K   1, A
    YOUPOP — YOUTH POPULATION
    PU   — POTENTIAL USERS
    USERS — USERS
    ALLADP — ALL ADDICTS, INCL. MAINT. PROG.

PU.K=PU.J+ (DT) (YPCR.JK–UCR.JK+UDO.JK)   2, L
PU=(IYPOP) (.8)   2.1, N
IYPOP=(.3) (IPOP)   2.2, N
IPOP=170E3   2.3, C
    PU   — POTENTIAL USERS
    YPCR   — YOUTH POPULATION CHANGE RATE
    UCR   — USER CHANGE RATE
    UDO   — USER DROPOUT
    IYPOP   — INITIAL YOUTH POPULATION
    IPOP   — INITIAL POPULATION

YPCR.KL=POPGRO   3, R
POPGRO=0   3.1, C
    YPCR   — YOUTH POPULATION CHANGE RATE
    POPGRO — POPULATION GROWTH/MO.

The youthful population in the community is made up of three groups:

1. *Potential Users* (PU)–all people between the ages of ten and thirty who do not currently use drugs;
2. *Users*–people who use drugs other than heroin or who use heroin on a less-than-daily basis; and
3. *Addicts* (ALLADP)–including those on the street, in prison, and in various treatment programs.

The size of the potential user group changes as the community's youthful population becomes larger or smaller (YPCR), declines as potential users become users (UCR), and grows as users stop using drugs and drop out of the user group (UDO). Potential users are initially assumed to be 80 percent of the community's youthful population. The youthful population—people between ten and thirty—comprises roughly 30 percent of the community's total population of 170,000, or about 50,000. The youthful population remains the same during the simulations (YPCR = POPGRO = 0) to reflect the actual situation in the community being modelled.

UCR.KL=((YOUPOP.K*PMUP.K)-(USERS.K+ALLADP.K))/TGMP.K   4, R
    UCR   — USER CHANGE RATE
    YOUPOP — YOUTH POPULATION
    PMUP   — POTEN. MAXIMUM USER PERCENT
    USERS — USERS
    ALLADP — ALL ADDICTS, INCL. MAINT. PROG.
    TGMP   — TIME TO GROW TO MAXIMUM PERCENT

PMUP.K=(SPEUSE.K) (ADU.K) (EDF.K) (PAAU.K)   5, A
    PMUP   — POTEN. MAXIMUM USER PERCENT
    SPEUSE — SOCIAL POSITION EFFECT ON USE
    ADU   — APPEAL OF DRUG USAGE
    EDF   — EDUCATION FACTOR
    PAAU   — POLICE ACTION AGAINST USERS

The user change rate causes the user population to grow toward the number of users that might be expected in the community, based on prevailing socioeconomic, cultural and other environmental conditions. The expected number of users is expressed as the product of an expected user percentage (PMUP) and the youthful population. Addicts are assumed to be a subset of users for the purposes of this calculation. The rate increases as the difference between expected and actual numbers of users becomes larger and decreases toward zero as the actual value comes into line with the expected. The time over which the actual user population grows to its expected value (TGMP) is a function of soft-drug availability in the community.

The potential maximum user percentage (PMUP) is a function of four factors:

1. Social Position Effect (SPEUSE) reflecting the socioeconomic character of the community;
2. Appeal of Drug Usage (ADU) reflecting various cultural aspects of drug use;
3. Education Factor (EDF) representing the impact of drug education on drug use; and

4. Police Action Against Users (PAAU) representing the impact of enforcement efforts.

Of these four, the social position and appeal factors are assumed to have a dominant effect while the other two have only marginal effects.

```
SPEUSE.K=TABLE (SPEUTB,FDL.K,0,1,.2)                              6, A
SPEUTB=.25,.2,.25,.3,.37,.4                                       6.1, T
      SPEUSE  — SOCIAL POSITION EFFECT ON USE
      SPEUTB  — SOCIAL POSITION EFFECT ON USE TABLE
      FDL     — FUTILITY-DESPAIR LEVEL

ADU.K=TABHL (ADUTB,DAC.K/YOUPOP.K,0,1,.2)                         7, A
ADUTB=1,1.2,1.6,2,2.4,2.5                                         7.1, T
      ADU     — APPEAL OF DRUG USAGE
      ADUTB   — APPEAL OF DRUG USAGE TABLE
      DAC     — DRUG ASSOCIATED CULTURE
      YOUPOP  — YOUTH POPULATION
TGMP.K=(BTC) (SDAF.K)                                             8, A
BTC=15                                                           8.1, C
      TGMP    — TIME TO GROW TO MAXIMUM PERCENT
      BTC     — BASE TIME CONSTANT
      SDAF    — SOFT DRUG AVAIL. FACTOR
```

The social position effect is a function of the community's futility despair level (FDL) characteristic of its socioeconomic status. A very wealthy community with a futility despair level close to zero is assumed to have 25 percent of its youthful population involved in drug use solely as a function of its futility despair level (first term in table SPEUTB). A less wealthy community would have a 20 percent involvement (reflecting a "boredom" factor in the very wealthy community) and progressively poorer communities (with futility despair levels approaching 1) have up to a 40 percent involvement in drug use solely as a function of futility despair levels (the latter terms in SPEUTB).

The expected or potential user percentage is principally determined by multiplying SPEUSE by a factor (ADU) representing the cultural impact of drug use. Appeal of drug usage is a function of both the number of users in a community and the impact those users have had on the perceived attractiveness of drug use. The drug-associated culture term is expressed in user equivalents and represents the actual number of users in the community inflated by a factor (explained later) reflecting the impact on youth culture of the use of drugs by that many individuals. As this number of user equivalents goes from zero toward a level equaling the entire youthful population, the appeal of drug usage moves (in ADUTB) from having no effect (a multiplier of 1) to having an effect that multiplies the potential number of users 2.5 times. In a wealthier, low futility despair community, this unrealistically high an appeal would

produce a user group encompassing 62.5 percent of the youthful population
(0.25 X 2.5). A community with a high futility despair level and an unrealistically high drug appeal multiplier would have its entire youthful population
ultimately included in the user group.

The social position and appeal factors primarily determine the level
to which a community's user population will grow. However, the time over
which that growth takes place (TGMP) is assumed to be a function of soft-drug
availability. An abundant or moderately good supply of soft drugs in the community causes that time to be a little less than or equal to a base value of 15
months, while a relatively scarce supply lengthens that time to twice the base, or
30 months.

```
DAC.K=DAC.J+(DT) (CSR.JK)                                    9, L
DAC=CRU                                                      9.1, N
        DAC    — DRUG ASSOCIATED CULTURE
        CSR    — CULTURE SPREAD RATE
        CRU    — CULTURE RELATED USAGE


CSR.KL=(CRU.K–DAC.K)/TCS                                     10, R
TCS=12                                                       10.1, C
        CSR    — CULTURE SPREAD RATE
        CRU    — CULTURE RELATED USAGE
        DAC    — DRUG ASSOCIATED CULTURE
        TCS    — TIME FOR CULTURE SPREAD


CRU.K=(USERS.K) (CMF.K)                                      11, A
        CRU    — CULTURE RELATED USAGE
        USERS  — USERS
        CMF    — CULTURE MULTIPLIER FACTOR


CMF.K=TABHL (CMFTB,USERS.K/YOUPOP.K,0,.8,.1)                 12, A
CMFTB=1,1.2,1.8,2.4,3,3.4,3.7,3.9,4                          12.1, T
        CMF    — CULTURE MULTIPLIER FACTOR
        CMFTB  — CULTURE MULTIPLIER FACTOR TAB
        USERS  — USERS
        YOUPOP — YOUTH POPULATION
```

As indicated above, the level of drug-associated culture is expressed
in user equivalents and reflects amplification of an actual number of users based
on their expected cultural impact. This level changes at a rate (CSR) that adjusts
drug-associated culture toward a quantity of culture-related usage (CRU) based
on the current number of users and the value of a culture multiplier factor
(CMF). This adjustment is assumed to take place over a period of twelve months
(TCS), representing the lag between the time a change takes place in usage levels
and the time new usage patterns are perceived as cultural phenomena. The
culture multiplier factor causes users to have an impact on the appeal of drug

usage that grows at a greater rate than the number of users itself. This factor begins to have a pronounced amplifying effect when users make up more than 10 percent of the youthful population (shown in CMFTB) and reaches a fourfold multiplicative effect when 80 percent of the youthful population are users. The most important effect of this factor is to make it seem as if, in terms of appeal, "everyone is using drugs", when only 40 percent of the youthful population is actually using drugs (0.4 × 3.0 = 1.2).

```
SDAF.K=TABHL (SDAFTB,SDA.K/USERS.K,2,4,.5)                    13, A
SDAFTB=2,1.5,1,.9,.8                                         13.1, T
      SDAF    — SOFT DRUG AVAIL. FACTOR
      SDAFTB  — SOFT DRUG AVAIL. FACTOR TABLE
      SDA     — SOFT DRUG AVAILABILITY
      USERS   — USERS


SDA.K=SDA.J+(DT) (SDSGR.JK)                                   14, L
SDA=(USERS) (UN)                                            14.1, N
      SDA     — SOFT DRUG AVAILABILITY
      SDSGR   — S D SUPPLY GROWTH RATE
      USERS   — USERS
      UN      — USER NEEDS


SDSGR.KL=( (USERS.K*UN*PASD.K)-SDA.K)/TGSDS                   15, R
UN=4                                                        15.1, C
TGSDS=6                                                     15.2, C
      SDSGR   — S D SUPPLY GROWTH RATE
      USERS   — USERS
      UN      — USER NEEDS
      PASD    — POLICE ACTION ON S D
      SDA     — SOFT DRUG AVAILABILITY
      TGSDS   — TIME FOR GROWTH OF S D SUPPLY
```

As described above, the soft-drug availability factor causes a reduction in the user population's growth rate in situations of extreme scarcity. For purposes of this formulation, "normal" usage is set arbitrarily at three units of soft drugs per user per month. When only half that is available, expected growth in the user population takes twice as long to occur (because existing users are much less willing to share their drugs with friends interested in becoming users, and dealers only have enough for their steady customers). When four units (instead of three) are available, new users can find drugs easily. Under these conditions, expected growth in the user population is assumed to take place over only twelve months. Soft-drug availability changes at a rate (SDSGR) determined by changes in the number of users (representing demand in the soft-drug market), and the impact of police action against soft drugs. Actual soft-drug availability adjusts to the level determined by demand and police action over a period of six months (TGSDS). In the main this represents the amount of time necessary to establish distribution channels necessary for serving new users. Soft-drug availability is initially assumed (in equation 14.1, N) to be equal to four units per user per month.

PASD.K=TABHL (PASDTB,PEDSD.K/USERS.K,0,.01,.002)   16, A
PASDTB=1,.95,.9,.86,.82,.8   16.1, T
     PASD   – POLICE ACTION ON S D
     PASDTB – PASD TABLE
     PEDSD – POLICE EFFORT DIRECTED AT SOFT DRUGS
     USERS – USERS

PAAU.K=PASD.K   17, A
     PAAU   – POLICE ACTION AGAINST USERS
     PASD   – POLICE ACTION ON S D

PEDSD.K=(CAPF.K) (FDSD.K)   18, A
     PEDSD – POLICE EFFORT DIRECTED AT SOFT DRUGS
     CAPE   – CUMULATIVE ADDITIONAL POLICE EFFORT
     FDSD   – FRACTION OF EFFORT DIRECTED AT SOFT DRUGS

EDSD.K=(1–PAAA.K) (SDE.K)   19, A
     FDSD   – FRACTION OF EFFORT DIRECTED AT SOFT DRUGS
     PAAA   – POLICE ACTION AGAINST ADDICTS
     SDE   – SOFT DRUG EFFORT OF POLICE

SDE.K=TABHL (SDETB,CATT.K,0,1,.2)   20, A
SDETB=.5,.5,.5,.5,.5,.5   20.1, T
     SDE   – SOFT DRUG EFFORT OF POLICE
     SDETB – SOFT DRUG EFFORT TABLE
     CATT   – COMMUNITY ATTITUDE

The extent to which police action against soft drugs can reduce soft-drug supplies is represented as a function of the ratio of police effort directed at soft drugs (PEDSD) (expressed in man-equivalents) to the number of users in the community. If the number of police officers working against the supply of soft drugs is miniscule compared to the number of users, the police are assumed to have practically no effect. At the other extreme—one officer for every hundred users (a relatively massive police presence)—police effort has the effect of reducing soft-drug supplies by only 20 percent (the 0.8 in PASDTB). This reflects the difficulty of detecting and seizing large quantities of soft drugs.

Police action against users (PAAU) is assumed to be equivalent to the effort that is directed against soft-drug supply. Police effort directed at soft drugs (PEDSD) is a fraction of the cumulative additional police effort (CAPE) directed at all aspects of heroin and soft-drug use, and is part of the residual after officers have been allocated to direct action against addicts [thus the (1–PAAA) term in equation 19]. The fraction of this residual effort that is directed at soft drugs as opposed to heroin (SDE) is assumed to be a function of community attitudes toward (or definition of) the drug problem. A more medical rather than criminal problem definition (CATT near 1) causes a larger fraction of the total residual effort directed at supply to be aimed at heroin. For simplicity's sake, though, a 50–50 split between effort directed at heroin and soft drugs is assumed in most of the simulations.

```
EDF.K=1-(PIES.K) (CF.K)                                        21, A
     EDF     — EDUCATION FACTOR
     PIES    — POTEN IMPCT OF EDUC ON SD
     CF      — CREDIBILITY FACTOR


PIES.K=TABHL (PIESTB,EDEF.K/EDUNED.K,0,1,.2)                   22, A
PIESTB=0,0,.01,.03,.05,.06                                     22.1, T
     PIES    — POTEN IMPCT OF EDUC ON SD
     PIESTB  — POTENTIAL IMPACT OF EDUCATION TABLE
     EDEF    — EDUCATION EFFORT
     EDUNED  — EDUCATION NEEDED


CF.K=TABHL (CFTB,CEDEF.K/EDEF.K,0,1,.2)                        23, A
CFTB=0,0,0,.5,.8,1                                             23.1, T
     CF      — CREDIBILITY FACTOR
     CFTB    — EDUCATIONAL CREDIBILITY FACTOR TABLE
     CEDEF   — CREDIBLE EDUCATION EFFORT
     EDEF    — EDUCATION EFFORT
```

The model assumes a minimal impact, at best, of education on soft-drug use (EDF). The potential impact educational programs can have on soft-drug use (PIES) is assumed to be a function of the adequacy of budgeted educational programs (EDEF, expressed in dollars), given the community's need for educational programs (EDUNED, expressed in dollars, as the product of users and potential users in the youthful population and the cost of an adequate program for a member of each group). Even when the budgeted effort completely satisfies this computed need, it can only effect a 6 percent reduction (PIESTB) in the number of users. This small impact is reduced even further if a substantial number of the educational programs are not credible and use scare tactics rather than an objective examination of drug use. This credibility factor (CF) is a function of the fraction of a community's total budget for drug education devoted to credible programs (CEDEF/EDEF). It causes the impact of education to be halved when that fraction is equal to 0.6 (from CFTB), and practically eliminates any impact at all when the fraction has a lower value.

```
SDAEDO.K=TABHL (SDDOTB,SDA.K/USERS.K,2,4,.5)                   25, A
SDDOTB=2,1.8,1.5,1.2,1                                         25.1, T
     SDAEDO — SOFT DRUG AVAILABILITY EFFECT ON DROPOUT
     SDDOTB — SOFT DRUG DROPOUT TABLE
     SDA    — SOFT DRUG AVAILABILITY
     USERS  — USERS
```

EDEDO.K=1+(PIES.K) (CF.K)   26, A
    EDEDO   — EDUCATION EFFECT ON DROPOUT
    PIES   — POTEN IMPCT OF EDUC ON SD
    CF   — CREDIBILITY FACTOR

UDO.KL=(USERS.K) (NUDO) (SDAEDO.K) (EDEDO.K)   24, R
NUDO=.01   24.1, C
    UDO   — USER DROPOUT
    USERS   — USERS
    NUDO   — NORMAL USER DROPOUT/MO.
    SDAEDO — SOFT DRUG AVAILABILITY EFFECT ON DROPOUT
    EDEDO — EDUCATION EFFECT ON DROPOUT

      At least 1 percent of the user group is assumed to drop out each month (NUDO). This represents the people who simply become tired of using drugs and halt their use, at least temporarily. The dropout rate (UDO) may be as much as double this number if soft drugs are quite scarce (as indicated by SDAEDO). Drug education can also have a minor effect on the dropout rate, with up to a 6 percent increase if budgeted programs completely satisfy the community's needs and are substantially credible.

USERS.K=USERS.J+(DT) (UCR.JK–AR.JK–UDO.JK)   27, L
USERS=(.2) (IYPOP)   27.1, N
    USERS — USERS
    UCR   — USER CHANGE RATE
    AR   — ADDICTION RATE
    UDO   — USER DROPOUT
    IYPOP — INITIAL YOUTH POPULATION

      The size of the user population at the beginning of each month is equal to the number of users at the beginning of the previous month plus the number of people who became users during the previous month minus the number of people who became addicts and the number that dropped out during that month. Users are assumed to comprise 20 percent of the youthful population at the beginning of each simulation.

Addict Sector

AR .KL=(YOUPOP .K*PMAP .K–ALLADP .K)/TGMPA .K   28, R
    AR   — ADDICTION RATE
    YOUPOP — YOUTH POPULATION
    PMAP   — POTL MAX ADDICT PRCT
    ALLADP — ALL ADDICTS, INCL. MAINT. PROG.
    TGMPA — TIME TO GROW TO MAXIMUM PERCENT OF ADDICTS

```
TADPRS.K=ADDICT.K+PRISON.K                                              29, A
     TADPRS  — TOTAL ADDICTS IN PRISON AND ON STREET
     ADDICT  — ADDICTS
     PRISON  — PRISON ADDICTS


ALLADD.K=TADPRS.K+ADDINP.K                                              30, A
     ALLADD  — ALL ADDICTS
     TADPRS  — TOTAL ADDICTS IN PRISON AND ON STREET
     ADDINP  — ADDICTS IN TREATMENT PROGRAMS


ADDINP.K=COMRHB.K+RBOCOM.K+METHDN.K+HERMNT.K+ANTAG.K                    31, A
     +DETOX.K+REENT.K
     ADDINP  — ADDICTS IN TREATMENT PROGRAMS
     COMRHB  — COMMUNITY REHABILITATION
     RBOCOM  — ADDICTS IN REHABILITATION OUTSIDE THE
                  COMMUNITY
     METHDN  — ADDICTS IN METHADONE PROGRAMS
     HERMNT  — ADDICTS IN HER MAINT
     ANTAG   — ADDICTS IN ANTAGONIST PROGRAMS
     DETOX   — ADDICTS IN DETOX PROGRAM
     REENT   — ADDICTS IN RE-ENTRY PROCESS


ADDTMP.K=ADDINP.K+MMP.K                                                 32, A
     ADDTMP  — ADDICTS IN TREATMENT AND MAIN PROG
     ADDINP  — ADDICTS IN TREATMENT PROGRAMS
     MMP     — EX-ADDICTS IN METHADONE MAINTENANCE PROG
ALLADP.K=ALLADD.K+MMP.K                                                 33, A
     ALLADP  — ALL ADDICTS, INCL. MAINT. PROG.
     ALLADD  — ALL ADDICTS
     MMP     — EX-ADDICTS IN METHADONE MAINTENANCE PROG
```

The rate at which people become addicts is formulated in a manner similar to the user change rate discussed earlier. The number of addicts that can be expected in a community, based on prevailing conditions, is computed as a product of the youthful population and the percentage of the population expected to be addicts (**PMAP**). This formulation of the rate causes the actual number of addicts in the community (including those currently in prisons or in programs) to grow toward this expected number at a decreasing rate as actual approaches expected. The time over which this adjustment takes place (**TGMPA**) is similarly affected by the availability of heroin in the community.

Equations 29–33 shown above aggregate various addict sub-populations that are used in a number of different model sectors.

```
PMAP.K=PMAP.J+(DT) (1/TCPA) (TMAP.J–PMAP.J)                             34, L
PMAP=.003                                                              34.1, N
TCPA=24                                                                34.2, C
     PMAP    — POTL MAX ADDICT PRCT
     TCPA    — TIME FOR CHANGING POTL ADDICTS
     TMAP    — TARGET MAXIMUM ADDICT PERCENTAGE
```

```
TMAP.K=(FDEADD.K) (AH.K) (EDFH.K) (SDAFH.K) (SDEUBA.K)          35, A
   (SREA.K) (PDEA.K) (PAH.K)
      TMAP     — TARGET MAXIMUM ADDICT PERCENTAGE
      FDEADD  — FUTILITY-DESPAIR EFFECT
      AH       — ATTRACTIVENESS OF HEROIN
      EDFH     — EDUCATION FACTOR FOR HEROIN
      SDAFH    — S D AVAILABILITY ON H
      SDEUBA  — SOCIAL DISTANCE EFFECT ON USERS BECOMING
                   ADDICTS
      SREA     — SUCCESSFUL REHAB EFFECT ON ADDICT
      PDEA     — POLICE DETERRENT EFFCT
      PAH      — PRICE ATTRACTIVENESS OF HEROIN
```

The percentage of a community's population expected to be addicted (PMAP) lags behind changes in conditions responsible for that addiction by a period of 24 months (TCPA). Adjustment of PMAP to changing conditions is accomplished by equation 34. Addicts are assumed initially to comprise 0.3 percent of the youthful population.

As with the percentage of the youthful population in the user group, the addict percentage is principally determined by a futility-despair effect (FDEADD) and a cultural appeal factor (AH). Several other factors have effects on the addict percentage including:

1. an Education Factor (EDFH),
2. a Soft Drug Availability Factor (SDAFH),
3. a Social Distance Effect (SDEUBA),
4. a Success of Rehabilitation Effect (SREA),
5. a Police Deterrent Effect (PDEA),
6. and an effect of the Price Attractiveness of Heroin (PAH).

```
FDEADD.K=TABLE (FDETB,FDL.K,0,1,.2)                             36, A
FDETB=.01,.0125,.0175,.0225,.0275,.03                          36.1, T
      FDEADD  — FUTILITY-DESPAIR EFFECT
      FDETB    — FUTILITY-DESPAIR EFF TAB
      FDL      — FUTILITY-DESPAIR LEVEL


AH.K=( (AW*AEH.K)+ (DACW*CEH.K) )+1                             37, A
      AH       — ATTRACTIVENESS OF HEROIN
      AW       — ADDICT WEIGHT
      AEH      — ADDICT EFFECT ON H
      DACW     — DRUG CULTURE WEIGHT
      CEH      — CULTURE EFFECT


AEH.K=TABHL (AEHTB,ALLADD.K/YOUPOP.K,0,.05,.01)                 38, A
AEHTB=0, 1.2,2.4,3.2,3.6,4                                     38.1, T
AW=.5                                                          38.2, C
      AEH      — ADDICT EFFECT ON H
      AEHTB    — ATTRACTIVENESS EFFECT TAB
```

```
        ALLADD  −  ALL ADDICTS
        YOUPOP  −  YOUTH POPULATION
        AW       −  ADDICT WEIGHT
```

CEH.K=TABHL (CEHTB,DAC.K/YOUPOP.K,0,1,.1)   39, A
CEHTB=0,.6,1.2,1.8,2.6,3.6,4.6,5.4,6,6.4,6.8   39.1, T
DACW=.5   39.2, C

```
        CEH      −  CULTURE EFFECT
        CEHTB    −  CULTURE EFF TAB
        DAC      −  DRUG ASSOCIATED CULTURE
        YOUPOP   −  YOUTH POPULATION
        DACW     −  DRUG CULTURE WEIGHT
```

Futility-despair is modeled as having a greater range of effect upon heroin addiction than upon soft-drug usage. While involvement in drug use varied from 20 percent to 40 percent over the range of socioeconomic levels (a factor of 2), involvement in addiction varies over a factor of 3, from 1 percent to 3 percent (in FDETB), going from the lowest to highest socio-economic levels.

The futility-despair effect is multiplied by an appeal factor that determines the percentage of a community's youths that are likely to become addicts. The appeal factor (AH) has two components. One derives from the mere presence of addicts in a community (AEH) and the effect they have in introducing new people to heroin. This factor has its highest value of 4 (in AEHTB) when 5 percent or more of a community's youths are addicted. The other component derives from the presence of a particular level of drug-associated culture (CEH) created by some number of users and addicts and the process of cultural amplification described earlier. High levels of drug associated culture are likely to make experimentation with heroin more acceptable and cause more people to become involved. When the amplified number of user-equivalents represented by drug-associated culture is greater than or equal to the community's youthful population, this factor has its maximum value of 6.8 (in CEHTB).

Each of the factors is given an equal weight and is multiplied by 0.5 in computing AH. The sum of these two weighted factors is added to 1 so that AH has, at the very least, a neutral effect. In communities with extremely serious drug problems, AH has a maximum multiplicative effect of $[1 + (4)(0.5) + (6.8)(0.5)]$, or 6.4.

EDFH.K=1−(PIEH.K) (CF.K)   40, A

```
        EDFH     −  EDUCATION FACTOR FOR HEROIN
        PIEH     −  POTEN. IMPACT OF EDUC.
        CF       −  CREDIBILITY FACTOR
```

PIEH.K=TABHL (PIEHTB,EDEF.K/EDUNED.K,0,1,.2)   41, A
PIEHTB=0,.05,.12,.16,.18,.2   41.1, T

```
PIEH      — POTEN. IMPACT OF EDUC.
PIEHTB    — POTENTIAL IMPACT OF EDUCATION TABLE
EDEF      — EDUCATION EFFORT
EDUNED    — EDUCATION NEEDED
```

```
SDAFH.K=TABHL (SDHTB,SDA.K/USERS.K,2,4,.5)                    42, A
SDHTB=1.2,1.1,1,.95,.9                                       42.1, T
    SDAFH   — S D AVAILABILITY ON H
    SDHTB   — S D AVAILABILITY TABLE
    SDA     — SOFT DRUG AVAILABILITY
    USERS   — USERS
```

```
SDEUBA.K=TABHL (UBATB,PHE.K,.5,1,.1)                         43, A
UBATB=1,1.02,1.05,1.1,1.15,1.2                               43.1, T
    SDEUBA  — SOCIAL DISTANCE EFFECT ON USERS BECOMING
              ADDICTS
    UBATB   — USERS BECOMING ADDICTS TABLE
    PHE     — POLICE HARASSMENT EFF.
```

The impact of drug education on addiction (EDFH) operates in the same manner as its impact on soft-drug use. Impact is a function of the adequacy of budgeted education programs (EDEF) given the computed need (EDUNED) (also expressed in dollars) and the same credibility factor described earlier (CF). An educational effort that fully satisfies the community's need and is substantially credible is assumed to effect a 20 percent reduction in the size of the addict population (in PIEHTB), all other things held equal. This is a much greater impact than is assumed for soft drugs, but still reflects pessimism about the ultimate impact education programs can have by themselves.

Poor availability of soft drugs is seen as a factor (SDAFH) that can make heroin relatively more attractive. For extremely low supply levels, in which only half the desired amount of soft drugs is available, a 20 percent increase is assumed in the size of the potential addict population (in SDHTB). When a fully adequate supply is available, a 10 percent reduction in that population is assumed.

Another factor captures the effect of society's designation of heroin addiction as a highly deviant activity on the appeal of addiction to youths seeking outlets for rebellious, antisocial tendencies. This factor, referred to in Chapter 3 as an aspect of psychopathology and in equation 43 as the social distance effect (SDEUBA), is assumed to make a greater contribution to heroin's appeal as the community's actions against addicts are intensified. The police harassment effect (PHE), a derivative of the average rate at which street addicts are arrested, serves as a measure of the community's negative reaction to addiction. When the harassment effect has a value of 1—equivalent to 10 percent of the street addicts being arrested each month—this factor causes a 20 percent increase in the community's addict population. The effect of this factor is balanced by a police deterrent effect described later.

SREA.K=TABHL (SREATB,CESR.K,0,1,.2)   44, A
SREATB=1,1.02,1.06,1.12,1.18,1.2   44.1, T
    SREA   – SUCCESSFUL REHAB EFFECT ON ADDICT
    SREATB – SUCCESSFUL REHAB EFFEC TAB
    CESR   – COLL EFF OF SUCC

CESR.K=CRSF .K*CRR+ORSF .K*ORR+MPSF .K*CMPR+HPSF .K*CHPR   45, A
    CESR   – COLL EFF OF SUCC
    CRSF   – COMMUNITY REHABILITATION SUCCESS FACTOR
    CRR   – COMMUNITY REHABILITATION RESPONSIBILITY
    ORSF   – OUTSIDE REHABILITATION SUCCESS FACTOR
    ORR   – OUTSIDE REHAB RESPONSIBILITY
    MPSF   – METHADONE PROGRAM SUCCESS FACTOR
    CMPR – COMMUNITY METHADONE PROGRAM RESPONSIBILITY
    HPSF   – HEROIN MAINTENANCE PROGRAM SUCCESS FACTOR
    CHPR   – COMMUNITY HEROIN PROGRAM RESPONSIBILITY

CRSF.K=TABHL (RSTB,FTBRC.K*COMRHB.K/ALLADP.K,0,.125,.025)   46, A
RSTB=0,.1,.3,.6,.9,1   46.1, T
    CRSF   – COMMUNITY REHABILITATION SUCCESS FACTOR
    RSTB   – REHABILITATION SUCCESS TABLE
    FTBRC – FRACT TO BE REHABILITATED IN COMMUNITY
    COMRHB – COMMUNITY REHABILITATION
    ALLADP – ALL ADDICTS, INCL. MAINT. PROG.

ORSF.K=TABHL(RSTB,FTBRO.K*RBOCOM.K/ALLADP.K,0,.125,.025)   47, A
    ORSF   – OUTSIDE REHABILITATION SUCCESS FACTOR
    RSTB   – REHABILITATION SUCCESS TABLE
    FTBRO – FRACTION TO BE REHABILITATED OUTSIDE
    RBOCOM – ADDICTS IN REHABILITATION OUTSIDE THE
             COMMUNITY
    ALLADP – ALL ADDICTS, INCL. MAINT. PROG.

MPSF.K=TABHL(RSTB,METHDN.K*(1-FTDOM.K)/ALLADP.K,0,.25,.05)   48, A
    MPSF   – METHADONE PROGRAM SUCCESS FACTOR
    RSTB   – REHABILITATION SUCCESS TABLE
    METHDN – ADDICTS IN METHADONE PROGRAMS
    FTDOM – FRACTION TO DROP OUT OF METHADONE PROGRAMS
    ALLADP – ALL ADDICTS, INCL. MAINT. PROG.

HPSF.K=TABHL (RSTB,HERMNT.K*(1-FTDOH.K)/ALLADP.K,0,.25,.05)   49, A
    HPSF   – HEROIN MAINTENANCE PROGRAM SUCCESS FACTOR
    RSTB   – REHABILITATION SUCCESS TABLE
    HERMNT – ADDICTS IN HER MAINT
    FTDOH – FRACTION TO DROP OUT OF HEROIN PROGRAMS
    ALLADP – ALL ADDICTS, INCL. MAINT. PROG.

       The success of rehabilitation effect on addiction (SREA) is a
function of the collective success of rehabilitation programs operating in the

community (CESR). This collective effect is the sum of success effects for individual programs weighted by the fraction of the addict population that each program is aimed at rehabilitating. Each of the individual success factors is based on the fraction of the addicts enrolled in a program that are rehabilitated successfully. The relationships are the following:

1. When the fraction of addicts to be rehabilitated in community rehabilitation drug-free programs is 12.5% or greater (the number of addicts in this category being the product of a fraction to be rehabilitated successfully (FTBRC) and number of addicts in community programs (COMRHB)), this success factor (CRSF) has its maximum value of one (from RSTB).

2. The outside-of-community rehabilitation success factor (ORSF) is determined in a manner identical to CRSF.

3. When the fraction of addicts successfully maintained in methadone programs [the product of the number of addicts in methadone programs (METHDN) and one minus the fraction to drop out (1 - FTDOM)] is greater than or equal to 25% of the total addict population, this success factor (MPSF) has its maximum value of one (again from RSTB).

4. The heroin maintenance program success factor (HPSF) is determined in a manner identical to MPSF.

The closer each of these individual factors is to 1, the closer to 1 is CESR. At its maximum value of 1, this collective effect of successful rehabilitation causes the addict population to be 20 percent larger (from SREATB) because addiction is not as threatening as when it appears to be a permanent affliction. Under such a condition, heroin seems more attractive (actually, less unattractive).

```
PDEA.K=TABHL (PDEATB,AVARR.K/ADDICT.K,0,.1,.02)              50, A
PDEATB=1,.95,.9,.8,.75,.7                                    50.1, T
      PDEA    — POLICE DETERRENT EFFCT
      PDEATB  — POLICE DETERRENCE EFFECT TABLE
      AVARR   — AVERAGE ARREST RATE
      ADDICT  — ADDICTS


PAH.K=TABHL (PAHTB,RHP.K,0,60,10)                            51, A
PAHTB=3,2,1.5,1,.8,.6,.5                                     51.1, T
      PAH     — PRICE ATTRACTIVENESS OF HEROIN
      PAHTB   — PRICE ATTRACTIVENESS TABLE
      RHP     — RECENT HP

TGMPA.K=(BTCA) (HAF.K)                                       52, A
BTCA=15                                                      52.1, C
      TGMPA   — TIME TO GROW TO MAXIMUM PERCENT OF ADDICTS
      BTCA    — BASE TIME CONSTANT
      HAF     — HEROIN AVAILABILITY FACTOR
```

HAF.K=TABHL (HAFTB,PAAP.K/(YOUPOP.K*PMAP.K-ALLADP.K),0,1,.2)   53, A
HAFTB=2,1.8,1.5,1.2,1,.8   53.1, T
    HAF   — HEROIN AVAILABILITY FACTOR
    HAFTB — HEROIN AVAILABILITY TABLE
    PAAP   — PERCEIVED ADDITIONAL ADDICT POTENTIAL
    YOUPOP — YOUTH POPULATION
    PMAP   — POTL MAX ADDICT PRCT
    ALLADP — ALL ADDICTS, INCL. MAINT. PROG.

The police deterrent effect (PDEA) causes addiction to be less attractive when a large number of addicts is being arrested. A decrease in the potential addict population of 30 percent is assumed when the police are arresting 10 percent or more of the street addict group each month (in **PDEATB**).

The price attractiveness of heroin (PAH), as it affects the number of people who become addicts, is dependent on the recent price of a mature addict's average daily habit. As the price tends toward zero, it makes heroin competitive with various "soft" drugs and is assumed in the extreme to cause up to a tripling in the attractiveness of addiction because heroin then offers a much greater effect per dollar. Prices of around $30 per day are assumed to have a neutral effect since they represent presumably accustomed price levels. A price as high as $60 per day for the average habit causes a 50 percent reduction in the number of potential addicts.

The time over which a community's addict population grows toward the expected number (TGMPA) is a function of the availability of heroin. The heroin availability factor (HAF) reflects the effect of availability on the ease with which people having potential for addiction can actually become addicted. If the perceived additional addict potential (PAAP, actually the number of new addicts that could be supported on the existing surplus of heroin) is miniscule compared to the number of people who might potentially become addicts [that is, the ratio PAAP/(YOUPOP*PMAP-ALLADP) is near zero], HAF provides a value of 2. This produces a growth time of 30 months when multiplied by the base time constant (BTCA) of 15 months. On the other hand, if the number of addicts that can be supported on the existing surplus (PAAP) is equal to or greater than the computed number of potential addicts, HAF provides a value of 0.8, which causes TGMPA to equal 12 months.

PHP.K=TABHL (HPTB, (HA.K/URA.K)/(YOUPOP.K*PMAP.K-   54, A
   ADDTMP.K),0,2,.2)
HPTB=60,55,50,40,30,30,25,20,15,10,5   54.1, T
    PHP   — POTENTIAL HEROIN PRICE
    HPTB   — HEROIN PRICE TABLE
    HA   — HEROIN AVAILABILITY
    URA   — USAGE RATE PER ADDICT
    YOUPOP — YOUTH POPULATION
    PMAP   — POTL MAX ADDICT PRCT
    ADDTMP — ADDICTS IN TREATMENT AND MAINT PROG

```
HP.K=HP.J+(DT) (1/TCPR) (PHP.J-HP.J)                          55, L
HP=30                                                         55.1, N
TCPR=12                                                       55.2, C
        HP      — HEROIN PRICE
        TCPR    — TIME FOR CHANGING PRICE
        PHP     — POTENTIAL HEROIN PRICE


RHP.K=SMOOTH(HP.K,3)                                          56, A
        RHP     — RECENT HP
        HP      — HEROIN PRICE
```

The potential heroin price (PHP) depends on the ratio of the number of addicts that can be supported each month by the available supply (HA in average daily doses/URA in daily doses per addict per month) to the total number of people that represent the community's potential demand for heroin. This demand includes people who are already addicts and people who can potentially become addicts, but excludes those currently in treatment and maintenance programs (as indicated by the difference between YOUPOP*PMAP and ADDTMP). When the number of addicts that can be supported is very small compared to the potential demand for heroin, that ratio is close to zero and the potential heroin habit price approaches $60 per day (from HPTB). When the ratio has a value near 1, a habit price of around $30 is assumed to prevail. Abundant supply situations bring much lower prices; down to $5 per day in the extreme if available supply exceeds potential demand by 100 percent (that is, a ratio equal to 2).

The actual heroin price (HP) prevailing in a community adjusts to the potential price over a period of 12 months (TCPR). The initial daily heroin habit price is set at $30. Heroin availability is set initially at a level (in equation 62.1) that causes the price to be in equilibrium at the beginning of each simulation. The recent heroin price (RHP) used in calculating the price attractiveness of heroin (PAH) in equation 56 is the actual price lagged by a period of 3 months to represent a delay in the perception of new prices.

```
PAAP.K=SMOOTH(AAP.K,TPAAP)                                    57, A
TPAAP=8                                                       57.1, C
        PAAP    — PERCEIVED ADDITIONAL ADDICT POTENTIAL
        AAP     — ADDITIONAL ADDICT POTENTIAL
        TPAAP   — TIME TO PERCEIVE A A P


AP.K=(HA.K-URA.K*EHA.K-URNA*NADD.K)/URNA                      58, A
        AAP     — ADDITIONAL ADDICT POTENTIAL
        HA      — HEROIN AVAILABILITY
        URA     — USAGE RATE PER ADDICT
        EHA     — EXPERIENCED HEROIN ADDICTS
        URNA    — USAGE RATE OF NEW ADDICTS
        NADD    — NEW ADDICTS
```

EHA.K=ADDICT.K-NADD.K+FMMC*METHDN.K+FHMC*HERMNT.K   59, A
     EHA   — EXPERIENCED HEROIN ADDICTS
     ADDICT   — ADDICTS
     NADD   — NEW ADDICTS
     FMMC   — FRAC OF METH. MAINT. ALSO STREET HEROIN
                  CRIMINALS
     METHDN — ADDICTS IN METHADONE PROGRAMS
     FHMC   — FRAC OF HEROIN MAINT. ALSO STREET HEROIN
                  CRIMINALS
     HERMNT — ADDICTS IN HER MAINT

NADD.K=(TDUR)*SMOOTH(AR.JK,TDUR)   60, A
NADD=0   60.1, N
TDUR=6   60.2, C
     NADD   — NEW ADDICTS
     TDUR   — TIME TO DEVELOP USAGE RATE
     AR   — ADDICTION RATE

URA,K=30*(1-DEMRED.K)   61, A
URNA=30   61.1, C
     URA   — USAGE RATE PER ADDICT
     DEMRED — STREET DEMAND EFFECT OF REDUCTION
     URNA   — USAGE RATE OF NEW ADDICTS

The additional addict potential (PAAP) is, as mentioned earlier, the number of new addicts that can be supported on the surplus heroin existing in the community (after the needs of current addicts have been satisfied). It is computed by subtracting heroin needed by experienced addicts (EHA*URA) and by new addicts (NADD*URNA) from total heroin availability to get the surplus and dividing by the usage rate of new addicts to get the number of new addicts that can be supported (AAP). Experienced heroin addicts (EHA) consist of all street addicts, except those considered to be "new addicts", and some fraction of the addicts enrolled in methadone and heroin maintenance programs who continue to engage in street addict behavior. "New" addicts (NADD) are those who have become addicts in the last six months. Their number is calculated by multiplying 6 months (TDUR) times the average rate at which new people become addicts each month. The usage rate per addict (URA) used in these calculations is the monthly total of 30 daily doses reduced by an amount reflecting the impact on habit size of detoxification programs, if any, operating in the community. PAAP, the quantity used in calculations such as the one for the heroin availability factor, is the additional addict potential subjected to a perception delay of 8 months (TPAAP).

HA.K=HA.J+(DT) (RCHA.JK)   62, L
HA=(PMAP*YOUPOP) (URA)   62.1, N
     HA   — HEROIN AVAILABILITY
     RCHA   — RATE OF CHNG OF HA

```
PMAP     – POTL MAX ADDICT PRCT
YOUPOP – YOUTH POPULATION
URA      – USAGE RATE PER ADDICT
```

```
RCHA.KL=LEAKAG.K+METHLK.K+( (PHA.K–HA.K)/TCHS)                    63, R
TCHS=6                                                           63.1, C
    RCHA     – RATE OF CHNG OF HA
    LEAKAG – LEAKAGE OF HER
    METHLK – METHADONE LEAKAGE
    PHA      – POTEN. H AVAILABILITY
    HA       – HEROIN AVAILABILITY
    TCHS     – TIME TO CHANGE HEROIN SUPPLY
```

```
PHA.K=(PAOP.K) (SPTSA.K) (URA.K) (EPA.K)                          64, A
    PHA      – POTEN. H AVAILABILITY
    PAOP     – PERC ATTR OF PUSHING
    SPTSA    – SMOOTHED POTENTIAL STREET ADDICT ADDITIONS
    URA      – USAGE RATE PER ADDICT
    EPA      – EFF POLICE ACTION
```

```
SPTSA.K=SMOOTH(PMAP.K*YOUPOP.K–ADDTMP.K, TCSPTA)                  65, A
SPTSA=150                                                        65.1, N
TCSPTA=36                                                        65.2, C
    SPTSA    – SMOOTHED POTENTIAL STREET ADDICT ADDITIONS
    PMAP     – POTL MAX ADDICT PRCT
    YOUPOP – YOUTH POPULATION
    ADDTMP – ADDICTS IN TREATMENT AND MAINT PROG
    TCSPTA – TIME FOR CHANGING SPTSA
```

Heroin availability (HA) is a level that changes as a result of various supply, demand, and enforcement factors in the community. It is initially equal to the community's total potential demand for heroin. Change in the level of heroin availability (RCHA) comes about due to leakage from heroin maintenance and methadone (heroin substitute) programs, if any, and the adjustment of actual heroin availability to a potential level created by market conditions and affected by enforcement efforts. This adjustment takes place over a period of 6 months (TCHS).

Potential heroin availability is primarily a function of the potential market, represented here in terms of smoothed potential street addict additions (SPTSA). This group includes people who may eventually become addicts and addicts already on the street or in prison, but excludes addicts in treatment and maintenance programs. SPTSA initially includes 150 addicts and potential addicts. Changes in the size of this group, as it affects the perceived potential market, are assumed to take place over a period of 36 months (TCSPTA). This number of people is multiplied by the usage rate per addict to get the basis for potential heroin availability in terms of daily dosages.

The product of these two numbers provides the exact level of supply needed to satisfy the potential market. Two other factors are assumed to affect potential heroin availability. One, representing the economic attractiveness of pushing (PAOP), can effect substantial increases in potential availability. The other, effect of police action (EPA), can reduce availability somewhat.

```
PAOP.K=SMOOTH(AOP.K,TPAOP)*HPF.K*EPA.K                    66, A
TPAOP=8                                                   66.1, C
     PAOP    - PERC ATTR OF PUSHING
     AOP     - ATTRACTIVENESS OF PUSH
     TPAOP   - TIME TO PERCEIVE A O P
     HPF     - HEROIN PRICE FACTOR
     EPA     - EFF POLICE ACTION


HPF.K=TABHL (HPFTB,RHP.K,0,60,10)                         67, A
HPFTB=1,1,1,1,1,1,1                                       67.1, T
     HPF     - HEROIN PRICE FACTOR
     HPFTB   - HEROIN PRICE FACTOR TABLE
     RHP     - RECENT HP


AOP.K=TABHL (AOPTB,SPTSA.K/YOUPOP.K,0,.1,.02)             68, A
AOPTB=1,1.1,1.3,1.5,1.7,1.8                               68.1, T
     AOP     - ATTRACTIVENESS OF PUSH
     AOPTB   - ATTR OF PUSHING TABLE
     SPTSA   - SMOOTHED POTENTIAL STREET ADDICT ADDITIONS
     YOUPOP  - YOUTH POPULATION
```

Perceived attractiveness of pushing (PAOP) is based on the actual attractiveness of pushing subjected to an 8-month perception delay (TPAOP), a heroin price factor (HPF), and the effect of police action (EPA). Police action is seen to have its effect here in terms of the perceived risk of pushing, while it is assumed to have a direct supply-reducing effect in the determination of potential availability (equation 64). The heroin price factor makes pushing more attractive if prices are high and less attractive if prices are low, but was assigned a neutral effect (HPFTB) in the simulations.

Attractiveness of pushing (AOP) itself is a function of the fraction of a community's youthful population in the potential street-addict additions group. This is a measure of the market's magnitude as perceived by drug dealers, and essentially determines their willingness to invest in establishing and maintaining distribution channels. Establishment of extensive distribution channels in a community is assumed to increase potential heroin availability by up to 80 percent (in AOPTB) (due to inventories in the supply pipeline) if 10 percent or more of the youth population falls into the SPTSA group.

```
EPA.K=TABHL(EPATB,PEDH.K/(HA.K/URA.K),0,.1,.02)          69, A
EPATB=1,.9,.85,.8,.75,.7                                 69.1, T
     EPA     - EFF POLICE ACTION
     EPATB   - EFF OF POLICE ACTION TAB
```

```
     PEDH   – POLICE EFFORT DIRECTED AT HEROIN
     HA     – HEROIN AVAILABILITY
     URA    – USAGE RATE PER ADDICT
```

PEDH.K=(CAPE.K) (EDH.K)   70, A
```
     PEDH   – POLICE EFFORT DIRECTED AT HEROIN
     CAPE   – CUMULATIVE ADDITIONAL POLICE EFFORT
     EDH    – FRACTION OF EFFORT DIRECTED AT HEROIN
```

EDH.K=(1–PAAA.K) (HE.K)   71, A
```
     EDH    – FRACTION OF EFFORT DIRECTED AT HEROIN
     PAAA   – POLICE ACTION AGAINST ADDICT
     HE     – HEROIN EFFORT
```

HE.K=TABHL(HFTB,CATT.K,0,1,.2)   72, A
HETB=.5,.5,.5,.5,.5,.5   72.1, T
```
     HE     – HEROIN EFFORT
     HETB   – HEROIN EFFORT TABLE
     CATT   – COMMUNITY ATTITUDE
```

Police action is assumed to have an effect (EPA) of up to 30 percent in reducing both potential heroin availability and the perceived attractiveness of pushing. The magnitude of this reduction is dependent on the ratio of police effort directed at heroin supply (in men) to the community's heroin availability expressed in addict-equivalents (HA/URA). The maximum 30 percent reduction is only attainable if one officer is assigned to supply reduction for each ten addict-equivalents of supply, that is, a really massive police effort. A much smaller impact could therefore be expected in most communities. A possible exception might be a community with a limited distribution system in which one dealer controlled a large portion of the total supply.

Police effort directed at heroin (PEDH) is part of the fraction of total effort directed at drugs and drug-related crime (CAPE) left over after effort is allocated to action against addicts themselves (1 – PAAA). In the base model it shares the residual effort equally with activity against soft drugs (HETB = 0.5, . . ,), though the possibility of distributing effort between the two based on community attitudes is represented in equation 72.

AMR.KL=(ATAON.K) (ADDICT.K) (NAM)   73, R
```
     AMR      – ADDICT MIGRATION RATE
     ATAON    – ATTRAC. TO ADDICTS FROM OTHER NEIGH
     ADDICT   – ADDICTS
     NAM      – NORMAL ADDICT MIGRATION/MO.
```

ATAON.K=(WDA) (DAF.K) – (WPH) (EPH.K)   74, A
```
     ATAON    – ATTRAC. TO ADDICTS FROM OTHER NEIGH
     WDA      – WEIGHT OF DRUG AVAILABILITY
     DAF      – DRUG AVAILABILITY FACTOR
     WPH      – WEIGHT OF POLICE HARASSMENT
     EPH      – EFF OF POLICE HARASSMENT
```

```
DAF.K=TABHL(DAFTB,PAAP.K/ADDICT.K,-.4,.8,.4)                    75, A
DAFTB=-2,0.1,2                                                 75.1, T
WDA=.5                                                         75.2, C
       DAF     – DRUG AVAILABILITY FACTOR
       DAFTB   – DRUG AVAILABILITY TABLE
       PAAP    – PERCEIVED ADDITIONAL ADDICT POTENTIAL
       ADDICT  – ADDICTS
       WDA     – WEIGHT OF DRUG AVAILABILITY


EPH.K=TABHL (EPHTB,AVARR.K/ADDICT.K,0,.1,.02)                   76, A
EPHTB=-.2,.2,.8,1.4,1.8,2                                      76.1, T
WPH=.5                                                         76.2, C
NAM=.02                                                        76.3, C
       EPH     – EFF OF POLICE HARASSMENT
       EPHTB   – EFF OF POLICE HARASSMENT TABLE
       AVARR   – AVERAGE ARREST RATE
       ADDICT  – ADDICTS
       WPH     – WEIGHT OF POLICE HARASSMENT
       NAM     – NORMAL ADDICT MIGRATION/MO.


ADO.KL=ADDICT.K/TADO                                           77, R
TADO=120                                                      77.1, C
       ADO     – ADDICT DROPOUT RATE
       ADDICT  – ADDICTS
       TADO    – TIME FOR ADDICT DROPOUT
```

The rate at which addicts migrate in and out of a community (AMR) is based on the assumption that some "normal" migration occurs (due, for example, to addicts' families moving) and involves 2 percent of the street addict population each month (NAM). An attractiveness factor (ATAON) can make actual migration greater or less than 2 percent and determines whether migration is positive or negative (i.e., in or out). This factor has two components with equal weights of 0.5 (WDA, WPH). One of these, the drug availability factor (DAF), causes out-migration when heroin is extremely scarce and in-migration when heroin is abundant. When only enough heroin is available to satisfy 60 percent of current needs (i.e., the "additional" addict potential is -0.4 in that 40 percent of existing needs are unsatisfied), this factor alone produces an out-migration rate of $-2 \times 0.5 \times 0.02 = 2$ percent per month (DAF $\times$ WDA $\times$ NAM). On the other extreme, when surplus heroin is available, exceeding current needs by 80 percent, DAF alone produces a net in-migration rate of 2 percent.

A very low arrest rate causes the police harassment effect (EPH) to have a slightly positive effect and to encourage in-migration of $-0.5 \times -0.2 \times 0.02 = 0.2$ percent per month. At the other extreme, this factor, by itself, can cause an out-migration of $-0.5 \times 2 \times 0.02 = -2$ percent per month when 10 percent or more of the addict population is being arrested each month. Very low drug availability and a high arrest rate have additive effects and produce a total out-migration rate of 4 percent per month.

The addict dropout rate (ADO) represents the "burn-out" phenomenon in which addicts stop being addicts because they are tired of the hassle of getting drugs and money to buy drugs. This process is assumed to take an average of 10 years (120 months) from the time a person becomes an addict (TADO). Therefore, 1/120 of the addict population is assumed to drop out each month.

```
ADDICT.K=ADDICT.J+ (DT) (AR.JK+AMR.JK-ADO.JK-STPR.JK-              78, L
    INTAKE.JK-COMR.JK-STMR.JK+PRTS.JK+DFCR.JK+
    DFOR.JK+MPDO.JK+DORP.JK-STHR.JK+HPDO.JK-
    GANTAG.JK+ANTAGD.JK-DETCR.JK)
ADDICT=(.003) (IYPOP)                                             78.1, N
```

ADDICT	–	ADDICTS
AR	–	ADDICTION RATE
AMR	–	ADDICT MIGRATION RATE
ADO	–	ADDICT DROPOUT RATE
STPR	–	STREET TO PRISON RATE
INTAKE	–	INTAKE
COMR	–	OUTSIDE COMM RATE
STMR	–	STREET TO METH
PRTS	–	PRISON RELEASE TO STREET
DFCR	–	DROPOUT RATE FROM COMMUNITY REHAB
DFOR	–	DROPOUTS FROM OUTSIDE REHAB.
MPDO	–	METHADONE PROGRAM DROPOUT RATE
DORP	–	DROPOUT FROM RE-ENTRY
STHR	–	STR TO HER MAINT
HPDO	–	HEROIN PROGRAM DROPOUT RATE
GANTAG	–	GROWTH OF ANTAGONIST LEVEL
ANTAGD	–	ANTAGONIST DROPOUT RATE
DETCR	–	DETOX CHANGE
IYPOP	–	INITIAL YOUTH POPULATION

The level of addicts on the street is added to and depleted by the rates of flow indicated in equation 78. Addicts on the street are initially assumed to be 0.3 percent of the youthful population and initially comprise almost all the community's addicts. All of the definitions shown are self-explanatory with the exception of INTAKE which is the rate of flow from the street into in-community, drug-free rehabilitation programs. Additions to and deletions from the street addict level are indicated by plus and minus signs, respectively.

Community Response Sector

CRIME.KL=(THIEV.K) (PCRSH.K) (HPE.K) (1–DRCU.K)   79, R
    CRIME   – CRIME RATE
    THIEV   – THIEVES
    PCRSH   – PROP CRIME REQ TO SUPPORT HABIT/MO
    HPE   – HEROIN PRICE EFFECT
    DRCU   – DETOX REDUCTION OF CRIME AND USAGE

THIEV.K=(ADDICT.K+FMMC*METHDN.K+FHMC*HERMNT.K)*   80, A
  CRIMF.K*PROPF.K
FMMC=0   80.1, C
FHMC=0   80.2, C
    THIEV   – THIEVES
    ADDICT – ADDICTS
    FMMC   – FRAC OF METH. MAINT. ALSO STREET HEROIN
                 CRIMINALS
    METHDN – ADDICTS IN METHADONE PROGRAMS
    FHMC   – FRAC OF HEROIN MAINT. ALSO STREET HEROIN
                 CRIMINALS
    HERMNT – ADDICTS IN HER MAINT
    CRIMF   – CRIMINAL FRACTION OF ADDICTS
    PROPF   – PROPERTY CRIMINALS FRACTION

HPE.K=TABHL (HPETB,HP.K,0,60,10)   81, A
HPETB=.1,.7,1.3,2,2.5,2.8,3   81.1, T
    HPE   – HEROIN PRICE EFFECT
    HPETB   – HEROIN PRICE EFFECT TAB
    HP   – HEROIN PRICE

PCRSH.K=TABHL (PCRTB,SEL.K,0,1,.2)   82, A
PCRTB=12,11,9,7,6,5   82.1, T
    PCRSH   – PROP CRIME REQ TO SUPPORT HABIT/MO.
    PCRTB   – PROP CRIME REQS TABLE
    SEL   – SOCIO-ECONOMIC LEVEL

CRIMF.K=TABHL (CRIMTB,SEL.K,0,1,.2)   83, A
CRIMTB=1,.9,.8,.6,.4,.3   83.1, T
    CRIMF   – CRIMINAL FRACTION OF ADDICTS
    CRIMTB – CRIME FRACTION TABLE
    SEL   – SOCIO-ECONOMIC LEVEL

PROPF.K=TABHL (PROPTB,SEL.K,0,1,.2)   84, A
PROPTB=.4,.45,.5,.4,.35,.3   84.1, T
    PROPF   – PROPERTY CRIMINALS FRACTION
    PROPTB – PROPERTY CRIME TABLE
    SEL   – SOCIO-ECONOMIC LEVEL

The monthly property crime rate in a community attributable to its addicts (CRIME) is the product of the number of addicts actually committing crimes (THIEV), the number of property crimes required to support the average habit each month (PCRSH), a heroin price effect that raises or lowers the number of crimes required as a function of heroin price and its impact on daily habit cost (HPE), and a factor that reduces property crimes required as a result of decreases in average habit size achieved by detoxification programs (1 − DRCU). Calculation of THIEV begins with street addicts plus some fraction of the addicts in methadone and heroin maintenance programs that continue to commit crimes as a basis, but only draws on the fraction committing crimes to support their habits (CRIMF) and, of those, only the fraction committing property crimes (PROPF) are actually included.

The number of property crimes committed by each of these THIEVs each month (PCRSH) is assumed to be a function of the community's socioeconomic level (SEL). This represents the differential value of crime opportunities in poor and wealthy communities. Addicts in the poorest communities must commit twelve crimes per month to support the same sized habit (in dollars per day) as an addict in a wealthy community can support with only five crimes (in PCRTB; where SEL = 0 represents extreme poverty and SEL = 1 represents extreme wealth). The heroin price effect (HPE) can reduce the required number of crimes to an extreme of 10 percent of its SEL-based value if the average daily habit approaches zero, and as much as triple the required number as the price approaches $60 per day. This effect has an initial value of 2 because the initial price is $30.

The fraction of addicts committing crimes and the subset of those addicts committing property crimes are also both considered to be functions of community socioeconomic level. The fraction involved in some sort of criminal activity grows as socioeconomic level drops, reflecting reduced opportunities for raising money from employment, family and friends in poorer communities, and goes from 30 percent in the wealthiest community to complete crime involvement in the poorest community (CRIMTB). The fraction of this group committing property crimes reflects opportunities for consensual crime (such as prostitution, con games, selling drugs) as a function of socioeconomic level. The greater the opportunity for consensual crime, the less need for property crime. PROPTB was given an inverted "U" shape for this reason with the middle-class community having the largest fraction of its criminal addicts involved in property crime (50 percent) because it lacks the wealthy community's ready availability of money to finance consensual crime and the poor community's tolerance of it. Multiplying CRIMF and PROPF yields fractions of addicts engaging in property crime of 9 percent when the community is extremely wealthy and 40 percent for the extremely poor community.

SFC.K=SFC.J+ (DT) (1/ROS.J) (CRIME.JK–SFC.J)   85, L
SFC=(CRIME) (.6)   85.1, N
    SFC   – STANDARD FOR CRIME
    ROS   – RIGIDITY OF STANDARD (IN MOS. ADJUST)
    CRIME – CRIME RATE

ROS.K=TABHL (ROSTB,CS.K,0,1,.25)   86, A
ROSTB=20,24,30,36,40   86.1, T
    ROS   – RIGIDITY OF STANDARD (IN MOS. ADJUST)
    ROSTB – RIGIDITY OF STNDS TABLE
    CS   – COMMUNITY STRUCTURE

      A community's standard for crime is the basis against which it compares current crime rates. This standard is the level of crime to which the community becomes accustomed. As shown in equation 85, the standard for crime is assumed to follow current crime rates, adjusting to them (as they become accustomed crime rates) over a period of time characteristic for the community. This characteristic is referred to as the rigidity of standard (ROS) and is measured by the months it takes for the standard to adjust to changes in crime rates. This rigidity is assumed to be a function of a community's structural attributes including the strength of its institutions and its population's average length of residence. A community with weak structure (CS = 0) may see its standards change in as little as 20 months, while one with a strong structure may see that change take 40 months (in ROSTB). SFC is initially set at 60 percent of the current crime rate (in equation 85.1), implying what is believed to be a realistic degree of alarm about crime.

AAC.K=AAC.J+ (DT) (1/TBA) (CRIME.JK–AAC.J)   87, L
AAC=CRIME   87.1, N
TBA=3   87.2, C
    AAC   – AWARENESS OF ADDICT CRIME
    TBA   – TIME TO BECOME AWARE
    CRIME – CRIME RATE

ADP.K= (AAC.K) (EPAAAC.K)   88, A
    ADP   – AWARENESS OF DRUG PROBLEM
    AAC   – AWARENESS OF ADDICT CRIME
    EPAAAC – EFFECT OF PERVASIVENESS IN AMPLIFYING
                  AWARENESS OF ADDICT CRIME

EPAAAC.K=TABHL (EPRTB,PERINV.K/YOUPOP.K,0,.1,.02)   89, A
EPRTB=1,1.05,1.1,1.2,1.4,1.5   89.1, T
    EPAAAC – EFFECT OF PERVASIVENESS IN AMPLIFYING
                  AWARENESS OF ADDICT CRIME
    EPRTB – EFF OF PERVASIVENESS TABLE
    PERINV – PERSONS INVOLVED
    YOUPOP – YOUTH POPULATION

A community's awareness of addict crime (AAC) is assumed to follow the actual crime rate with a delay of three months (TBA). Its awareness of the drug problem (ADP) is based on awareness of addict crime, which is then inflated (multiplying by EPAAAC) to reflect the pervasiveness of drug use in the community.

The number of people the community perceives as being involved in drug use, PERINV, is assumed to be equal to the number of addicts it has plus one-tenth the number of other drug users (they are seen as part of the problem, but have much lower visibility than addicts). When PERINV, computed in this manner, reaches 10 percent or more of the youthful population, EPAAAC inflates the community's awareness of addict crime by 50 percent (from EPRTB) in producing its awareness of the drug problem (also expressed in crimes per month).

```
GDP.KL=( ( ( (ADP.K/AEC) - (POLPRD.K*CAPE.K*CONRAT*                    90, R
   TTBREL))/(POLPRD.K*CONRAT*TTBREL) )*ALF.K-DAPE.K)
AEC=5                                                                  90.1, C
   GDP      - GROWTH OF DESIRED ADDITIONAL POLICE EFFORT
   ADP      - AWARENESS OF DRUG PROBLEM
   AEC      - ADDITIONAL POLICE EFFECT ON CRIMES
   POLPRD   - POLICE PRODUCTIVITY
   CAPE     - CUMULATIVE ADDITIONAL POLICE EFFORT
   CONRAT   - CONVICTION RATE (PRCT)
   TTBREL   - TIME TO BE RELEASED
   ALF      - ALARM FACTOR
   DAPE     - DESIRED ADDITIONAL POLICE EFFORT


ALF.K=TABHL (ALFTB,CA.K,1,4,.5)                                        91, A
ALFTB=0,.1,.2,.4,.6,.75,.8                                             91.1, T
   ALF      - ALARM FACTOR
   ALFTB    - ALARM FACTOR TABLE
   CA       - COMMUNITY ALARM


DAPE.K=DAPE.J+(DT) (GDP.JK-GPE.JK)                                     92, L
DAPE=0                                                                 92.1, N
   DAPE     - DESIRED ADDITIONAL POLICE EFFORT
   GDP      - GROWTH OF DESIRED ADDITIONAL POLICE EFFORT
   GPE      - GROWTH OF POLICE EFFORT


GPE.KL=DAPE.K/TRDEL.K                                                  93, R
   GPE      - GROWTH OF POLICE EFFORT
   DAPE     - DESIRED ADDITIONAL POLICE EFFORT
   TRDEL    - TRAINING DELAY


TRDEL.K=TABHL (TRDTB,DAPE.K/CAPE.K,0,.5,.1)                            94, A
```

```
TRDTB=6,8,12,16,17,18                                         94.1, T
    TRDEL   — TRAINING DELAY
    TRDTB   — TRAINING DELAY TABLE
    DAPE    — DESIRED ADDITIONAL POLICE EFFORT
    CAPE    — CUMULATIVE ADDITIONAL POLICE EFFORT


CAPE.K=CAPE.J+(DT) (GPE.JK)                                    95, L
CAPE=1.5                                                       95.1, N
    CAPE    — CUMULATIVE ADDITIONAL POLICE EFFORT
    GPE     — GROWTH OF POLICE EFFORT
```

The community makes its decision about the number of additional police officers to deploy against addict crime and the supplies of heroin and soft drugs based on two criteria. One is the "ideal" number of officers that appears to be sufficient to put all addict criminals in prison. The additional number of officers desired is computed by finding the difference between the estimated number of addict criminals (estimated by dividing the perceived monthly crime rate [ADP] by five crimes per addict per month [AEC]) and the estimated number that can be put in jail by the existing police effort (estimated as the product of men [CAPE], arrests/man/month [POLPRD], convictions/ arrest [CONRAT], and months of imprisonment [TTBREL]). The difference, in maximum convictions obtainable, is then divided by the estimated number of convictions each officer can obtain (POLPRD∗CONRAT∗TTBREL) to get the number of additional officers needed to achieve that goal.

The desired number of additional officers computed in this manner is likely to be far greater than most communities can or will support. The fraction of this desired number of officers actually hired is a function of an alarm factor (ALF), the other criterion used. This factor, based on the ratio of current awareness of the drug problem (ADP, in crimes per month) to the standard for monthly crime rate (SFC) as a measure of alarm, causes none of the officers to be hired if the ratio is around 1 (crime is at accustomed levels) and as many of 80 percent of these officers to be hired if this ratio reaches or exceeds a value of 4 (in ALFTB).

The number of additional police to be hired (DAPE) increases to include additional hiring requirements produced by this calculation (of GDP). DAPE is reduced as the new officers are hired and placed on the street (GPE). The rate at which new officers are placed on the street (GPE) is proportional to the number to be hired, but is subject to a training delay (TRDEL). The training delay is based on the ratio of new officers to be hired to officers already working on drug-related crimes and drug enforcement (CAPE). If new hires represent only a small fraction of CAPE, a 6-month delay is assumed. If, on the other hand, new hires reach or exceed 50 percent of those already working, an 18-month delay is used (TRDTB). CAPE merely accumulates new officers that are hired and deployed and is initially given a value of 1.5 officers.

```
EPCR.K=TABHL (EPCRTB, (ADP.K/AEC)/CAPE.K,0,50,10)                    96, A
EPCRTB=.8,.7,.6,.45,.35,.3                                          96.1, T
        EPCR    — EXPECTED PERCENTAGE CRIME REDUCTION
        EPCRTB  — EXP POLICE CRIME REDUCTION TABLE
        ADP     — AWARENESS OF DRUG PROBLEM
        AEC     — ADDITIONAL POLICE EFFECT ON CRIMES
        CAPE    — CUMULATIVE ADDITIONAL POLICE EFFORT


EPE.K=(ADP.K) (1–EPCR.K)                                             97, A
        EPE     — EXPECTED POLICE EFFECT
        ADP     — AWARENESS OF DRUG PROBLEM
        EPCR    — EXPECTED PERCENTAGE CRIME REDUCTION


AEPE.K=SMOOTH(EPE.K,TAE)                                             98, A
TAE=36                                                             98.1, C
        AEPE    — AVERAGED EXPECTED POLICE EFFECT
        EPE     — EXPECTED POLICE EFFECT
        TAE     — TIME TO AVERAGE EXPECTATIONS


GFRUST.KL=( (ADP.K–AEPE.K)–FRUST.K)/TGF                              99, R
TGF=24                                                             99.1, C
        GFRUST  — GROWTH OF FRUSTRATION
        ADP     — AWARENESS OF DRUG PROBLEM
        AEPE    — AVERAGED EXPECTED POLICE EFFECT
        FRUST   — FRUSTRATION WITH POLICE APPROACH
        TGF     — TIME FOR GROWTH OF FRUSTRATION


FRUST.K=FRUST.J+(DT) (GFRUST.JK)                                    100, L
FRUST=0                                                            100.1, N
        FRUST   — FRUSTRATION WITH POLICE APPROACH
        GFRUST  — GROWTH OF FRUSTRATION


FREFF.K=TABHL (FRETB,FRUST.K/ADP.K,0,1,.2)                          101, A
FRETB=.1,.4,.7,.9,.95,1                                            101.1, T
        FREFF   — FRUSTRATION EFFECT
        FRETB   — FRUST EFFECT TABLE
        FRUST   — FRUSTRATION WITH POLICE APPROACH
        ADP     — AWARENESS OF DRUG PROBLEM
```

An important factor affecting the community's definition of the narcotics problem is its perception of police success in coping with drug-related crime. Poor performance may suggest that the problem is not exclusively one of a criminal nature, but instead requires a sociomedical solution. The community is assumed to judge police performance in terms of performance against an expected percentage reduction in crime (EPCR). This expectation is based on the ratio of perceived addict-criminals (ADP/AEC) to officers devoted to pursuing drug-related crime (CAPE). An 80 percent reduction is expected when there are few addict-criminals relative to the police effort directed against them (EPCRTB). Only a 30 percent reduction is expected if there are 50 or more addict-criminals per officer. The expected effect of police effort (EPE), in terms of crimes that should be expected after police effort has its effect, is the product of perceived crimes (ADP) and 1 minus the expected percentage reduction (1 - EPCR). The expectation is subjected to a 36-month delay (TAE) before it enters into the community's evaluation of police performance to allow time for police effort to have its effect.

The difference between perceived crime and crime expected as a result of police effort forms the basis for the community's frustration with police inability to "solve" the narcotics problem. The community's frustration (FRUST), in terms of the number of crimes it feels should have been avoided, grows to match this difference over a period of 24 months (TGF). The frustration level is assumed initially to be zero. Frustration's effect (FREFF) in changing the community's definition of the narcotics problem (from criminal to sociomedical in nature) is based on the fraction of perceived crime the community feels should have been avoided (FRUST/ADP). If little crime is perceived as avoidable due to police effort, the effect of frustration on attitude change is minimal (FREFF = 0.1). If most of the perceived crime is thought to be avoidable, frustration with the police has its maximum effect in changing community attitudes (FREFF = 1).

```
POLPRD.K=TABHL (PRODTB,PAAA.K*CAPE.K,0,50,10)              102, A
PRODTB=2.5,2.2,1.6,1,1,1                                   102.1, T
      POLPRD  —  POLICE PRODUCTIVITY
      PRODTB  —  PRODUCTIVITY TABLE
      PAAA    —  POLICE ACTION AGAINST ADDICTS
      CAPE    —  CUMULATIVE ADDITIONAL POLICE EFFORT


ARREST.KL=(CAPE.K) (POLPRD.K) (PAAA.K) (ASEA.K)            103, R
      ARREST  —  ARRESTS
      CAPE    —  CUMULATIVE ADDITIONAL POLICE EFFORT
      POLPRD  —  POLICE PRODUCTIVITY
      PAAA    —  POLICE ACTION AGAINST ADDICTS
      ASEA    —  ADDICT SCARCITY EFFECT ON ARRESTS


PAAA.K=TABHL(PAAATB,FREFF.K,0,1,.2)*AE.K                   104, A
PAAATB=.6,.65,.7,.8,.85,.9                                 104.1, T
      PAAA    —  POLICE ACTION AGAINST ADDICTS
      PAAATB  —  POLICE ACTION TABLE
      FREFF   —  FRUSTRATION EFFECT
      AE      —  ATTITUDE EFFECT ON DEPLOYMENT


AE.K=TABHL(AEFTB,CATT.K,0,1,.2)                            105, A
AEFTB=1,1,1,1,1,1                                          105.1, T
      AE      —  ATTITUDE EFFECT ON DEPLOYMENT
      AEFTB   —  ATTITUDE EFFECT TABLE
      CATT    —  COMMUNITY ATTITUDE
```

```
ASEA.K=TABHL(ASEATB,ADDICT.K/YOUPOP.K,0,.1,.02)              106, A
ASEATB=.4,.5,.7,.9,1,1                                       106.1, T
      ASEA    — ADDICT SCARCITY EFFECT ON ARRESTS
      ASEATB  — ADDICT SCARCITY EFFECT TABLE
      ADDICT  — ADDICTS
      YOUPOP  — YOUTH POPULATION
```

```
AVARR.K=SMOOTH(ARREST.JK,TAAR)                               107, A
TAAR=3                                                       107.1, C
      AVARR   — AVERAGE ARREST RATE
      ARREST  — ARRESTS
      TAAR    — TIME TO AVERAGE ARREST RATE
```

Police productivity, in arrests per man per month, is assumed to diminish as more officers are concentrated against addicts. When only a few officers are working on drug-related crime, each can make up to 2.5 arrests per month because each has a large number of addict criminals as potential arrestees. When 30 or more officers are concentrating on drug-related crime, each officer is assumed to produce only one arrest per month because of fewer addict-criminals per officer. The arrest rate achieved by these officers is the product of the number directing their efforts against addicts themselves (**CAPE*PAAA**), arrest productivity per man, and a factor (**ASEA**) that reduces arrest productivity when addicts make up a very small part of the youthful population and are harder to find.

The fraction of police effort directed against addicts (**PAAA**) is represented as a function of frustration with police performance against addict crime. Sixty percent is allocated if frustration is low (**FREFF** near zero), and 90 percent if frustration is extremely high (**FREFF** close to 1). Allocation of police against addict crime can also be a function of the community's definition of the problem (criminal vs. sociomedical) (**AE**), though this factor was given a neutral effect in the simulations.

The addict-scarcity effect on arrests (**ASEA**) causes the arrest rate to be reduced by up to 60 percent if very few addicts exist, and restores arrests to their normal value (based on numbers of men and their assumed productivity) if street addicts make up 8–10 percent or more of the youthful population. The average arrest rate (**AVARR**), used in many of the model's equations, is the arrest rate averaged over a period of 3 months (**TAAR**).

```
PRELAR.K=PRELAR.J+(DT) (FREQEF.J/TAPREL) (AVARR.J-           108, L
      PRELAR.J)
PRELAR=AVARR                                                 108.1, N
TAPREL=60                                                    108.2, C
      PRELAR — PERSONAL RELEVANCE OF ARRESTS
      FREQEF — FREQUENCY EFFECT
      TAPREL — TIME TO ADJUST FOR PERSONAL RELEVANCE
      AVARR  — AVERAGE ARREST RATE
```

```
FREQEF.K=TABHL(FREQTB,AVARR.K/YOUPOP.K,0,.01,.002)          109, A
FREQTB=1,5,10,15,18,20                                      109.1, T
     FREQEF  —  FREQUENCY EFFECT
     FREQTB  —  FREQUENCY TABLE
     AVARR   —  AVERAGE ARREST RATE
     YOUPOP  —  YOUTH POPULATION
```

```
PRELEF.K=TABHL(PRELTB,PRELAR.K/YOUPOP.K,0,.001,.0002)       110, A
PRELTB=.1,.4,.7,.8,.9,1                                     110.1, T
     PRELEF  —  PERS. RELEV EFF
     PRELTB  —  PERSONAL RELEVANCE TABLE
     PRELAR  —  PERSONAL RELEVANCE OF ARRESTS
     YOUPOP  —  YOUTH POPULATION
```

Arrests for drug-related crimes are assumed to change the community's definition of the narcotics problem when they involve youths known to people in the community. Such arrests prevent residents from blaming the problem on "outsiders" and influence them to perceive a need for social and medical solutions. The number of arrests that is seen as "personally relevant" (PRELAR) is assumed to lag as far as 60 months (TAPREL) behind the total number being arrested when only a miniscule fraction of the youthful population is being arrested for addiction-related crimes each month (because FREQEF = 1). But when the average number being arrested each month reaches 1 percent or more of the entire youthful population, FREQEF takes on a value of 20 and causes the period between an increase in arrests and the time it takes for a perception to develop that "our neighbors' kids are being arrested" to be reduced to as little as 3 months (FREQEF(20)/TAPREL (60) = 1/3). Personal relevance of arrests has its full effect in changing the community's definition of the problem (PRELEF = 1) when the number of "personally relevant" arrests equals or exceeds 0.1 percent of the youthful population each month.

```
PERVEF.K=TABHL(PERTB,PERINV.K/YOUPOP.K,0,.1,.02)           111, A
PERTB=1,1.1,1.3,1.7,1.9,2                                  111.1, T
     PERVEF   —  PERVASIVENESS EFFECT
     PERTB    —  PERVASIVENESS TABLE
     PERINV   —  PERSONS INVOLVED
     YOUPOP   —  YOUTH POPULATION
```

```
PERINV.K=(USERS.K) (.1)+ALLADP.K                           112, A
     PERINV   —  PERSONS INVOLVED
     USERS    —  USERS
     ALLADP   —  ALL ADDICTS, INCL. MAINT. PROG.
```

```
AGEEFF.K=TABHL(AGETB,COMMED.K,0,.06,.01)                   113, A
AGETB=1,1.1,1.3,1.5,1.7,1.9,2                              113.1, T
     AGEEFF   —  AGENCY ENABLING EFF.
     AGETB    —  AGENCY ENABLING EFFECT TABLE
     COMMED   —  COMMUNITY EDUCATION EFFORT
```

```
COMMED.K=COMEDC*CEPOL.K                                    114, A
COMEDC=0                                                  114.1, C
    COMMED  – COMMUNITY EDUCATION EFFORT
    COMEDC  – COMMUNITY EDUC CONTROL SWITCH
    CEPOL   – COMMUNITY EDUCATION POLICY


CEPOL.K=TABHL(CEPTB,PCATT.K,0,1,1/6)                       115, A
CEPTB=.06,.05,.04,.03,.02,.01,0                          115.1, T
    CEPOL   – COMMUNITY EDUCATION POLICY
    CEPTB   – COMMUNITY EDUCATION TABLE
    PCATT   – PERCEIVED COMMUNITY ATTITUDE


MEDEFF.K=CME                                               116, A
CME=.01                                                  116.1, C
    MEDEFF  – MEDIA EFFECT
    CME     – CONTINUING MEDIA EFFECT
```

Another factor contributing to changes in community-problem definition is the perceived pervasiveness of drug problems in the community (PERVEF). This factor has no effect when few young people are involved, but can double the rate at which community attitudes toward the problem change when the number of persons perceived as involved equals or is greater than 10 percent of the youthful population. As explained earlier, the PERINV term includes all of a community's addicts and one person-equivalent for each ten users of other drugs.

An agency enabling effect (AGEEFF), representing the impact of local human service agencies in conveying the sociomedical nature of addiction to community residents, also affects the rate of attitude change. The magnitude of this effect is based on the size of community education programs in progress (COMMED). Community education programs are described in terms of the percentage change they can effect each month in the community's attitudes toward addiction (where the full range of attitudes from all-criminal to all-sociomedical is covered by a 0-to-1 scale). The agency enabling effect can, at most, double the rate of attitude change when ongoing community education programs are geared up to achieve a 6 percent change per month in community attitudes (in AGETB).

Community education programs, measured in terms of the percentage change in attitudes that can be achieved each month, are based on a community education policy (CEPOL). The model user can include these programs in simulations by changing the constant COMEDC from its nonoperative value of zero to a value of 1. The community education policy, when functioning, is designed to allocate effort to community education programs in proportion to need. When community attitude is perceived to be very low (PCATT near zero; indicative of a solely criminal definition of addiction), an effort is maintained that is capable of achieving a change of 6 percent per month (from CEPTB).

The media are also assumed to have an effect (MEDEFF) in achieving attitude change by providing information about addiction's socio-medical character. Media are assumed to have a continuing effect (CME) in achieving a change of 1 percent per month.

```
GCATT.KL=( (FREFF.K) (PRELEF.K) (PERVEF.K) (AGEEFF.K)            117, R
   (COMMED.K+MEDEFF.K) (1–CATT.K) )
      GCATT   – GROWTH OF COMMUNITY ATTITUDE ON DRUG
                 ADDICTION
      FREFF   – FRUSTRATION EFFECT
      PRELEF  – PERS. RELEV EFF
      PERVEF  – PERVASIVENESS EFFECT
      AGEEFF  – AGENCY ENABLING EFF.
      COMMED  – COMMUNITY EDUCATION EFFORT
      MEDEFF  – MEDIA EFFECT
      CATT    – COMMUNITY ATTITUDE
```

```
CATT.K=CATT.J+(DT) (GCATT.JK–DCATT.JK)                           118, L
CATT=.1                                                          118.1, N
      CATT    – COMMUNITY ATTITUDE
      GCATT   – GROWTH OF COMMUNITY ATTITUDE ON DRUG
                 ADDICTION
      DCATT   – DETERIORATION OF COMMUNITY ATTITUDE
```

```
PCATT.K=SMOOTH(CATT.K,TPCATT)                                    119, A
TPCATT=12                                                        119.1, C
      PCATT   – PERCEIVED COMMUNITY ATTITUDE
      CATT    – COMMUNITY ATTITUDE
      TPCATT  – TIME TO PERCEIVE COMMUNITY ATTITUDE
```

```
DCATT.KL=CATT.K/(TDCATT*RSFEFF.K)                                120, R
TDCATT=60                                                        120.1, C
      DCATT   – DETERIORATION OF COMMUNITY ATTITUDE
      CATT    – COMMUNITY ATTITUDE
      TDCATT  – TIME FOR DETERIORATION OF COMMUNITY
                 ATTITUDE
      RSFEFF  – RE-ENTRY SUCCESS-FAILURE EFFECT
```

```
RSFEFF.K=TABHL(RSFTB,FTSR.K,0,.8,.2)                             121, A
RSFTB=.8,1,1.2,1.5,1.6                                           121.1, T
      RSFEFF  – RE-ENTRY SUCCESS-FAILURE EFFECT
      RSFTB   – RE-ENTRY SUCCESS-FAILURE TABLE
      FTSR    – FRACTION TO SUCCESSFULLY RE-ENTER
```

Community attitude toward addiction grows at a rate (GCATT) that is driven by community education and media exposure (both expressed in percent change per month) and constrained (FREFF and PRELEF) or accelerated (PERVEF and AGEEFF) by the other factors that have been described.

The two contraining factors have their effect by preventing attitude change until community residents become sufficiently frustrated with a police-oriented solution. The (1 - CATT) factor causes attitude change to slow as a substantially sociomedical attitude level is approached.

CATT grows and deteriorates (moves back toward a criminal definition) in response to GCATT and DCATT respectively. CATT begins each simulation with a value of 0.1, representing a primarily criminal definition. Perceived community attitude follows its actual attitude with a delay of 12 months (TPCATT).

Community attitude, unless continually bolstered by exposure to media and community education programs, can return to a criminal problem definition over a period of 60 months (TDCATT). The time over which deterioration takes place is assumed to be affected by the success or failure of addicts reentering the community from rehabilitation programs. If only a few reenter successfully (FTSR near zero), RSFEFF can cause a 20 percent reduction in the deterioration time and lead to a more rapid deterioration in community attitude (over only 48 months). If, on the other hand, 80 percent of those in rehabilitation programs reenter successfully, the community can be convinced that sociomedical solutions are feasible and RSFEFF will cause a doubling in the deterioration time. Deterioration in attitude would then take place much more slowly over a period of 120 months.

```
AERHB.K=TABHL(AERTB,CATT.K,0,.6,.1)                          122, A
AERTB=0,.1,.2,.4,.6,.9,1                                     122.1, T
      AERHB  — ATTITUDE EFFECT ON REHABILITATION
      AERTB  — ATTITUDE EFFECT ON REHAB TABLE
      CATT   — COMMUNITY ATTITUDE


RHBPP.K=RHBPRG*RHBPOL.K                                      123, A
RHBPRG=0                                                     123.1, C
      RHBPP  — REHABILITATION PROGRAM PLANNED
      RHBPRG — REHAB PROGRAM CONTROL SWITCH
      RHBPOL — REHABILITATION POLICY


RHBPOL.K=(DRHER.K) (EADRH.K) (RCPA.K)                        124, A
      RHBPOL — REHABILITATION POLICY
      DRHER  — DESIRED REHAB. ENTRY RATE
      EADRH  — EXP AVG DURATION IN REHAB
      RCPA   — TOTAL REHAB COST PER ADDICT


DRHER.K=( (ADDICT.K+PRISON.K)/TCFA)*CRR                      125, A
      DRHER  — DESIRED REHAB. ENTRY RATE
      ADDICT — ADDICTS
      PRISON — PRISON ADDICTS
      TCFA   — TIME TO CARE FOR ALL ADDICTS (GOAL)
      CRR    — COMMUNITY REHABILITATION RESPONSIBILITY
```

```
EADRH.K=(FTBRC.K) (TTBRHB) + (1-FTBRC.K) (TTDO)          126, A
TCFA=48                                                  126.1, C
COSTPA=250                                               126.2, C
      EADRH  - EXP AVG DURATION IN REHAB
      FTBRC  - FRACT TO BE REHABILITATED IN COMMUNITY
      TTBRHB - TIME TO BE REHABILITATED
      TTDO   - TIME TO DROP OUT
      TCFA   - TIME TO CARE FOR ALL ADDICTS (GOAL)
      COSTPA - COST PER ADDICT


RCPA.K=COSTPA+ROC.K                                      127, A
      RCPA   - TOTAL REHAB COST PER ADDICT
      COSTPA - COST PER ADDICT
      ROC    - REHAB OVH COST


GRP.KL=(RHBPP.K-RHBEF.K)*AERHB.K/TIRP                    128, R
TIRP=12                                                  128.1, C
      GRP    - GROWTH-REHABILITATION PROGRAM
      RHBPP  - REHABILITATION PROGRAM PLANNED
      RHBEF  - REHABILITATION EFFORT
      AERHB  - ATTITUDE EFFECT ON REHABILITATION
      TIRP   - TIME TO IMPLEMENT REHABILITATION PROGRAM


RHBEF.K=RHBEF.J+(DT) (GRP.JK)                            129, L
RHBEF=0                                                  129.1, N
      RHBEF  - REHABILITATION EFFORT
      GRP    - GROWTH-REHABILITATION PROGRAM
```

Community attitudes are presumed to have their primary effect on a community's willingness to accept in-community programs. The attitude effect on rehabilitation (AERHB) acts as a barrier to in-community programs when CATT has a value below 0.5 (in AERTB). This range is indicative of a primarily criminal definition of addiction and causes residents to reject in-community programs because they are thought to bring criminals into the neighborhood. Attitude levels at or above 0.5 cause this barrier to be lowered and enable in-community programs to be established.

A model user has the option of including in-community programs in a simulation by giving RHBPRG a value of 1 rather than zero. Inclusion of in-community programs produces a budget that provides for sufficient program capacity at each point in time (RHBPOL). Required capacity is determined by multiplying a desired entry rate for addicts (DRHER, in addicts/month) by an expected average duration in the program (EADRH, in months). Desired entry rate is based on the fraction of the addict population deemed eligible for in-community drug-free programs (ADDICT + PRISON)*CRR and the time after which all eligible addicts should have been treated (TCFA). In this case, the community tries to treat all of its eligible addicts by the end of 48 months (from the current month in which the plan is being made). CRR, the community rehabilitation responsibility, is set at the discretion of the model user. Expected average duration in programs is the average of program completion time and time after which dropouts occur, weighted by the fraction to successfully complete the program (FTBRC) and the fraction to drop out (1 - FTBRC), respectively. This allows places vacated by dropouts to be anticipated and included in planning calculations.

The required budget (in dollars per month) is computed by multiplying this number of places by the cost per month for each addict in the program. Cost per addict is the sum of a direct cost of $250 per month and an overhead cost dependent on the number in the program.

The rate at which the community implements this program plan is proportional to the difference between the sizes of the planned and existing programs and is constrained by the attitude effect described earlier. Implementation is assumed to take place over a period of 12 months (TIRP). Rehabilitation effort (RHBEF) (stated in dollars budgeted per month) grows as a result of this rate and is initially assumed to be zero.

```
MPP.K=METHPR*MTHPOL.K                                          130, A
METHPR=0                                                       130.1, C
      MPP      — METHADONE PROGRAM PLANNED
      METHPR   — METHADONE PROGRAM CONTROL SWITCH
      MTHPOL   — METH POLICY


MTHPOL.K=MTHNED.K*BUDF.K                                       131, A
      MTHPOL   — METH POLICY
      MTHNED   — METHADONE PROGRAM NEED
      BUDF     — BUDGET FACTOR–METH
BUDF.K=TABHL(BUDFTB,PERINV.K/YOUPOP.K,0,.25,.05)               132, A
BUDFTB=0,.05,.1,.3,.7,.9                                       132.1, T
      BUDF     — BUDGET FACTOR–METH
      BUDFTB   — BUDGET FACTOR–METH TABLE
      PERINV   — PERSONS INVOLVED
      YOUPOP   — YOUTH POPULATION


MTHNED.K=( (ADDICT.K+PRISON.K)*CMPR+METHDN.K)*CMPA.K           133, A
      MTHNED   — METHADONE PROGRAM NEED
      ADDICT   — ADDICTS
      PRISON   — PRISON ADDICTS
      CMPR     — COMMUNITY METHADONE PROGRAM RESPONSIBILITY
      METHDN   — ADDICTS IN METHADONE PROGRAM
      CMPA     — TOTAL COST OF METHADONE MAINTENANCE PER
                 ADDICT


GMP.KL=(MPP.K–METHEF.K)*AEMP.K/TIMP                            134, R
TIMP=12                                                        134.1, C
      GMP      — GROWTH OF METHADONE PROGRAM
      MPP      — METHADONE PROGRAM PLANNED
      METHEF   — METHADONE EFFORT
      AEMP     — ATTITUDE EFFECT ON METHADONE PROG
      TIMP     — TIME TO IMPLEMENT METHADONE PROGRAM
```

AEMP.K=TABHL(AEMPTB,CATT.K,0,.6,.1)   135, A
AEMPTB=0,.1,.2,.4,.65,.85,1   135.1, T
    AEMP   — ATTITUDE EFFECT ON METHADONE PROG
    AEMPTB — ATTITUDE EFFECT TAB
    CATT   — COMMUNITY ATTITUDE

METHEF.K=METHEF.J+(DT) (GMP.JK)   136, L
METHEF=1   136.1, N
    METHEF — METHADONE EFFORT
    GMP   — GROWTH OF METHADONE PROGRAM

Methadone programs are planned in a slightly different manner. They are included in a simulation by setting METHPR to 1 rather than zero. Because methadone programs can potentially serve so many addicts and represent an indeterminate commitment to addicts who enter, a budget factor (BUDF) intervenes between the computed need for methadone program budget (MTHNED) and the amount actually budgeted (MTHPOL). This factor causes only a small fraction of the need to be budgeted for, if relatively few people are perceived to be involved (where PERINV again is ALLADP + (0.1) (USERS)). When PERINV equals or exceeds 25 percent of the youthful population, 90 percent of the needed amount is budgeted (from BUDFTB).

Need for methadone programs is computed differently from the need for drug-free programs because perpetual maintenance makes concepts of average time in program and time over which all eligible addicts should be treated irrelevant. Methadone program need is instead determined by adding the number of addicts eligible for, but not yet in, methadone programs [(ADDICT + PRISON)∗CMPR] to the number currently enrolled and continuing in the community's methadone programs. CMPR is set at the discretion of the model user. The number of places required is multiplied by the cost per addict per month (CMPA) to get the monthly budget needed.

Growth of methadone programs (GMP) also occurs at a rate proportional to the difference between planned and existing budgets, is constrained by community attitudes (AEMP), and takes place over 12 months (TIMP). The attitude effect is very similar to the one on in-community drug-free programs.

EDUCPP.K=EDUCAT∗EDUPOL.K   137, A
EDUCAT=0   137.1, C
    EDUCPP — EDUCATION PROGRAM PLANNED
    EDUCAT — EDUCATION PROGRAM SWITCH
    EDUPOL — EDUCATIONAL POLICY

EDUPOL.K=EDUNED.K   138, A
    EDUPOL — EDUCATIONAL POLICY
    EDUNED — EDUCATION NEEDED

```
EDUNED.K=(PU.K) (CEPU+OCEPU.K) + (USERS.K) (CEU+OCEU.K)          139, A
CEPU=1.25                                                        139.1, C
CEU=3.4                                                          139.2, C
        EDUNED   – EDUCATION NEEDED
        PU       – POTENTIAL USERS
        CEPU     – COST OF EDUCATING POTENTIAL USERS
        OCEPU    – OVH COST OF EDUC POTL USERS
        USERS    – USERS
        CEU      – COST OF EDUCATING USERS
        OCEU     – OVH COST OF EDUC USERS


GEDEF.KL=(EDUCPP.K–EDEF.K)/(TDEDEF*(1/PERVEF.K) )                140, R
TDEDEF=36                                                        140.1, C
        GEDEF    – GRWTH OF EDUC EFFORT
        EDUCPP   – EDUCATION PROGRAM PLANNED
        EDEF     – EDUCATION EFFORT
        TDEDEF   – TIME TO DEVELOP EDUCATION EFFORT
        PERVEF   – PERVASIVENESS EFFECT


EDEF.K=EDEF.J+(DT) (GEDEF.JK)                                    141, L
EDEF=(EDUPOL/2)*EDUCAT+1                                         141.1, N
        EDEF     – EDUCATION EFFORT
        GEDEF    – GRWTH OF EDUC EFFORT
        EDUPOL   – EDUCATIONAL POLICY
        EDUCAT   – EDUCATION PROGRAM SWITCH
```

Drug education programs for the community are also planned on the basis of a computed need and can be included in a simulation by setting EDUCAT to 1 rather than zero. Potential users and users are considered separately in determining need. The model assumes that potential users can be reached less expensively through mass communication techniques while users require more intensive approaches, such as small group sessions, if education is to be at all effective. Total required budget is the sum of the numbers of potential users and users multiplied by their respective direct monthly costs ($1.25 for potential users and $3.40 for users) and overhead costs. Growth in educational programs is again proportional to the difference between budgeted and existing programs. Perceived pervasiveness also affects the rate at which education programs are implemented. This results in an implementation time of 36 months (TDEDEF) if pervasiveness is perceived as low (again based on the PERINV variable) and one of 18 months if pervasiveness is high (and PERVEF = 2). The community's education effort (in dollars per month) is assumed initially to be half of what is needed when education programs are included in simulations.

```
AECEDP.K=TABHL(AECTB,CATT.K,0,1,.2)                              142, A
AECTB=0,.1,.3,.5,.8,1                                            142.1, T
        AECEDP   – ATTITUDE EFFECT ON CREDIBLE EDUCATION
                       PROGRAM
        AECTB    – ATTITUDE EFFECT ON CREDIBILITY TABLE
        CATT     – COMMUNITY ATTITUDE
```

```
GCEDEF.KL=(EDEF.K-CEDEF.K)*AECEDF.K/TICP                143, R
TICP=24                                                 143.1, C
    GCEDEF  -  GROWTH OF CREDIBLE PROGRAM
    EDEF    -  EDUCATION EFFORT
    CEDEF   -  CREDIBLE EDUCATION EFFORT
    AECEDP  -  ATTITUDE EFFECT ON CREDIBLE EDUCATION
               PROGRAM
    TICP    -  TIME TO IMPLEMENT CREDIBLE PROGRAM

CEDEF.K=CEDEF.J+(DT) (GCEDEF.JK)                         144, L
CEDEF=0                                                 144.1, N
    CEDEF   -  CREDIBLE EDUCATION EFFORT
    GCEDEF  -  GROWTH OF CREDIBLE PROGRAM
```

Education programs are presumed to be implementable with little community opposition since residents can adopt programs that reflect their own biases (that drugs are all bad). The amount of budget allocated to credible education programs is, however, affected by community attitudes. Low values of community attitude, corresponding to a criminal definition of addiction, will produce values of AECEDP that prevent credible education programs of any substance from being developed. Values of CATT between 60 percent and 80 percent are necessary before a major portion of the drug education budget can be devoted to credible programs. The rate at which credible programs develop (GCEDEF) is dependent on the fraction of the drug education budget that is not already invested in credible programs (EDEF–CEDEF), this attitude effect, and an implementation time of 24 months (TICP). The credible education budget is assumed initially to be zero.

Community-Change Sector
This sector deals with change in the community's socioeconomic level in response to addict crime and resultant migration. The community-change sector remained inactive during most of the simulations (socioeconomic level remained constant), but was allowed to behave dynamically during the set of simulations described in Section 6.7.

```
CA.K=(ADP.K/SFC.K) (SELCE.K)                            145, A
    CA      -  COMMUNITY ALARM
    ADP     -  AWARENESS OF DRUG PROBLEM
    SFC     -  STANDARD FOR CRIME
    SELCE   -  SOCIO-ECONOMIC LEVEL CHANGE EFFECT

SELCE.K=TABHL(SELCTB,AVRSEL.K,-.01,.01,.005)            146, A
SELCTB=2,1.4,1,.9,.8                                    146.1, T
    SELCE   -  SOCIO-ECONOMIC LEVEL CHANGE EFFECT
    SELCTB  -  SOCIO-ECONOMIC LEVEL CHANGE TABLE
    AVRSEL  -  AV R C OF S-E L
```

```
AVRSEL.K=AVRSEL.J+(DT) (1/TARSEL) (RCSEL.JK-AVRSEL.J)          147, L
AVRSEL=0                                                       147.1, N
TARSEL=12                                                      147.2, C
      AVRSEL − AV R C OF S-E L
      TARSEL − TIME OF AV R C OF S-E L
      RCSEL  − R C OF SOCIO-ECONOMIC L
```

Community alarm (CA) was introduced earlier as the factor affecting the strength of a community's police response, given some computed need for manpower. As stated then, alarm is principally a function of the ratio of perceived crime (ADP) to the community's accustomed standard for crime (SFC) and expressed as that ratio. Alarm is also affected by perceived changes in socioeconomic level (SELCE). A 1 percent per month shift downward in socioeconomic level causes increased concern about the impact of addiction on the community and doubles alarm (from SELCTB). No change has a neutral effect and positive socioeconomic change produces up to a 20 percent reduction in alarm when SEL is growing at 1 percent per month. The average rate of socioeconomic change (AVRSEL) upon which perceptions are based follows the actual rate (RCSEL) after a delay of 12 months (TARSEL).

```
PPM.K=CSEL.K-SEL.K                                            148, A
      PPM    − POTENTIAL PERCENTAGE MIGRATION
      CSEL   − COMPATIBLE SOCIO-ECON LEVEL
      SEL    − SOCIO-ECONOMIC LEVEL

CSEL.K=TABHL(CSELTB,CI.K,0,.08,.01)                           149, A
CSELTB=.8,.75,.7,.7,.7,.7,.7,.7,.7                            149.1, T
      CSEL    − COMPATIBLE SOCIO-ECON LEVEL
      CSELTB  − COMP SEL TABLE
      CI      − CRIME INCIDENCE

CI.K=LAC.K/POP                                                150, A
      CI     − CRIME INCIDENCE
      LAC    − LONG-TERM AWARENESS OF CRIME
      POP    − TOTAL POPULATION

LAC.K=LAC.J+(DT) (1/TPC) (ADP.J-LAC.J)                        151, L
LAC=ADP                                                       151.1, N
TPC=3                                                         151.2, C
      LAC    − LONG-TERM AWARENESS OF CRIME
      TPC    − TIME TO PERCEIVE CRIME
      ADP    − AWARENESS OF DRUG PROBLEM
```

The potential percentage migration (PPM) forms the basis for rates of migration into or out of the community. It is equal to the difference between the socioeconomic level compatible with current crime incidence and the community's current socioeconomic level. PPM can be expressed as a percentage because CSEL and SEL are both points on a 0-to-1 scale.

Compatible socioeconomic level (CSEL) is the level a community would be expected to have, given its per capita crime incidence. High crime incidence communities are assumed to have poorer residents who cannot afford to move to communities with less crime. For most of the simulations, though, CSELTB had the form shown in equation 149.1, which kept socioeconomic change from taking place due to addict crime. Only those simulations described in Section 6.7 included forms of CSELTB that had the socioeconomic level decreasing with higher crime incidence, permitting socioeconomic decline to take place. In these formulations socioeconomic level is lowest when crime incidence reaches 8 crimes per 100 residents each month. Crime incidence is simply the long-term awareness of crime (LAC) [ADP, in crimes per month, subjected to a 3-month delay for awareness of new crime rates to develop (TPC)] divided by the community's total population (POP).

```
OMIG.KL=CLIP(0,(PPM.K*POP/TM.K)*SE.K,CSEL.K,SEL,K)                    152, R
        OMIG   − OUT-MIG. RATE
        PPM    − POTENTIAL PERCENTAGE MIGRATION
        POP    − TOTAL POPULATION
        TM     − TIME TO MIGRATE
        SE     − STRUCTURAL EFFECT ON MIGRATION
        CSEL   − COMPATIBLE SOCIO-ECON LEVEL
        SEL    − SOCIO-ECONOMIC LEVEL


IMIG.KL=CLIP(PPM.K*POP/NTM,0,CSEL.K,SEL.K)                            153, R
NTM=48                                                              153.1, C
        IMIG   − IN-MIG. RATE
        PPM    − POTENTIAL PERCENTAGE MIGRATION
        POP    − TOTAL POPULATION
        NTM    − NORMAL TIME TO MIGRATE
        CSEL   − COMPATIBLE SOCIO-ECON LEVEL
        SEL    − SOCIO-ECONOMIC LEVEL


SE.K=TABHL(SETB,CS.K,0,1,.2)                                         154, A
SETB=1,.9,.8,.7,.4,.2                                              154.1, T
POP=170E3                                                          154.2, C
        SE     − STRUCTURAL EFFECT ON MIGRATION
        SETB   − STRUCTURAL EFFECT TABLE
        CS     − COMMUNITY STRUCTURE
        POP    − TOTAL POPULATION


TM.K=TABHL(TMTB,CA.K,1,3,.4)                                         155, A
TMTB=78,66,54,42,30,24                                             155.1, T
        TM     − TIME TO MIGRATE
        TMTB   − TIME FOR MIGRATION TABLE
        CA     − COMMUNITY ALARM
```

ARM.K=SMOOTH(OMIG.JK+IMIG.JK,TARM)   156, A
TARM=6   156.1, C

     ARM   – AVERAGE RATE OF MIGRATION
     OMIG   – OUT–MIG. RATE
     IMIG   – IN–MIG. RATE
     TARM   – TIME TO AVERAGE RATE OF MIGRAT.

          Out-migration from the community (OMIG) is basically a function of the number of people who would have to migrate to bring the community's economic level to one compatible with its crime incidence. This is formulated as the product of potential percentage migrating (PPM) and total population, where PPM is the size of the adjustment necessary to bring current socioeconomic level in line with CSEL. Migration by this number of people takes place over the number of months defined by the time to migrate (TM). This time period is assumed to be a function of community alarm. Out-migration may be sharply curtailed by a structural effect (SE) that causes community residents to hold fast in the face of growing crime incidence.

          The structural effect (SE) is based on the existing level of community structure (CS). Structure is represented by a 0-to-1 scale in which 1 corresponds to a very high degree of structure (very long length of residence and its effect on relationships among residents, strong community institutions and organizations), and zero corresponds to no real structure at all (highly transient community). Community socioeconomic level and structure are not wholly independent, since the out-migration that reduces socioeconomic level can also destroy structure. Values of CS close to zero do not inhibit outmigration at all, but values approaching 1 can reduce the out-migration rate by up to 80 percent (the 0.2 multiplier in SETB).

          In-migration is computed in a manner slightly different from the out-migration rate, though it is also based on the number of people who must migrate to bring SEL and CSEL into line. In this case, the structural effect is omitted, since community structure does not affect people not yet living in a community. Time to migrate is not a function of community alarm (not relevant to people seeing the community as relatively more attractive), and instead is given a constant value of 48 months (NTM). In-migration occurs at the rate indicated if CSEL is greater than SEL but does not otherwise occur.

          As indicated earlier, the community's total population, upon which the migration calculations are based, is 170,000. The average rate of migration (ARM) is calculated over a 6-month period (TARM).

FM.K=ARM.K/POP   157, A

     FM   – FRACTION MOVING
     ARM   – AVERAGE RATE OF MIGRATION
     POP   – TOTAL POPULATION

DCS.KL=(CS.K) (FM.K)   158, R
    DCS   – DETERIORATION OF COMMUNITY STRUCTURE
    CS   – COMMUNITY STRUCTURE
    FM   – FRACTION MOVING

CS.K=CS.J+(DT) (BCS.JK+DCS.JK)   159, L
CS=.9   159.1, N
    CS   – COMMUNITY STRUCTURE
    BCS   – BUILDING COMMUNITY STRUCTURE
    DCS   – DETERIORATION OF COMMUNITY STRUCTURE

BCS.KL=(REGEN.K) (COMDEV.K) (1–CS.K)   160, R
    BCS   – BUILDING COMMUNITY STRUCTURE
    REGEN   – REGENERATION OF STRUCTURE
    COMDEV – COMMUNITY DEVELOPMENT EFFORT
    CS   – COMMUNITY STRUCTURE

REGEN.K=TABHL(REGTB,CA.K,1,3,.4)   161, A
REGTB=0,.0015,.0025,.0035,.0045,.0050   161.1, T
    REGEN   – REGENERATION OF STRUCTURE
    REGTB   – REGENERATION TABLE
    CA   – COMMUNITY ALARM

COMDEV.K=CDEVEL*CDPOL.K   162, A
CDEVEL=0   162.1, C
    COMDEV – COMMUNITY DEVELOPMENT EFFORT
    CDEVEL – COMMUNITY DEVELOPMENT SWITCH
    CDPOL   – COMMUNITY DEVELOPMENT POLICY

CDPOL.K=TABHL(CDTB,CS.K,0,1,.25)   163, A
CDTB=10,6,5,4,3   163.1, T
    CDPOL   – COMMUNITY DEVELOPMENT POLICY
    CDTB   – COMMUNITY DEVELOPMENT TABLE
    CS   – COMMUNITY STRUCTURE

The fraction of people moving into or out of a community (FM) is
the average rate of migration divided by total population. Deterioration in
structure (CS) occurs at a rate proportional to the fraction moving and the level
of structure itself. Because structure is represented on a 0-to-1 scale, low values
of structure produce lower rates of deterioration when multiplied by the
fraction moving. High levels of CS (closer to one) deteriorate at a faster rate.
Community structure deteriorates at the rate shown or grows at the rate BCS.
CS is given an initial value of 0.9, representing a high degree of structure in
the community.

    Building of community structure is assumed to be the result of
internal regenerative forces (REGEN) and developmental efforts using outside
resources (COMDEV). The regenerative forces are stimulated by community
alarm (CA) and cause structure to grow at up to 0.5 percent per month when

alarm has a value of 3 (crime three times standard). This process corresponds to spontaneous organization among residents seeking better police protection and, possibly, various treatment and preventive programs. The effect of regenerative forces can be amplified up to tenfold by an explicit community development program if one is in operation (CDEVEL = 1 rather than zero). If operating, community development efforts counter deterioration in structure and intensify as the value of CS drops (CDPOL, CDTB). The (1 – CS) term in equation 160 causes it to be more difficult to build structure as CS approaches 1.

```
RCSEL.KL=CLIP(WORSEL.K,IMPSEL.K,0,AVRSEL.K)                      164, R
      RCSEL   – R C OF SOCIO-ECONOMIC L
      WORSEL – WORSENING OF SOCIO-ECONOMIC LEVEL
      IMPSEL  – IMPROVEMENT OF S-E L
      AVRSEL – AV R C OF S-E L


WORSEL.K=(SEL.K) (FM.K)                                          165, A
      WORSEL – WORSENING OF SOCIO-ECONOMIC LEVEL
      SEL      – SOCIO-ECONOMIC LEVEL
      FM       – FRACTION MOVING


IMPSEL.K=(FM.K) (1-SEL.K)                                        166, A
      IMPSEL  – IMPROVEMENT OF S-E L
      FM       – FRACTION MOVING
      SEL      – SOCIO-ECONOMIC LEVEL


SEL.K=SEL.J+(DT) (RCSEL.JK)                                      167, L
SEL=.7                                                           167.1, N
      SEL      – SOCIO-ECONOMIC LEVEL
      RCSEL   – R C OF SOCIO-ECONOMIC L
```

The rate of change of socioeconomic level takes on either of two values (WORSEL or IMPSEL) depending on the direction of change. If SEL is declining (AVRSEL less than zero), RCSEL will equal WORSEL and is slowed as SEL approaches zero. Similarly, if SEL is growing (AVRSEL greater than zero) RCSEL will equal IMPSEL and is slowed as SEL approaches 1 [and (1 – SEL) approaches zero]. These factors permit rapid change to take place in the mid-range of socioeconomic levels, but prevent unrealistically rapid change when SEL moves toward either end of the scale. SEL is initially set at 0.7, a value representative of the middle-income community that was modeled.

```
RCFDL.KL=( (1-SEL.K-FDL.K)/TCFDL)-CMHCEF.K*FDL.K                168, R
TCFDL=12                                                        168.1, C
      RCFDL  – RATE OF CHANGE OF FUTILITY-DESPAIR LEVEL
      SEL     – SOCIO-ECONOMIC LEVEL
      FDL     – FUTILITY-DESPAIR LEVEL
      TCFDL  – TIME TO CHANGE FUTILITY-DESPAIR LEVEL
      CMHCEF – CMHC PROG EFF
```

```
CMHCPR.K=MHEFF*MHPOL.K                                          169, A
MHEFF=0                                                         169.1, C
      CMHCPR  − COMM MENTAL HEALTH CENTER PROGRAM
      MHEFF   − MENTAL HEALTH EFFORT SWITCH
      MHPOL   − MENTAL HEALTH POLICY


MHPOL.K=(TFRAC.K) (PU.K+USERS.K) (TMHCST.K)                     170, A
      MHPOL   − MENTAL HEALTH POLICY
      TFRAC   − TROUBLED FRACTION
      PU      − POTENTIAL USERS
      USERS   − USERS
      TMHCST  − TOTAL MENTAL HEALTH COST/MO./PERSON


TFRAC.K=TABHL(TFTB,FDL.K,0,1,.2)                                171, A
TFTB=.1,.15,.2,.25,.28,.3                                       171.1, T
CCOST=40                                                        171.2, C
      TFRAC   − TROUBLED FRACTION
      TFTB    − TROUBLED FRACTION TABLE
      FDL     − FUTILITY−DESPAIR LEVEL
      CCOST   − CARE COST


TMHCST.K=CCOST+MHOCST.K                                         172, A
      TMHCST  − TOTAL MENTAL HEALTH COST/MO./PERSON
      CCOST   − CARE COST
      MHOCST  − MH OH COST


CMHCEF.K=TABHL(CMHCTB,CMHCPR.K/MHPOL.K,0,2,.5)                  173, A
CMHCTB=0,.005,.01,.02,.03                                       173.1, T
      CMHCEF  − CMHC PROG EFF
      CMHCTB  − CMHC EFFECTIVENESS TABLE
      CMHCPR  − COMM MENTAL HEALTH CENTER PROGRAM
      MHPOL   − MENTAL HEALTH POLICY


FDL.K=FDL.J+(DT) (RCFDL.JK)                                     174, L
FDL=1−SEL                                                       174.1, N
      FDL     − FUTILITY−DESPAIR LEVEL
      RCFDL   − RATE OF CHANGE OF FUTILITY−DESPAIR LEVEL
      SEL     − SOCIO−ECONOMIC LEVEL
```

The community's futility despair level (FDL) is essentially the inverse of its socioeconomic level; it follows the value of (1 − SEL) after a delay of 12 months. Futility despair can be reduced each month by the effects of community mental health center efforts (CMHCEF). Those effects are greater when futility despair is at higher values (near 1) because of the multiplicative formulation. Mental health programs are in effect when MHEFF is set at 1 rather than zero. The mental health policy (MHPOL) is designed to allocate resources for a troubled fraction (TFRAC) of the nonaddicted youthful population (PU + USERS). A direct cost of $40 per month (CCOST) and an overhead cost (inversely proportional to the number being served) is incurred for each person in this group. The troubled fraction is assumed to be proportional to the futility despair level and reaches 30 percent when FDL is at its highest value. Community mental health center programs have their maximum effect (CMHCEF) when the budgeted program is unrealistically equal to twice the total need [where need is (TFRAC) (PU + USERS) (TMHCST)] and, at that point, can reduce the futility despair level by 3 percent per month. The futility despair level is set initially equal to (1 – SEL) and remains at that level unless a change in SEL takes place.

Incarceration, Rehabilitation and Reentry Sector

```
PRTS.KL=(PRISON.K) (FPRTS.K)/TTBREL                              175, R
TTBREL=18                                                        175.1, C
      PRTS     – PRISON RELEASE TO STREET
      PRISON   – PRISON ADDICTS
      FPRTS    – FRAC PRISONERS TO STREET
      TTBREL   – TIME TO BE RELEASED

FPRTS.K=TABHL(FPTSTB,1–FPREH.K,0,1,.2)                           176, A
FPTSTB=.2,.35,.5,.66,.83,1.0                                     176.1, T
      FPRTS    – FRAC PRISONERS TO STREET
      FPTSTB   – FRAC PRIS TO STREET TABLE
      FPREH    – FRAC PRIS TO REHABS

FPREH.K=(ECSUS.K) (FPCR.K*RSEA.K+FPOR.K*ORSEA.K)                 177, A
      FPREH    – FRAC PRIS TO REHABS
      ECSUS    – EFFECT OF C R SUSCEPTIBILITY
      FPCR     – FRACTION FROM PRISON TO COMMUNITY REHAB
      RSEA     – REHABILITATION SUCCESS EFFECT ON ADMISSIONS
      FPOR     – FRAC FROM PRISON TO OUTSIDE REHAB
      ORSEA    – OUTSIDE REHAB SUCCESS EFFECT ON ADMISSIONS

PRISON.K=PRISON.J+(DT) (STPR.JK–PRTS.JK–PCR.JK–POR.JK)           178, L
PRISON=(IYPOP) (.001)                                            178.1, N
      PRISON   – PRISON ADDICTS
      STPR     – STREET TO PRISON RATE
      PRTS     – PRISON RELEASE TO STREET
      PCR      – PRISON TO COMMUN RE
      POR      – PRISON TO OUT REH
      IYPOP    – INITIAL YOUTH POPULATION

STPR.KL=AVARR.K*CONRAT                                           179, R
CONRAT=.25                                                       179.1, C
      STPR     – STREET TO PRISON RATE
      AVARR    – AVERAGE ARREST RATE
      CONRAT   – CONVICTION RATE (PRCT)
```

The number of addict prisoners released to the street (PRTS), rather than to rehabilitation programs, is equal to the product of the total number of addicts in prison who are being released (PRISON/TTBREL) and the fraction of those addicts ultimately released to the street (FPRTS). Because the average length of incarceration is assumed to be 18 months (TTBREL), one-eighteenth of the imprisoned addicts are released each month. The fraction released to the street is a function of the fraction not entering rehabilitation programs. When none of those released enters rehabilitation programs, all are assumed to return to the street. On the other hand, even if all are expected to enter programs, 20 percent are assumed to return to the street because all of those eligible will not enroll in programs (in FPTSTB, FPRTS = 0.2 when 1 - FPREH = 0).

The fraction entering rehabilitation programs from prison (FPREH) is subject to the effect of susceptibility to community rehabilitation programs (ECSUS). This effect reflects the fact that only a limited fraction of any addict population can benefit from a drug-free program. Many addicts are too accustomed to the addict life-style to make the behavioral changes necessary for success in this type of program. Entry into rehabilitation programs is also affected by the perceived success of those programs in rehabilitating addicts who enter. The success effect for drug-free programs within and outside the community is a composite of individual success effects (RSEA and ORSEA) weighted by the fractions of addicts (FRCR and FPOR) going into in-community and out-of-community programs, respectively.

The number of addicts in prison during any month (PRISON) grows as a result of additions from the street and declines due to releases to the street and to rehabilitation programs. Addicts in prison initially make up 0.1 percent of the community's youthful population. The rate at which addicts enter prison (STPR) is a fraction of the number arrested that are actually convicted and sentenced (CONRAT). This fraction is assumed to be 25 percent.

```
PCR.KL=(PRISON.K) (FPCR.K) (ECSUS.K) (RSEA.K)/TTBREL                  180, R
        PCR       — PRISON TO COMMUN RE
        PRISON    — PRISON ADDICTS
        FPCR      — FRACTION FROM PRISON TO COMMUNITY REHAB
        ECSUS     — EFFECT OF C R SUSCEPTIBILITY
        RSEA      — REHABILITATION SUCCESS EFFECT ON ADMISSIONS
        TTBREL    — TIME TO BE RELEASED

ECSUS.K=TABHL(ECSTB,CSUS.K,0,.4,.1)                                   181, A
ECSTB=.01,.05,.1,.3,.4                                               181.1, T
        ECSUS     — EFFECT OF C R SUSCEPTIBILITY
        ECSTB     — EFF OF C R SUSCEPTIBILITY TABLE
        CSUS      — COMM REHAB SUSC

CSUS.K=(CLFRAC*ALLADP.K–COMRHB.K–RBOCOM.K)/ALLADP.K                   182, A
CLFRAC=.4                                                            182.1, C
        CSUS      — COMM REHAB SUSC
        CLFRAC    — COMM REHAB LIMIT FRACTION
        ALLADP    — ALL ADDICTS, INCL. MAINT. PROG.
```

```
        COMRHB  — COMMUNITY REHABILITATION
        RBOCOM  — ADDICTS IN REHABILITATION OUTSIDE THE
                  COMMUNITY
```

```
FPCR.K=TABHL(FPRPTB, (RHBEF.K–COMRHB.K*RCPA.K)/              183, A
  (COMRHB.K*RCPA.K),–.5,.2,.1)
FPRPTB=0,.1,.2,.3,.5,.7,.9,1                                 183.1, T
CRR=.3                                                       183.2, C
        FPCR    — FRACTION FROM PRISON TO COMMUNITY REHAB
        FPRPTB  — FRAC FROM PRISON TO REHAB PROGRAM TABLE
        RHBEF   — REHABILITATION EFFORT
        COMRHB  — COMMUNITY REHABILITATION
        RCPA    — TOTAL REHAB COST PER ADDICT
        CRR     — COMMUNITY REHABILITATION RESPONSIBILITY
```

```
RSEA.K=TABHL(SEATB,COMRHB.K/ALLADP.K,.05,.3,.05)            184, A
SEATB=1,1.05,1.1,1.2,1.4,1.5                                 184.1, T
        RSEA    — REHABILITATION SUCCESS EFFECT ON ADMISSIONS
        SEATB   — SUCCESS EFFECT ON ADMISSIONS TABLE
        COMRHB  — COMMUNITY REHABILITATION
        ALLADP  — ALL ADDICTS, INCL. MAINT. PROG.
```

The rate at which addicts move from prison into in-community drug-free rehabilitation programs (PCR) is based on the number now in prison expected eventually to enter that type of program. That number is the product of addicts in prison, the fraction to enter community rehabilitation programs (FPCR), and multipliers reflecting the effects of susceptibility (ECSUS) and perceived success of rehabilitation (RSEA). Each month, one-eighteenth of that number (1/TTBREL) actually enters community rehabilitation programs from prison.

Susceptibility of an addict population to any form of rehabilitation is based on a judgment about the maximum fraction of the population for which that form is appropriate. The remaining fraction susceptible, at any point in time, is the total number susceptible (CLFRAC*ALLADP) less the number already in programs divided by the total number of addicts. In this case, the model initially assumes that a maximum of 40 percent of the community's addicts could be placed in in-community, drug-free programs (CLFRAC). ECSUS reduces movement from prison to rehabilitation when only a very small fraction of the addicts are still susceptible and allows the full fraction susceptible to enter when CSUS is near 0.4.

FPCR represents the effect of available capacity in rehabilitation programs on entry from prison into those programs. The difference between rehabilitation effort (RHBEF, dollars per month of budget allocated to in-community programs) and the product of the number of addicts currently in those programs and the monthly cost for each one (COMRHB*RCPA) represents the excess budget available for new addicts to be treated. Dividing that difference by the cost of treating addicts currently in those programs yields the programs' fractional excess capacity. If the number produced by that calculation is negative, inadequacy of resources is indicated and FPCR inhibits new entries by taking on a low value. "Excess" capacity that is zero or even slightly negative still allows some access to these programs because, as long as resources are at least sufficient to meet current needs, it is assumed that those resources can be stretched a bit to accommodate a few more addicts. An excess of 20 percent is required for FPCR to have no inhibiting effect at all. Community rehabilitation responsibility (CRR), the fraction of the addict population at which in-community drug-free programs are directed, was set at 0.3 in most of the simulations utilizing those programs.

The rehabilitation success effect (RSEA) is based on the fraction of the addict population in community rehabilitation programs (rather than the fraction successfully rehabilitated as in the success effect influencing addiction rate). This represents a critical mass factor in which entry of some number of addicts into a program makes that program less threatening and strange and encourages new addicts to enter. This enrollment effect gradually grows as program visibility increases, reaching its maximum ability to increase the entry rate to in-community programs, 50 percent in SEATB, when 30 percent of the addict population is in these programs.

```
INTAKE.KL=(ADDICT.K) (FACR.K) (ECSUS.K) (RSEA.K)/TTERP          185, R
TTERP=12                                                       185.1, C
      INTAKE   – INTAKE
      ADDICT   – ADDICTS
      FACR     – FRAC OF ADDICTS TO COMMUNITY REHAB
      ECSUS    – EFFECT OF C R SUSCEPTIBILITY
      RSEA     – REHABILITATION SUCCESS EFFECT ON ADMISSIONS
      TTERP    – TIME TO ENTER REHABILITATION PROGRAM


FACR.K=TABHL(FARPTB, (RHBEF.K–COMRHB.K*RCPA.K)/                 186, A
      (COMRHB.K*RCPA.K),–5,.2,.1)*PAFIC.K
FARPTB=0,.1,.2,.3,.5,.7,.9,1                                   186.1, T
      FACR     – FRAC OF ADDICTS TO COMMUNITY REHAB
      FARPTB   – FRAC ADDICTS TO REHAB PROGRAM TABLE
      RHBEF    – REHABILITATION EFFORT
      COMRHB   – COMMUNITY REHABILITATION
      RCPA     – TOTAL REHAB COST PER ADDICT
      PAFIC    – POLICE AND AVAILABILITY FACTORS IN
                 COMMUNITY


PAFIC.K=PHE.K+LDAF.K                                            187, A
      PAFIC    – POLICE AND AVAILABILITY FACTORS IN
                 COMMUNITY
      PHE      – POLICE HARASSMENT EFF.
      LDAF     – LOW DRUG AVAIL. FACTOR
```

```
PHE.K=TABHL(PHETB,AVARR.K/ADDICT.K,0,.1,.02)                    188, A
PHETB=.5,.6,.7,.8,.9,1                                         188.1, T
    PHE     — POLICE HARASSMENT EFF.
    PHETB   — POLICE HARASSMENT EFF TABLE
    AVARR   — AVERAGE ARREST RATE
    ADDICT  — ADDICTS


LDAF.K=TABHL(LDAFTB,AAP.K/ADDICT.K,-1,0,.2)                     189, A
LDAFTB=1,.9,.8,.6,.55,.5                                       189.1, T
    LDAF    — LOW DRUG AVAIL. FACTOR
    LDAFTB  — LOW DRUG AVAIL. FAC. TABLE
    AAP     — ADDITIONAL ADDICT POTENTIAL
    ADDICT  — ADDICTS


COMRHB.K=COMRHB.J+(DT) (INTAKE.JK+PCR.JK-CREHAB.JK-             190, L
    DFCR.JK)
COMRHB=1                                                       190.1, N
    COMRHB  — COMMUNITY REHABILITATION
    INTAKE  — INTAKE
    PCR     — PRISON TO COMMUN RE
    CREHAB  — COMMUNITY REHABILITATION RATE
    DFCR    — DROPOUT RATE FROM COMMUNITY REHAB
```

Entry to in-community programs directly from the street occurs at a rate (INTAKE) computed in a manner similar to, but different in two respects from, the computation of the entry rate from prison. First, the number of people now on the street who will enter the programs enter over a 12-month period (TTERP) rather than the 18 months determined by the time to be released from prison (TTBREL). Second, entry from the street is affected by conditions prevailing on the street that do not affect addicts in prison. This influence is composed of police and availability factors in the community (PAFIC). A police harrassment effect (PHE) varies between 0.5 and 1 as the average rate of addict arrests each month goes from zero to 10 percent of addicts on the street. The low drug-availability factor (LDAF) goes from 1 down to 0.5 as existing drug supplies increase in adequacy (AAP of zero means that availability is at least adequate for the existing addict group, while negative values indicate inadequate heroin availability). Because PHE and LDAF are additive, PAFIC ranges from a neutral value of 1 to a doubling effect on the entry rate as police harassment and low drug availability combine to make rehabilitation programs more attractive to the street addict.

Addicts in community rehabilitation (COMRHB) are added to as people enter from prison and the street. Their number is depleted as addicts are rehabilitated (enter a reentry phase) or drop out of programs.

CREHAB.KL=(COMRHB.K-PDFCR.K)/TTBRHB   191, R
TTBRHB=18   191.1, C
    CREHAB   – COMMUNITY REHABILITATION RATE
    COMRHB   – COMMUNITY REHABILITATION
    PDFCR   – POTENTIAL DROPOUTS FROM COMMUNITY REHAB
    TTBRHB   – TIME TO BE REHABILITATED

PDFCR.K=PDFCR.J+(DT) ((1-FTBRC.J) (INTAKE.JK+PCR.JK)-   192, L
   DFCR.JK)
PDFCR=0   192.1, N
    PDFCR   – POTENTIAL DROPOUTS FROM COMMUNITY REHAB
    FTBRC   – FRAC TO BE REHABILITATED IN COMMUNITY
    INTAKE   – INTAKE
    PCR   – PRISON TO COMMUN RE
    DFCR   – DROPOUT RATE FROM COMMUNITY REHAB

DFCR.KL=PDFCR.K/TTDO   193, R
    DFCR   – DROPOUT RATE FROM COMMUNITY REHAB
    PDFCR   – POTENTIAL DROPOUTS FROM COMMUNITY REHAB
    TTDO   – TIME TO DROP OUT

FTBRC.K=TABHL(FRTB,(CSUSEF.K*RHBEF.K)/(COMRHB.K*   194, A
   RCPA.K),0,2,.4)
FRTB=0,.05,.1,.2,.25,.3   194.1, T
    FTBRC   – FRACT TO BE REHABILITATED IN COMMUNITY
    FRTB   – FRACTION REHAB TABLE
    CSUSEF   – COMM SUSCEPT EFFECT ON SUCCESS
    RHBEF   – REHABILITATION EFFORT
    COMRHB   – COMMUNITY REHABILITATION
    RCPA   – TOTAL REHAB COST PER ADDICT

CSUSEF.K=TABHL(CSEFTB,CSUS.K,0,.4,.1)   195, A
CSEFTB=.1,.3,.5,1,1   195.1, T
TTDO=3   195.2, C
    CSUSEF   – COMM SUSCEPT EFFECT ON SUCCESS
    CSEFTB   – COMM SUSCEPT EFFECT TABLE
    CSUS   – COMM REHAB SUSC
    TTDO   – TIME TO DROP OUT

      The number of addicts now in community, drug-free programs who
will be successfully rehabilitated is the total number in those programs less the
number of potential dropouts. Because the rehabilitation process takes 18
months to complete (TTBRHB), one-eighteenth of that number is "graduated"
each month. The subset of addicts in rehabilitation programs who potentially
drop out (PDFCR) is determined by allocating some fraction of the addicts
entering each month (INTAKE + PCR) to the dropout group. That fraction
(1 - FTBRC) is a function of the adequacy of resources devoted to community
rehabilitation [RHBEF/(COMRHB*RCPA)], given the number of addicts
being treated, and of a susceptibility factor (CSUSEF).

The susceptibility factor represents a "creaming" phenomenon in which the first few addicts taken into a program are more likely to be highly motivated and rehabilitated successfully than addicts who enter only after many others have already entered. When CSUS is close to 0.4, a number of the addicts on the street and in prison are still susceptible to in-community programs. The addicts who do enter under these conditions are assumed to be highly motivated, and CSUSEF has a neutral effect (from CSEETB). In this case, the fraction to be rehabilitated successfully is determined entirely by resource adequacy. On the other hand, when CSUS is close to zero and few susceptible addicts remain outside of programs, CSUSEF reflects reaching "the bottom of the barrel" by a drastic but real reduction of FTBRC.

If resources are twice what is required and the addicts being treated represent a highly motivated segment, as much as 30 percent of those in community rehabilitation programs are assumed to be rehabilitated successfully (in FRTB). Poorer resource availability and/or lower motivation reduces this fraction substantially.

Addicts in these programs who eventually leave (DFCR) are assumed to drop out after an average of 3 months (TTDO). When they do, they are subtracted from PDFCR (in equation 192) as well as from the total number in in-community drug-free programs (COMRHB).

```
POR.KL=(PRISON.K) (FPOR.K) (ECSUS.K) (ORSEA.K)/TTBREL              196, R
        POR      — PRISON TO OUT REH
        PRISON   — PRISON ADDICTS
        FPOR     — FRAC FROM PRISON TO OUTSIDE REHAB
        ECSUS    — EFFECT OF C R SUSCEPTIBILITY
        ORSEA    — OUTSIDE REHAB SUCCESS EFFECT ON ADMISSIONS
        TTBREL   — TIME TO BE RELEASED


FPOR.K=TABHL(FPRPTB,(ORHBEF.K–RBOCOM.K*OCPA.K)/                    197, A
    (RBOCOM.K*OCPA.K), –5,.2,.1)
ORR=.4                                                            197.1, C
        FPOR     — FRAC FROM PRISON TO OUTSIDE REHAB
        FPRPTB   — FRAC FROM PRISON TO REHAB PROGRAM TABLE
        ORHBEF   — OUTSIDE REHABILITATION EFFORT
        RBOCOM   — ADDICTS IN REHABILITATION OUTSIDE THE
                     COMMUNITY
        OCPA     — OUTSIDE REHAB COST PER ADDICT/MO.
        ORR      — OUTSIDE REHAB RESPONSIBILITY


ORSEA.K=TABHL(SEATB,RBOCOM.K/ALLADP.K,.1,.2,.02)                  198, A
        ORSEA    — OUTSIDE REHAB SUCCESS EFFECT ON ADMISSIONS
        SEATB    — SUCCESS EFFECT ON ADMISSIONS TABLE
        RBOCOM   — ADDICTS IN REHABILITATION OUTSIDE THE
                     COMMUNITY
        ALLADP   — ALL ADDICTS, INCL. MAINT. PROG.
```

COMR.KL=(ADDICT.K) (FAOR.K) (ECSUS.K) (ORSEA.K)/TTERP   199, R

    COMR   — OUTSIDE COMM RATE
    ADDICT   — ADDICTS
    FAOR   — FRAC OF ADDICTS TO OUTSIDE REHAB
    ECSUS   — EFFECT OF C R SUSCEPTIBILITY
    ORSEA   — OUTSIDE REHAB SUCCESS EFFECT ON ADMISSIONS
    TTERP   — TIME TO ENTER REHABILITATION PROGRAM

FAOR.K=TABHL(FARPTB,(ORHBEF.K–RBOCOM.K*OCPA.K)/   200, A
    (RBOCOM.K*OCPA.K),–5,,2,.1)*PAFIC.K

    FAOR   — FRAC OF ADDICTS TO OUTSIDE REHAB
    FARPTB — FRAC ADDICTS TO REHAB PROGRAM TABLE
    ORHBEF — OUTSIDE REHABILITATION EFFORT
    RBOCOM — ADDICTS IN REHABILITATION OUTSIDE THE
                COMMUNITY
    OCPA   — OUTSIDE REHAB COST PER ADDICT/MO.
    PAFIC   — POLICE AND AVAILABILITY FACTORS IN
                COMMUNITY

Movement of addicts into and through outside-of-community programs is calculated in a manner similar to that for in-community programs. The calculation of the prison to outside rehabilitation flow rate (POR) is identical, even involving the same table functions for the availability of capacity (FPOR) and susceptibility factors (ECSUS). The success effect on rehabilitation (ORSEA) uses the same table function as the in-community success effect, but has its minimum effect when 10 percent and maximum effect when 20 percent of the community's addicts are in outside-of-community rehabilitation programs (as opposed to zero and 10 percent for in-community programs). Differences in entry rates to the two programs at each point in time are primarily a result of differences in numbers of addicts in those programs and budgets allocated to each one. In the simulations that included outside-of-community programs, they were generally given responsibility for 40 percent of a community's addicts (ORR).

The entry rate from the street (COMR, called commitment rate because of the nature of many entries to such programs) is also calculated in a manner identical to that for the INTAKE rate to in-community programs. Again, differences are due to numbers of addicts already in the two programs and amounts budgeted for them. Police and availability factors (PAFIC) also apply here to the determination of the fractional commitment rate (FAOR).

ORHBEF.K=ORHBEF.J+(DT) (1/TDORE) (ORPROG.J–ORHBEF.J)   201, L
ORHBEF=0   201.1, N
TDORE=12   201.2, C

    ORHBEF — OUTSIDE REHABILITATION EFFORT
    TDORE   — TIME TO DEVELOP OUTS REHAB EFFORT
    ORPROG — OUTSIDE REHAB PROGRAM

```
ORPROG.K=OCRHBP*ORPOL.K                                    202, A
OCRHBP=0                                                   202.1, C
     ORPROG  — OUTSIDE REHAB PROGRAM
     OCRHBP  — OUTSIDE OF COMM REHAB PROGRAM CONTROL
                 SWITCH
     ORPOL   — OUTSIDE REHAB POLICY


ORPOL.K=(DORHER.K) (EADRH.K) (OCPA.K)                      203, A
     ORPOL   — OUTSIDE REHAB POLICY
     DORHER  — DESIRED OUTS REHAB ENTRY RATE
     EADRH   — EXP AVG DURATION IN REHAB
     OCPA    — OUTSIDE REHAB COST PER ADDICT/MO.


DORHER.K=( (ADDICT.K+PRISON.K)/TCFA)*ORR                   204, A
     DORHER  — DESIRED OUTS REHAB ENTRY RATE
     ADDICT  — ADDICTS
     PRISON  — PRISON ADDICTS
     TCFA    — TIME TO CARE FOR ALL ADDICTS (GOAL)
     ORR     — OUTSIDE REHAB RESPONSIBILITY


OCPA.K=COSTPA+ROO.K                                        205, A
     OCPA    — OUTSIDE REHAB COST PER ADDICT/MO.
     COSTPA  — COST PER ADDICT
     ROO     — RATE OF OVH–OUTSIDE
```

      The budget for outside-community rehabilitation programs
(ORHBEF) is determined in the same manner as the budget for in-community
programs. Planned programs outside the community are assumed to take 12
months to be implemented (TDORE). To include these programs in a simulation, OCRHBP must be equal to 1 rather than zero. If included, the outside-
community program's magnitude is based on the same policy as that for the
in-community program with differences in program size arising from differences
in responsibilities given each program (ORR vs. CRR) and in each one's cost
per addict.

```
RBOCOM.K=RBOCOM.J+(DT) (POR.JK+COMR.JK–OREHAB.JK–          206, L
     DFOR.JK)
RBOCOM=5                                                   206.1, N
     RBOCOM  — ADDICTS IN REHABILITATION OUTSIDE THE
                 COMMUNITY
     POR     — PRISON TO OUT REH
     COMR    — OUTSIDE COMM RATE
     OREHAB  — OUTSIDE REHAB. RATE
     DFOR    — DROPOUTS FROM OUTSIDE REHAB.
```

OREHAB.KL=(RBOCOM.K-PDFOR.K)/TTBRHB   207, R
   OREHAB – OUTSIDE REHAB. RATE
   RBOCOM – ADDICTS IN REHABILITATION OUTSIDE THE
                 COMMUNITY
   PDFOR   – POTENTIAL DROPOUTS FROM OUTSIDE
                 REHABILITATION
   TTBRHB – TIME TO BE REHABILITATED

FTBRO.K=TABHL (FRTB,ORHBEF.K/(RBOCOM.K*OCPA.K),0,2,.4)   208, A
   FTBRO   – FRACTION TO BE REHABILITATED OUTSIDE
   FRTB   – FRACTION REHAB TABLE
   ORHBEF – OUTSIDE REHABILITATION EFFORT
   RBOCOM – ADDICTS IN REHABILITATION OUTSIDE THE
                 COMMUNITY
   OCPA   – OUTSIDE REHAB COST PER ADDICT/MO.

PDFOR.K=PDFOR.J+(DT) ((1-FTBRO.J) (COMR.JK+POR.JK)-   209, L
  DFOR.JK)
PDFOR=0   209.1, N
   PDFOR   – POTENTIAL DROPOUTS FROM OUTSIDE
                 REHABILITATION
   FTBRO   – FRACTION TO BE REHABILITATED OUTSIDE
   COMR   – OUTSIDE COMM RATE
   POR   – PRISON TO OUT REH
   DFOR   – DROPOUTS FROM OUTSIDE REHAB.

DFOR.KL=PDFOR.K/TTDO   210, R
   DFOR   – DROPOUTS FROM OUTSIDE REHAB.
   PDFOR   – POTENTIAL DROPOUTS FROM OUTSIDE
                 REHABILITATION
   TTDO   – TIME TO DROP OUT

Outside-of-community programs grow in the number of addicts they treat (RBOCOM) as new addicts enter from the street (COMR) and from prison (POR) and are depleted as addicts complete the programs (OREHAB) or drop out (DFOR). Five of the community's initial 150 addicts are assumed to be in this type of program at the beginning of each simulation.

The dropout rate from outside-community programs (DFOR) is computed in a manner identical to the rate from in-community programs, with one exception. The exception is that no susceptibility factor enters into the fraction to be rehabilitated successfully in outside-of-community programs. That fraction is based solely on resource adequacy. The time to drop out of these programs is, again, 3 months (TTDO).

Methadone Maintenance Program Sector

METHDN.K=METHDN.J+(DT) (STMR.JK-MPDO.JK-MPR.JK-   211, L
  AMMP.JK)

```
METHDN=1                                                           211.1, N
    METHDN  – ADDICTS IN METHADONE PROGRAMS
    STMR    – STREET TO METH
    MPDRO   – METHADONE PROGRAM DROPOUT RATE
    MPR     – METHADONE PROGRAM REHABILITATION
    AMMP    – ADDITIONS TO METH MAINT PRG


STMR.KL=(ADDICT.K) (EMSUS.K) (FAMP.K) (MPSEA.K)/TTEMP             212, R
TTEMP=12                                                          212.1, C
    STMR    – STREET TO METH
    ADDICT  – ADDICTS
    EMSUS   – EFF OF METH SUSC
    FAMP    – FRAC ATTRACTED TO METH PROG
    MPSEA   – METHADONE PROGRAM SUCCESS EFFECT ON
                 ADMISSIONS
    TTEMP   – TIME TO ENTER METHADONE PROGRAM


EMSUS.K=TABHL(EMSTB,MSUS.K,0,.6,.1)                               213, A
EMSTB=.01,.05,.1,.2,.4,.5,.6                                      213.1, T
    EMSUS   – EFF OF METH SUSC
    EMSTB   – EFF OF METH SUSC TABLE
    MSUS    – METH SUSCE


MSUS.K=(MLFRAC*ALLADP.K-METHDN.K-MMP.K-HERMNT.K)/                 214, A
    ALLADP.K
MLFRAC=.6                                                         214.1, C
    MSUS    – METH SUSCE
    MLFRAC  – METHADONE LIMIT FRACTION
    ALLADP  – ALL ADDICTS, INCL. MAINT. PROG.
    METHDN  – ADDICTS IN METHADONE PROGRAMS
    MMP     – EX-ADDICTS IN METHADONE MAINTENANCE PROG
    HERMNT  – ADDICTS IN HER MAINT


FAMP.K=TABHL(FAMPTB,( (METHEF.K/CMPA.K)–METHDN.K)/                215, A
    (METHEF.K/CMPA.K),-5,.2,.1)*AGEFAC.K*PAFAM.K
FAMPTB=0,.1,.2,.4,.7,.9,1,1                                       215.1, T
CMPR=.3                                                           215.2, C
COSTMM=60                                                         215.3, C
    FAMP    – FRAC ATTRACTED TO METH PROG
    FAMPTB  – FRAC ATTRACTED TO METH PROG TABLE
    METHEF  – METHADONE EFFORT
    CMPA    – TOTAL COST OF METHADONE MAINTENANCE PER
                 ADDICT
    METHDN  – ADDICTS IN METHADONE PROGRAMS
    AGEFAC  – AGE FACTOR METHADONE
    PAFAM   – POLICE AND AVAIL FACTORS AFFECTING
                 METHADONE
    CMPR    – COMMUNITY METHADONE PROGRAM RESPONSIBILITY
    COSTMM  – COST OF METHADONE MAINTENANCE
```

CMPA.K=COSTMM+ROM.K   216, A
    CMPA   — TOTAL COST OF METHADONE MAINTENANCE PER
                ADDICT
    COSTMM — COST OF METHADONE MAINTENANCE
    ROM   — RATE OF OVH FOR METH

The number of addicts in methadone programs (METHDN) is added
to each month by addicts entering from the street (it is assumed that none
enters directly from prison, but must go back to the street before entering) and
depleted by addicts dropping out, being rehabilitated (no longer needing even
methadone), or going into long-term maintenance programs (AMMP). The rate of
movement from the street into methadone programs (STMR) is formulated in a
manner similar to the other entry rates. The number of addicts to enter methadone programs is computed as the product of addicts on the street and a fraction
derived from susceptibility, available capacity, success of rehabilitation, and
other factors. One-twelfth of these addicts enters methadone programs each
month (TTEMP).

Susceptibility to methadone rehabilitation (EMSUS) and its effect
on entries to methadone programs are the same concepts that were applied
to drug-free programs. In this case, methadone is assumed initially to be an
appropriate form of treatment for 60 percent of a community's addict population at a maximum (MLFRAC). The addict population fraction that remains
susceptible to methadone programs at any point in time is equal to the difference
between the maximum number susceptible (MLFRAC*ALLADP) and the
number already in methadone, long-term methadone maintenance (MMP), and
heroin maintenance (HERMNT) programs divided by the total addict population. Low values of MSUS indicate that few motivated addicts remain on the
street who are susceptible to methadone programs, and thus cause EMSUS
to have a strongly inhibiting effect on STMR.

The fraction of addicts attracted to methadone programs (FAMP)
is a composite of three factors, reflecting the effects of available capacity,
average age of the addict population (AGEFAC), and police and availability
effects (PAFAM). The available capacity factor is based on a ratio of excess
capacity [difference between the number of addicts that can be supported
(METHEF/CMPA) and the number of addicts already in methadone programs
(METHDN)] to the number that can be supported by the budget. A negative
value from this calculation indicates that resources are already inadequate
for the current group of addicts being treated and causes a strong inhibiting
effect (from FAMPTB) on entry to methadone programs. Positive values
representing up to 20 percent excess capacity are reflected in the FAMPTB
table of values as presenting no barrier to entry.

In most of the simulations employing methadone programs, those
programs are given responsibility for 30 percent of the addict population

(CMPR). The cost of keeping an addict in one of these programs (CMPA) has a direct component (COSTMM) of $60 per month and an overhead component (ROM) that varies inversely with the number of addicts in methadone programs.

```
AGEFAC.K=TABHL(AGEFTB,AVAGE.K,168,408,60)                          217, A
AGEFTB=.3,.7,.9,.95,1                                             217.1, T
        AGEFAC  — AGE FACTOR METHADONE
        AGEFTB  — AGE FACTOR TABLE
        AVAGE   — AVERAGE AGE


AVAGE.K=AGTOT.K/ADDICT.K                                           218, A
        AVAGE   — AVERAGE AGE
        AGTOT   — AGE TOTAL FOR AVG AGE CALCULATION
        ADDICT  — ADDICTS


Z.K=TABHL(ZTB,AVAGE.K,168,288,30)                                 219, A
ZTB=1,1,1,1,1                                                     219.1, T
        Z       — Z FACTOR IN AVG AGE CALCULATION
        ZTB     — Z TABLE
        AVAGE   — AVERAGE AGE


AGTOT.K=AGTOT.J+(DT) (AVAGS.J*(AR.JK*Z.J+AMR.JK–                   220, L
    ADO.JK*1.4-STPR.JK-INTAKE. JK*.9-COMR.JK-STMR.JK*
    1.1+PRTS.JK*1.1+DFCR.JK+DFOR.JK*1.1+DORP.JK*1.1+
    MPDO.JK*1.2-DETCR.JK-GANTAG.JK+ANTAGD.JK-STHR.JK+
    HPDO.JK)+ADDICT.J)
AGTOT=(NAVAG) (ADDICT)                                            220.1, N
NAVAG=288                                                         220.2, C
        AGTOT   — AGE TOTAL FOR AVG AGE CALCULATION
        AVAGS   — AVG AGE, SMOOTHED
        AR      — ADDICTION RATE
        Z       — Z FACTOR IN AVG AGE CALCULATION
        AMR     — ADDICT MIGRATION RATE
        ADO     — ADDICT DROPOUT RATE
        STPR    — STREET TO PRISON RATE
        INTAKE  — INTAKE
        COMR    — OUTSIDE COMM RATE
        STMR    — STREET TO METH
        PRTS    — PRISON RELEASE TO STREET
        DFCR    — DROPOUT RATE FROM COMMUNITY REHAB
        DFOR    — DROPOUTS FROM OUTSIDE REHAB.
        DORP    — DROPOUT FROM RE-ENTRY
        MPDO    — METHADONE PROGRAM DROPOUT RATE
        DETCR   — DETOX CHANGE
        GANTAG  — GROWTH OF ANTAGONIST LEVEL
        ANTAGD  — ANTAGONIST DROPOUT RATE
        STHR    — STR TO HER MAINT
        HPDO    — HEROIN PROGRAM DROPOUT RATE
        ADDICT  — ADDICTS
        NAVAG   — INITIAL AVERAGE AGE
```

```
AVAGS.K=AVAGS.J+(DT) (1/TAVAG) (AVAGE.J-AVAGS.J)              221, L
AVAGS=NAVAG                                                  221.1, N
TAVAG=60                                                     221.2, C
    AVAGS   - AVG AGE, SMOOTHED
    TAVAG   - TIME FOR AVRGNG AGE
    AVAGE   - AVERAGE AGE
    NAVAG   - INITIAL AVERAGE AGE
```

The age factor affecting entry to methadone programs reflects an assumption that methadone maintenance is considered an appropriate treatment modality primarily for older addicts who have been addicted for several years, are somewhat set in their ways, and are not attracted to or amenable to the discipline of therapeutic community approaches. Therapeutic community programs are assumed to be preferred for younger addicts who are more impressionable and amenable to that approach, and for whom long-term methadone addiction may be avoided. When the average age of the street addict population (AVAGE) is above 24, the age factor (AGEFAC) has practically no effect in reducing the number of addicts entering methadone programs. Between 19 and 24, a moderate reduction (up to 30 percent) in entry rates takes place. When the average age of the street addict population falls below 19, AGEFAC reduces entry rates by as much as 70 percent (if an average age as low as 14 is reached).

Computation of average age is a complicated process because addicts are always entering and leaving the street addict population by a variety of routes. These movements are likely to have a systematic rather than random effect on average age. New addicts are usually of the average age or younger, while addicts such as those released from prison or dropping out of methadone programs are likely to be older than average. This phenomenon was dealt with by creating a "pool" of months of age attributable to all the addicts on the street (AGTOT). When an addict enters or reenters the street addict group, an appropriate number of months is added to the pool. If the addict entering is, for example, a dropout from a methadone program, he is assumed to be 20 percent older than average and AVAGS*MPDO*1.2 is added to AGTOT for all methadone program dropouts reentering during a given month. If the addict is migrating in from another community, he is assumed to be of average age and AVAGS*AMR(*1) is added to AGTOT to represent additions for all such addicts. Subtractions due to addicts leaving the street addict population are handled in the same manner. In addition to adding and subtracting months as addicts move in and out of the street population, that population is "aged" by adding a month to the pool for each addict on the street during a month in a simulation (the +ADDICT term at the end of equation 220).

Average age is then the total number of months in the pool divided by the number of addicts on the street. Average age is initially assumed to be

288 months or 24 years (equation 220.2C). The "Z" factor can be used to keep average age from going to unrealistically low levels, but was not required in the simulations that were done. AVAGS, the average age term used in the AGTOT equation, is simply the average age of the street addict population smoothed over a period of 60 months.

```
PAFAM.K=PHE.K+LDAFM.K                                                222, A
     PAFAM    — POLICE AND AVAIL FACTORS AFFECTING
                  METHADONE
     PHE      — POLICE HARASSMENT EFF.
     LDAFM    — LOW DRUG AVAIL FAC-METH


LDAFM.K=TABHL(LDAMTB,AAP.K/ADDICT.K,-1,0,.2)                         223, A
LDAMTB=2,1.8,1.5,1.1,.7,.5                                           223.1, T
     LDAFM    — LOW DRUG AVAIL FAC-METH
     LDAMTB   — LOW DRUG AVAIL FACTOR-METHADONE TABLE
     AAP      — ADDITIONAL ADDICT POTENTIAL
     ADDICT   — ADDICTS


MPSEA.K=TABHL(SEATB,(METHDN.K+MMP.K)/ALLADP.K,.05,                   224, A
     .3,.05)
     MPSEA    — METHADONE PROGRAM SUCCESS EFFECT ON
                  ADMISSIONS
     SEATB    — SUCCESS EFFECT ON ADMISSIONS TABLE
     METHDN   — ADDICTS IN METHADONE PROGRAMS
     MMP      — EX-ADDICTS IN METHADONE MAINTENANCE PROG
     ALLADP   — ALL ADDICTS, INCL. MAINT. PROG.
```

Police and availability factors affecting methadone (PAFAM) are similar to those affecting entry to drug-free programs. The police harassment component (PHE) is, in fact, the same one. The low drug availability factor (LDAFM) has a greater effect than the one affecting entry to drug-free programs because methadone represents a more attractive alternative (than drug-free programs) when street heroin supplies are low. Low drug availability by itself can have as much as a doubling effect on entry to methadone programs when heroin is extremely scarce (from LDAMTB). When supplies are adequate for the existing population (AAP = 0), LDAFM has a neutral effect since its value of 0.5 is added to the police harassment effect's minimum value of 0.5. PAFAM can have as high a value as 3 if there is a high average arrest rate coincident with low availability.

The success effect on admissions (MPSEA) is also similar to the one for drug-free programs and uses the same table function (SEATB). It has a neutral effect when 5 percent or less of the community's addicts are in methadone or long-term methadone maintenance programs, and causes up to a 50 percent increase in entry rates when 30 percent of the addicts have been enrolled.

MPDO.KL=PDFMP.K/TTDO   225, R
    MPDO   − METHADONE PROGRAM DROPOUT RATE
    PDFMP   − POTENTIAL DROPOUTS FROM METHADONE PROGRAMS
    TTDO   − TIME TO DROP OUT

PDFMP.K=PDFMP.J+(DT) ((FTDOM.J*STMR.JK)−MPDO.JK)   226, L
PDFMP=0   226.1, N
    PDFMP   − POTENTIAL DROPOUTS FROM METHADONE PROGRAMS
    FTDOM   − FRACTION TO DROP OUT OF METHADONE PROGRAMS
    STMR   − STREET TO METH
    MPDO   − METHADONE PROGRAM DROPOUT RATE

FTDOM.K=TABHL(DOMTB,(ESMEF.K*METHEF.K)/METHDN.K*   227, A
    CMPA.K),0,1,.2)
DOMTB=1,.9,.7,.5,.4,.35   227.1, T
    FTDOM   − FRACTION TO DROP OUT OF METHADONE PROGRAMS
    DOMTB   − DROPOUT FROM METHADONE TABLE
    ESMEF   − EFF OF SUSC ON METH SUCC FACTOR
    METHEF − METHADONE EFFORT
    METHDN − ADDICTS IN METHADONE PROGRAMS
    CMPA   − TOTAL COST OF METHADONE MAINTENANCE PER
                ADDICT

ESMEF.K=TABHL(ESMFTB,MSUS.K,0,.6,.1)   228, A
ESMFTB=.1,.3,.5,1,1,1,1   228.1, T
    ESMEF   − EFF OF SUSC ON METH SUCC FACTOR
    ESMFTB − ESMEF TABLE
    MSUS   − METH SUSCE

MPR.KL=PSMP.K/TTBRM   229, R
TTBRM=36   229.1, C
    MPR   − METHADONE PROGRAM REHABILITATION
    PSMP   − POTENTIAL SUCCESSES IN METHADONE PROGRAMS
    TTBRM   − TIME TO BE REHABILITATED–METHADONE

PSMP.K=PSMP.J+(DT) ((FTBRM.J*STMR.JK)−MPR.JK)   230, L
PSMP=0   230.1, N
    PSMP   − POTENTIAL SUCCESSES IN METHADONE PROGRAMS
    FTBRM   − FRACTION TO BE REHABILITATED–METHADONE
    STMR   − STREET TO METH
    MPR   − METHADONE PROGRAM REHABILITATION

FTBRM.K=TABHL(FRMTB,METHEF.K/METHDN.K*CMPA.K),1,2,   231, A
    .2)
FRMTB=.01,.02,.04,.07,.09,.1   231.1, T
    FTBRM   − FRACTION TO BE REHABILITATED–METHADONE
    FRMTB   − FRACTION REHABILITATED–METHADONE TABLE
    METHEF − METHADONE EFFORT
    METHDN − ADDICTS IN METHADONE PROGRAMS
    CMPA   − TOTAL COST OF METHADONE MAINTENANCE PER
                ADDICT

AMMP.KL=(METHDN.K-PDFMP.K-PSMP.K)/TMMP   232, R
TMMP=36   232.1, C
    AMMP   — ADDITIONS TO METH MAINT PRG
    METHDN — ADDICTS IN METHADONE PROGRAMS
    PDFMP — POTENTIAL DROPOUTS FROM METHADONE PROGRAMS
    PSMP   — POTENTIAL SUCCESSES IN METHADONE PROGRAMS
    TMMP   — TIME TO ENTER METHADONE MAINTENANCE PROG

MMP.K=MMP.J+(DT) (AMMP.JK)   233, L
MMP=0   233.1, N
    MMP   — EX-ADDICTS IN METHADONE MAINTENANCE PROG
    AMMP   — ADDITIONS TO METH MAINT PROG

Rates of dropout and "graduation" from methadone programs are also determined in a manner similar to that for drug-free programs. A fraction to drop out of methadone programs (FTDOM) directs the flow of that fraction of new entrants into the potential dropout category (PDFMP). Addicts actually dropping out (MPDO) are subtracted from the potential dropout category each month.

The fraction to drop out is a composite of susceptibility and budget adequacy components. The budget adequacy component, by itself, would cause all addicts to drop out if resources (METHEF) were insignificant compared to needs (METHDN*CMPA), and results in a minimum of 35 percent dropout rate if resources are completely adequate. The susceptibility factor (ESMEF) reduces the value of the independent variable in equation 227 and thereby increases the fraction to drop out when MSUS—the fraction of addicts remaining susceptible to methadone treatment—encompasses less than 30 percent of the total addict population. When there are almost no susceptible addicts left, ESMEF reduces the independent variable to 10 percent of the budget/need ratio's value, and almost all addicts in methadone programs drop out. Dropout is assumed to take place over an average period of 3 months (TTDO) in a program.

Most addicts who remain in methadone programs must continue to receive methadone if they are to remain heroin-free. Some small fraction, however, become rehabilitated (MPR) in the sense that they no longer need methadone and avoid readdiction without it. This rehabilitation comes about as addicts become involved in school, jobs and family relationships once methadone relieves them of their need to spend considerable time finding and raising money for heroin. The number of addicts rehabilitated each month is equal to the number now in methadone programs who will eventually be rehabilitated (PSMP) divided by the 36 months over which rehabilitation takes place (TTBRM). The number that will eventually be rehabilitated is determined in the same manner as the dropout segments in the methadone and other programs. A fraction to be rehabilitated (FTBRM) is diverted into the potential successes in the methadone programs group (**PSMP**) from the stream of entering addicts. That fraction is a function of budget adequacy alone and can reach 10 percent of the addicts entering methadone programs when the budget (**METHEF**) is twice what is required for current needs (**METHDN∗CMPA**). This formulation is based on the assumption that greater resources per addict increase the likelihood that some addicts in methadone programs become involved in "straight" lifestyles and do not require further methadone maintenance to avoid readdiction to heroin. Addicts actually achieving this sort of rehabilitation each month are subtracted from **PSMP** (in equation 230) as well as from **METHDN**.

Addicts who neither drop out from methadone treatment nor are completely rehabilitated fall into a third category, possibly the largest. These addicts continue to require methadone, but are assumed to be "safe" from readdiction to heroin so long as they are on methadone maintenance. This group is assumed to "graduate" into a long-term maintenance status (**MMP**) after a period of 36 months (**TMMP**) of continuous enrollment in a methadone program. The rate at which addicts enter the long-term maintenance status each month (**AMMP**) is equal to the number of addicts who will eventually enter (**METHDN–PDFMP–PSMP**, the difference between the total number in methadone programs and the number who will either drop out or be rehabilitated) divided by the 36 months (**TMMP**) required to achieve this status. **MMP** accumulates addicts advancing into long-term maintenance, and assumes permanence of this status, i.e., no further dropout or drug-free rehabilitation.

$$\text{METHLK.K=TABHL(MTHLKT,((METHEF.K/CMPA.K)–METHDN.K)/} \qquad \text{234, A}$$
$$\text{(METHEF.K/CMPA.K),–5,.2,.1)*METHDN.K*30}$$
$$\text{MTHLKT=.2,.18,.15,.12,.09,.06,.04,.02} \qquad\qquad \text{234.1, T}$$

METHLK — METHADONE LEAKAGE
MTHLKT — METH LEAK TABLE
METHEF — METHADONE EFFORT
CMPA   — TOTAL COST OF METHADONE MAINTENANCE PER
                     ADDICT
METHDN — ADDICTS IN METHADONE PROGRAMS

Leakage from methadone programs can, and has, become a major secondary source of illicit narcotics. The volume of methadone (in daily dosages) leaking to the street (**METHLK**) is assumed primarily to be a function of resource adequacy. If the number of addicts that can be supported by a methadone program budget (**METHEF/CMPA**) is greater than or equal to the number already in programs, leakage is assumed to be negligible—not more than 6 percent of the total amount of methadone distributed. Resource levels inadequate for the current group of addicts are likely to lead to much larger leakage rates, presumably because too few personnel cannot provide necessary monitoring and safeguards. When resources are only 50 percent of what is needed, leakage is assumed to reach its maximum of 20 percent. Monthly leakage (daily dosage additions to the street narcotic supply) is calculated by multiplying this percentage by the number of addicts in methadone programs (METHDN) and their product by the 30 days in a month. The model simply treats this methadone leakage as additions to the equivalent heroin supply in the street.

```
REENT.K=REENT.J+(DT) (CREHAB.JK+OREHAB.JK-RREENT.JK-          235, L
     DORP.JK)
REENT=1                                                      235.1, N
     REENT  − ADDICTS IN RE-ENTRY PROCESS
     CREHAB − COMMUNITY REHABILITATION RATE
     OREHAB − OUTSIDE REHAB. RATE
     RREENT − RATE OF RE-ENTRY
     DORP   − DROPOUT FROM RE-ENTRY


RREENT.KL=(REENT.K) (FTSR.K)/TRE                             236, R
TRE=12                                                       236.1, C
     RREENT − RATE OF RE-ENTRY
     REENT  − ADDICTS IN RE-ENTRY PROCESS
     FTSR   − FRACTION TO SUCCESSFULLY RE-ENTER
     TRE    − TIME TO RE-ENTER


DORP.KL=PDRP.K/TDOR                                          237, R
     DORP   − DROPOUT FROM RE-ENTRY
     PDRP   − POTENTIAL DROPOUTS FROM RE-ENTRY PROCESS
     TDOR   − TIME FOR DROPOUT FROM RE-ENTRY


PDRP.K=PDRP.J+(DT) ( (CREHAB.JK+OREHAB.JK) (1-FTSR.J)−       238, L
     DORP.JK)
PDRP=0                                                       238.1, N
TDOR=3                                                       238.2, C
     PDRP   − POTENTIAL DROPOUTS FROM RE-ENTRY PROCESS
     CREHAB − COMMUNITY REHABILITATION RATE
     OREHAB − OUTSIDE REHAB. RATE
     FTSR   − FRACTION TO SUCCESSFULLY RE-ENTER
     DORP   − DROPOUT FROM RE-ENTRY
     TDOR   − TIME FOR DROPOUT FROM RE-ENTRY
```

Addicts completing in-community or out-of-community drug-free programs enter a reentry phase in which they are no longer addicted, but still vulnerable to readdiction (REENT). The number in this phase is added to as addicts successfully complete drug-free programs (CREHAB and OREHAB) and is depleted as addicts either complete this phase successfully (RREENT) or drop out and become readdicted (DORP). The number of addicts successfully reentering each month is the fraction of those now in reentry who will success- fully reenter (REENT*FTSR) divided by the 12 months (TRE) attributed to the reentry phase. Dropouts from reentry are determined in the same manner as dropouts from the various rehabilitation programs. A fraction of the addicts entering the reentry phase (CREHAB + OREHAB) (1 – FTSR) are diverted into a group that will drop out and become readdicted sometime during the reentry process (PDRP). That fraction is 1 minus the fraction that will success-fully reenter. Ex-addicts who drop out of the reentry phase and become readdicted do so over an average of three months (TDOR).

```
FTSR.K=(ATTEF.K) (FDER.K) (HAR.K) (RECEF.K) (PEFOR.K)          239, A
     FTSR    — FRACTION TO SUCCESSFULLY RE-ENTER
     ATTEF   — COMMUNITY ATTITUDE EFFECT
     FDER    — FUTILITY-DESPAIR EFFECT ON RE-ENTRY
     HAR     — HEROIN AVAILABILITY EFFECT ON RE-ENTRY
     RECEF   — PRISON RECORD EFFECT ON RE-ENTRY
     PEFOR   — PROGRAM EFFECT


ATTEF.K=TABHL(ATTTB,CATT.K,.4,1,.1)                            240, A
ATTTB=.1,.2,.4,.5,.55,.6,.65                                   240.1, T
     ATTEF   — COMMUNITY ATTITUDE EFFECT
     ATTTB   — ATTITUDE EFFECT TABLE
     CATT    — COMMUNITY ATTITUDE


FDER.K=TABHL(FDERTB,FDL.K,0,1,.2)                              241, A
FDERTB=1.1,1,.9,.5,.3,.1                                       241.1, T
     FDER    — FUTILITY-DESPAIR EFFECT ON RE-ENTRY
     FDERTB  — FUTILITY-DESPAIR EFFECT TABLE
     FDL     — FUTILITY-DESPAIR LEVEL


HAR.K=TABHL(HARTB,AAP.K/ADDICT.K,0,2,.4)                       242, A
HARTB=1.2,1.1,1,.9,.7,.6                                       242.1, T
     HAR     — HEROIN AVAILABILITY EFFECT ON RE-ENTRY
     HARTB   — HEROIN AVAILABILITY EFFECT TABLE
     AAP     — ADDITIONAL ADDICT POTENTIAL
     ADDICT  — ADDICTS


RECEF.K=TABHL(RECTB,SPR.K,0,1,.2)                              243, A
RECTB=1,.95,.9,.7,.65,.6                                       243.1, T
     RECEF   — PRISON RECORD EFFECT ON RE-ENTRY
     RECTB   — RECORD EFFECT TABLE
     SPR     — SMOOTHED PRISON/ADDICT RATIO


SPR.K-SMOOTH(PRISON.K/ADDICT.K,TPRE)                           244, A
TPRE=36                                                        244.1, C
     SPR     — SMOOTHED PRISON/ADDICT RATIO
     PRISON  — PRISON ADDICTS
     ADDICT  — ADDICTS
     TPRE    — TIME FOR PRISON RECORD EFFECT


PEFOR.K=TABHL(PEFTB,RENEFF.K/(REENT.K*RENC.K),0,1,.2)          245, A
PEFTB=1,1.1,1.2,1.4,1.5,1.6                                    245.1, T
```

```
CREENT=40                                                    245.2, C
    PEFOR   − PROGRAM EFFECT
    PEFTB   − PROGRAM EFFECT ON RE-ENTRY TABLE
    RENEFF  − RE-ENTRY EFFORT
    REENT   − ADDICTS IN RE-ENTRY PROCESS
    RENC    − TOTAL RE-ENTRY COST
    CREENT  − COST OF RE-ENTRY


RENC.K=CREENT+RENOH.K                                        246, A
    RENC    − TOTAL RE-ENTRY COST
    CREENT  − COST OF RE-ENTRY
    RENOH   − RE-ENTRY OVH
```

The fraction to re-enter successfully (FTSR) is assumed to be a function of five different factors. These are:

1. An attitude effect (ATTEF) based on the community's attitude toward addiction (CATT);
2. A futility–despair effect (FDER) based on FDL;
3. A heroin availability effect (HAR) based on the additional addict potential heroin supply (AAP);
4. An effect of the likelihood that a reentering addict has a prison record (RECEF); and
5. A reentry program effect (PEFOR).

These factors are multiplicative with the basic fraction being determined by the attitude effect and increased or decreased by the other factors.

The attitude effect is given a central role in this calculation because of the critical impact a community's attitudes have on its behavior toward addicts and, in turn, on ex-addicts' perceptions of the value to them of remaining "straight". A low value of CATT, representing a generally held view that "once an addict, always an addict" and of the addict as a criminal, reflects attitudes that deny ex-addicts opportunities for jobs, housing and friendship, thereby making readdiction a difficult-to-escape alternative. As few as 10 percent of the ex-addicts can successfully reenter if the community's attitude is extremely negative (in ATTTB). If, on the other hand, people see ex-addicts as formerly sick, but now cured, they are more likely to extend those opportunities and make remaining heroin-free an attractive proposition. A value of CATT near 1 enables as many as 65 percent of the ex-addicts to reenter successfully.

A high futility-despair level, deriving from a low socioeconomic level, reduces that fraction substantially. The perceived and actual lack of opportunities for youths from poorer neighborhoods make readdiction more likely. A futility-despair level close to 1 allows only 10 percent of those ex-addicts who would otherwise reenter successfully to do so. A very low level, typical of a wealthy community, has a neutral effect or may even increase the fraction by as much as 10 percent.

Heroin availability in the community is assumed to affect reentry in that a very low level helps to enforce abstinence, while a very high level makes heroin easily available to addicts who are having difficulty adjusting to a "straight" lifestyle. If availability is twice again what is needed by the current addict population (AAP = 2), this effect can reduce the fraction successfully reentering by as much as 40 percent (value of 0.6 in HARTB). The absence of any additional heroin beyond what is needed for existing addicts (AAP = 0) can increase the fraction to reenter successfully by as much as 20 percent.

The prison record effect reflects the additional difficulty encountered by addicts who have been in prison. This difficulty stems primarily from reduced job opportunities. If, at an extreme, as many addicts have been in prison as on the street over a period of time (SPR = 1), this effect reduces the fraction to reenter successfully by 40 percent (0.6 in RECTB). An absence of prison records among addicts has a neutral effect. The ratio of addicts in prison to street addicts is averaged over a period of 36 months (TPRE) in computing SPR.

The reentry program effect can increase the fraction to reenter successfully by as much as 60 percent (1.6 in PEFTB) if sufficient resources are devoted to helping ex-addicts in the reentry phase. This aid can take the form of job training and placement, adjustment counseling, assistance in finding housing or placement in half-way houses, and other services. Resource levels (RENEFF) less than what is needed (REENT*RENC) produce proportionally smaller increases in FTSR.

The monthly cost of keeping an ex-addict in a (completely adequate) reentry program is structured in the same manner as other program costs, with a direct component of $40 (CREENT) and an overhead component (RENOH) inversely proportional to the number in reentry programs.

```
RENPRG.K=RENTRY*RENPOL.K                              247, A
RENTRY=0                                              247.1, C
     RENPRG  — RE-ENTRY PROGRAM
     RENTRY  — RE-ENTRY PROGRAM CONTROL SWITCH
     RENPOL  — RE-ENTRY POLICY

RENPOL.K=(REENT.K) (RENC.K)                           248, A
     RENPOL  — RE-ENTRY POLICY
     REENT   — ADDICTS IN RE-ENTRY PROCESS
     RENC    — TOTAL RE-ENTRY COST

RENEFF.K=RENEFF.J+(DT) (1/TDREN) (RENPRG.J−RENEFF.J)  249, L
RENEFF=0                                              249.1, N
```

```
TDREN=12                                                        249.2, C
     RENEFF  −  RE-ENTRY EFFORT
     TDREN   −  TIME TO DEVELOP RE-ENTRY EFFORT
     RENPRG  −  RE-ENTRY PROGRAM
```

      Reentry programs are included in a simulation when RENTRY is given a value of 1 rather than zero. The reentry program is based on a policy that, when in effect, provides enough resources to give each ex-addict in reentry the maximum benefit from the program effect. The actual reentry program (RENEFF) follows the planned program (RENPRG) after an implementation delay of 12 months (TDREN).

Heroin Maintenance Program Sector

```
HERMNT.K=HERMNT.J+(DT) (STHR.JK−HPDO.JK−AOHM.JK)                250, L
HERMNT=1                                                       250.1, N
     HERMNT  −  ADDICTS IN HER MAINT
     STHR    −  STR TO HER MAINT
     HPDO    −  HEROIN PROGRAM DROPOUT RATE
     AOHM    −  RATE OF AGING OUT OF HEROIN MAINT
```

```
STHR.KL=(ADDICT.K) (EHSUS.K) (FAHP.K) (HPSEA.K)/TTEHP          251, R
TTEHP=12                                                       251.1, C
     STHR    −  STR TO HER MAINT
     ADDICT  −  ADDICTS
     EHSUS   −  EFFECT OF HEROIN MAINT SUSCEPT
     FAHP    −  FRACTION OF ADDICTS TO HEROIN PROG
     HPSEA   −  HEROIN PROGRAM SUCCESS EFFECT ON ADMISSIONS
     TTEHP   −  TIME TO ENTER HEROIN PROGRAM
```

```
EHSUS.K=TABHL(EHSTB,HSUS.K,0,.8,.1)                            252, A
EHSTB=0,.05,.1,.2,.4,.5,.6,.7,.8                               252.1, T
     EHSUS   −  EFFECT OF HEROIN MAINT SUSCEPT
     EHSTB   −  HEROIN MAINT SUSCEPTIBILITY TABL
     HSUS    −  HER MAINT SUSCEPTIBILITY
```

```
HSUS.K=(HLFRAC*ALLADP.K−HERMNT.K−METHDN.K−MMP.K)/              253, A
   ALLADP.K
HLFRAC=.8                                                      253.1, C
     HSUS    −  HER MAINT SUSCEPTIBILITY
     HLFRAC  −  HEROIN MAINTENANCE LIMITING FRACTION
     ALLADP  −  ALL ADDICTS, INCL. MAINT. PROG.
     HERMNT  −  ADDICTS IN HER MAINT
     METHDN  −  ADDICTS IN METHADONE PROGRAMS
     MMP     −  EX-ADDICTS IN METHADONE MAINTENANCE PROG
```

```
FAHP.K=TABHL(FAHPTB,( (HERNEF.K/CHPA.K)−HERMNT.K)/             254, A
   (HERNEF.K/CHPA.K),−5,.2,.1)*AGFACH.K*PAFAH.K
FAHPTB=0,.3,.7,.9,1,1,1,1                                      254.1, T
```

```
CHPR=.4                                                      254.2, C
     FAHP    – FRACTION OF ADDICTS TO HEROIN PROG
     FAHPTB  – FRAC ADD TO HER PROG TABLE
     HERNEF  – HEROIN MAINT EFFORT
     CHPA    – TOTAL COST OF HEROIN MAINTENANCE PER ADDICT
     HERMNT  – ADDICTS IN HER MAINT
     AGFACH  – AGE FACTOR–HEROIN
     PAFAH   – POLICE AND AVAILABILITY FACTORS–HEROIN
     CHPR    – COMMUNITY HEROIN PROGRAM RESPONSIBILITY


PAFAH.K=PAFAM.K                                              255, A
COSTHM=180                                                   255.1, C
     PAFAH   – POLICE AND AVAILABILITY FACTORS–HEROIN
     PAFAM   – POLICE AND AVAIL FACTORS AFFECTING
               METHADONE
     COSTHM  – COST OF HEROIN MAINTENANCE


CHPA.K=COSTHM+ROHP.K                                         256, A
     CHPA    – TOTAL COST OF HEROIN MAINTENANCE PER ADDICT
     COSTHM  – COST OF HEROIN MAINTENANCE
     ROHP    – RATE OF OVH IN HER PROG


AGFACH.K=TABHL(AGFHTB,AVAGE.K,168,408,60)                    257, A
AGFHTB=.5,.9,.95,1,1                                         257.1, T
     AGFACH  – AGE FACTOR–HEROIN
     AGFHTB  – AGE FACTOR–HEROIN TABLE
     AVAGE   – AVERAGE AGE


HPSEA.K=TABHL(SEATB,HERMNT.K/ALLADP.K,.05,.3,.05)            258, A
     HPSEA   – HEROIN PROGRAM SUCCESS EFFECT ON ADMISSIONS
     SEATB   – SUCCESS EFFECT ON ADMISSIONS TABLE
     HERMNT  – ADDICTS IN HER MAINT
     ALLADP  – ALL ADDICTS. INCL. MAINT. PROG.
```

Heroin maintenance programs are included in the model as a substitute for or complement to the other treatment modalities. Because these programs are formulated in a manner almost identical to methadone programs, they are described only briefly. Only the differences between the methadone and heroin maintenance formulations are discussed in detail.

Addicts enter heroin maintenance (HERMNT) from the street (STHR) and leave by either dropping out (HPDO) or by aging out of their need for heroin (AOHM) in the same way that street addicts age out. The entry rate is made up of the same factors as the methadone entry rate. Here, the susceptibility effect allows up to 80 percent (in EHSTB) of the community's addicts to enter because a larger maximum susceptibility (HLFRAC = 0.8) is assumed for heroin maintenance than for methadone. The fraction of addicts still susceptible to heroin maintenance (HSUS) is equal to 80 percent of the addict population (HLFRAC*ALLADP) less those addicts already in heroin maintenance, divided by the total addict population.

The fraction of addicts going to heroin programs (FAHP) has the same three components as the corresponding variable affecting methadone program entry (FAMP). The available capacity factor, one of those three components, permits easier entry to heroin maintenance for a given level of available capacity than is possible for methadone programs with the same level of capacity available. For example, a heroin maintenance program with 20 percent less budget than actually required for the current number of addicts (((HERNEF /CHPA)-HERMNT)/(HERNEF/CHPA) = -0.2) can still admit 90 percent (0.9 in FAHPTB) of the otherwise eligible addicts, while a methadone program with the same capacity situation can admit only 40 percent (0.4 in FAMPTB). This reflects the assumption that heroin maintenance programs can tolerate less resources per addict than methadone programs because the drug they offer is perceived as more attractive to addicts and makes it easier to retain them in a program.

The age factor for heroin (AGFACH) is based on the same average age variable (AVAGE) affecting the methadone entry rate. The factor for heroin maintenance causes a smaller reduction in flow from the street when average age goes quite low than the same factor for methadone causes for those programs. The heroin maintenance age factor allows 50 percent and 90 percent of the otherwise eligible addicts to enter that type of program when the average age is 14 and 19, respectively, while the methadone age factor allows only 30 percent and 70 percent to enter for the same average age levels. This reflects an assumption that a community adopting heroin maintenance would prefer that its younger addicts received "legal" heroin in programs rather than facing the dangers of heroin overdoses, dirty needles and impure drugs on the street and having to commit crime in support of their habits.

The police and availability factors (PAFAH) and success effect on admissions (HPSEA) for heroin maintenance programs are identical to the corresponding factors for methadone programs. The monthly cost per addict of these (heroin) programs (CHPA) is equal to a direct component of $180 (COSTHM) (more expensive than the methadone program to cover heroin's higher costs) and an overhead component that goes down as the number in heroin maintenance increases (ROHP).

```
HPDO.KL=PDFHP.K/TTDO                                         259, R
     HPDO   — HEROIN PROGRAM DROPOUT RATE
     PDFHP  — POTENTIAL DROPOUTS FROM HEROIN PROGRAMS
     TTDO   — TIME TO DROP OUT


PDFHP.K=PDFHP.J+(DT) ( (FTDOH.J*STHR.JK)-HPDO.JK)           260, L
PDFHP=0                                                     260.1, N
     PDFHP  — POTENTIAL DROPOUTS FROM HEROIN PROGRAMS
     FTDOH  — FRACTION TO DROP OUT OF HEROIN PROGRAMS
     STHR   — STR TO HER MAINT
     HPDO   — HEROIN PROGRAM DROPOUT RATE
```

```
FTDOH.K=TABHL (DOHTB,(ESHEF.K*HERNEF.K)/HERMNT.K*          261, A
   CHPA.K),0,1,.2)
DOHTB=.8,.5,.2,.15,.1,.05                                   261.1, T
      FTDOH   — FRACTION TO DROP OUT OF HEROIN PROGRAMS
      DOHTB   — DROPOUT FROM HEROIN TABLE
      ESHEF   — EFFECT OF SUSCEPT ON HER DROP
      HERNEF  — HEROIN MAINT EFFORT
      HERMNT  — ADDICTS IN HER MAINT
      CHPA    — TOTAL COST OF HEROIN MAINTENANCE PER ADDICT


ESHEF.K=TABHL (ESHFTB,HSUS.K,0,.8,.1)                       262, A
ESHFTB=.1,.3,.5,1,1,1,1,1,1                                 262.1, T
      ESHEF   — EFFECT OF SUSCEPT ON HER DROP
      ESHFTB  — ESHEF TABLE
      HSUS    — HER MAINT SUSCEPTIBILITY


AOHM.KL=DELAY3(STHR.JK,TAOHM)                               263, R
TAOHM=180                                                   263.1, C
HERPRG=0                                                    263.2, C
      AOHM    — RATE OF AGING OUT OF HEROIN MAINT
      STHR    — STR TO HER MAINT
      TAOHM   — TIME TO AGE OUT OF HER MAINT
      HERPRG  — HEROIN PROGRAM CONTROL SWITCH
```

Dropout from heroin maintenance programs (HPDO) is again determined in the same manner as dropout from methadone and other programs. As with the other programs, a fraction of the entering addicts are diverted into a potential dropout category (PDFHP). That fraction (FTDOH) is also a composite of susceptibility and budget adequacy factors. The susceptibility factors for methadone (ESMEF) and heroin maintenance (ESHEF) are the same. The budget adequacy factor for heroin maintenance, however, produces a lower dropout rate for a given ratio of budget (HERNEF) to need (HERMNT*CHPA) than the methadone budget adequacy factor produces for the same ratio. Heroin maintenance's budget adequacy effect on dropout produces a maximum dropout rate of 80 percent and a minimum rate of 5 percent, while the same effect for methadone program dropout produces maximum and minimum dropout rates of 100 percent and 35 percent, respectively. This again assumes that heroin maintenance programs can tolerate less resources per addict (than methadone) and still retain addicts, because the drug they administer is perceived as more attractive by addicts.

Addicts are assumed to "age out" (AOHM) of their need for heroin maintenance 180 months (TAOHM) after they have entered that type of program.

```
HERPOL.K=HERNED.K*BUDFH.K                                   264, A
      HERPOL  — HEROIN MAINT POLICY
      HERNED  — HEROIN PROGRAM NEED
      BUDFH   — BUDGET FACTOR-HER
```

```
BUDFH.K=TABHL (BUDHTB,PERINV.K/YOUPOP.K,0,.25,.05)        265, A
BUDHTB=0,.05,.1,.3,.7,.9                                  265.1, T
     BUDFH    — BUDGET FACTOR-HER
     BUDHTB   — BUDGET FACTOR-HEROIN TABLE
     PERINV   — PERSONS INVOLVED
     YOUPOP   — YOUTH POPULATION


HERNED.K=( (ADDICT.K+PRISON.K)*CHPR+HERMNT.K)*CHPA.K      266, A
     HERNED   — HEROIN PROGRAM NEED
     ADDICT   — ADDICTS
     PRISON   — PRISON ADDICTS
     CHPR     — COMMUNITY HEROIN PROGRAM RESPONSIBILITY
     HERMNT   — ADDICTS IN HER MAINT
     CHPA     — TOTAL COST OF HEROIN MAINTENANCE PER ADDICT


GHP.KL=(HERPOL.K-HERNEF.K)*AEHP.K*HERPRG/TIHP             267, R
TIHP=12                                                   267.1, C
     GHP      — GROWTH OF HEROIN PROG
     HERPOL   — HEROIN MAINT POLICY
     HERNEF   — HEROIN MAINT EFFORT
     AEHP     — ATTITUDE EFFECT ON HEROIN PROG
     HERPRG   — HEROIN PROGRAM CONTROL SWITCH
     TIHP     — TIME TO IMPLEMENT HEROIN PROGRAM


AEHP.K=TABHL(AEHPTB,CATT.K,0,1,.2)                        268, A
AEHPTB=0,.05,.1,.4,.8,1                                   268.1, T
     AEHP     — ATTITUDE EFFECT ON HEROIN PROG
     AEHPTB   — ATTITUDE EFFECT ON HER PROG TAB
     CATT     — COMMUNITY ATTITUDE


HERNEF.K=HERNEF.J+(DT) (GHP.JK)                           269, L
HERNEF=1                                                  269.1, N
     HERNEF   — HEROIN MAINT EFFORT
     GHP      — GROWTH OF HEROIN PROG
```

The size of the heroin maintenance effort mounted by a community is determined in the same way as the methadone effort's size. The planned heroin program (HERPOL) is the product of a computed need and a budget factor. The need (HERNED) encompasses a fraction (CHPR) of the addicts on the street and in prison as well as the addicts already in heroin maintenance programs. The budget factor (BUDFH) allows up to 90 percent of this need to be funded if the perceived involvement in drug use and addiction [PERINV = ALLADP + (USERS) (0.1)] reaches 25 percent of the youthful population. Much smaller fractions are funded (in BUDHTB) if PERINV has lower values.

Implementation of plans takes 12 months (TIHP) and is subject to the effect of community attitudes. A high value of CATT, corresponding to a predominantly medical definition of addiction, is assumed to be necessary for the implementation of heroin maintenance programs. While methadone programs require a value of CATT equal to 0.6 for full implementation and 0.4

to be implemented substantially, heroin maintenance programs cannot be implemented in a substantial manner until CATT reaches 0.8 and cannot be fully implemented until CATT reaches its maximum value of 1. This assumes that most communities abhor the idea of dispensing the drug they consider "responsible" for the addiction problem and that only communities with extreme attitudes will consider this treatment modality.

Heroin maintenance programs are added to simulations by setting HERPRG to 1 rather than zero.

```
TAHM.K=TAHM.J+(DT) (HERMNT.J-HPDO.JK*TTDO-AOHM.JK*          270, L
   TAOHM)
TAHM=0                                                     270.1, N
       TAHM    — TIME OF ADDICTS IN HEROIN MAINTENANCE
       HERMNT  — ADDICTS IN HER MAINT
       HPDO    — HEROIN PROGRAM DROPOUT RATE
       TTDO    — TIME TO DROP OUT
       AOHM    — RATE OF AGING OUT OF HEROIN MAINT
       TAOHM   — TIME TO AGE OUT OF HER MAINT


AVTIME.K=TAHM.K/HERMNT.K                                    271, A
       AVTIME  — AVG TIME IN HER MAINT
       TAHM    — TIME OF ADDICTS IN HEROIN MAINTENANCE
       HERMNT  — ADDICTS IN HER MAINT


DOSAGE.K=TABHL(DOSETB,AVTIME.K,0,60,12)                     272, A
DOSETB=1,1.2,1.8,2.4,2.8,3                                  272.1, T
       DOSAGE  — DOSAGE IN HEROIN MAINT
       DOSETB  — DOSAGE TABLE
       AVTIME  — AVG TIME IN HER MAINT


LEAKAG.K=TABHL(LEAKTB,DOSAGE.K,0,3,.5)*HERMNT.K*30          273, A
LEAKTB=.1,.2,.4,.8,.9,1,1                                   273.1, T
       LEAKAG  — LEAKAGE OF HER
       LEAKTB  — LEAKAGE TABLE
       DOSAGE  — DOSAGE IN HEROIN MAINT
       HERMNT  — ADDICTS IN HER MAINT


ROHP.K=TABHL(ROHPTB,HERMNT.K,0,8000,1600)                   274, A
ROHPTB=80,60,40,30,20,10                                    274.1, T
       ROHP    — RATE OF OVH IN HER PROG
       ROHPTB  — RATE OF OVH IN HER PROG TABLE
       HERMNT  — ADDICTS IN HER MAINT
```

Leakage from heroin maintenance programs to street supplies is determined in a manner different from methadone leakage because of differences in pharmacological characteristics of the two drugs. Addicts on methadone can receive the same dosage for a long period of time. Those receiving heroin maintenance, however, require larger dosages as time goes on and their tolerance increases. Rates of tolerance increase are different for each individual and it is difficult to tell how much heroin an addict really needs and whether he is requesting more primarily to sell it on the street. As average time spent in heroin maintenance increases and dosage increases with it, the potential for leakage becomes greater, because each addict is receiving more heroin.

Average time in heroin maintenance (AVTIME) is derived from a "pool" similar to the one used to determine the addict population's average age. The "pool" contains the total number of months spent in heroin maintenance by addicts now in those programs (TAHM) and is added to each month by the number of addicts spending another month in them (the HERMNT term in equation 270). Addicts dropping out each month "take the number of months they have spent in heroin maintenance with them" (HPDO*TTDO) and addicts aging out do the same (AOHM*TAOHM). The average time spent in heroin maintenance is found by dividing the pool of total months spent (TAHM) by the number of addicts in heroin maintenance (HERMNT). Daily dosage in heroin maintenance (DOSAGE) is assumed to reach a maximum of three times the daily dosage required by street addicts as the average time approaches 60 months. When that dosage level is reached, an average of one street addict dosage is assumed to be leaked to the street each day (1 in LEAKTB) per addict in heroin maintenance. Lower heroin maintenance dosages produce correspondingly smaller leakage rates (shown in LEAKTB). The total monthly volume of leakage to the street (LEAKAG) is computed by multiplying this daily leakage per addict in heroin maintenance by HERMNT and by the 30 days in a month.

Detoxification Program

```
SWD=0                                                        274.2, C
      SWD    — SWITCH FOR DETOX PROGRAM

DETOX.K=DETOX.J+(DT) (DETCR.JK)                              275, L
DETOX=0                                                      275.1, N
      DETOX  — ADDICTS IN DETOX PROGRAM
      DETCR  — DETOX CHANGE

DETCR.KL=( (DETCAP.K) (PAFICD.K)–DETOX.K)*DSUS.K*SWD/        276, R
   TTEDX
TTEDX=3                                                      276.1, C
      DETCR  — DETOX CHANGE
      DETCAP — DETOX CAPACITY
      PAFICD — POLICE AND AVAILABILITY FACTORS–DETOX
      DETOX  — ADDICTS IN DETOX PROGRAM
      DSUS   — DETOX SUSCEPTIBILITY FACTOR
      SWD    — SWITCH FOR DETOX PROGRAM
      TTEDX  — TIME TO ENTER DETOX
```

```
PAFICD.K=.5*PHE.K+1.5*LDAF.K                                      277, A
    PAFICD  — POLICE AND AVAILABILITY FACTORS-DETOX
    PHE     — POLICE HARASSMENT EFF.
    LDAF    — LOW DRUG AVAIL. FACTOR


DSUS.K=TABHL (DSUSTB,DETOX.K/(CRIMF.K*LDAF.K*2*                   278, A
    ADDICT.K),0,2,.5)
DSUSTB=1,.8,.5,.3,.1                                              278.1, T
    DSUS    — DETOX SUSCEPTIBILITY FACTOR
    DSUSTB  — DETOX SUSCEPTIBILITY TABLE
    DETOX   — ADDICTS IN DETOX PROGRAM
    CRIMF   — CRIMINAL FRACTION OF ADDICTS
    LDAF    — LOW DRUG AVAIL. FACTOR
    ADDICT  — ADDICTS
```

Detoxification programs have their impact by temporarily keeping addicts from using heroin and thereby reducing average habit size. A smaller average habit means that addicts support their addiction while committing less crime. The number of addicts actually in detox programs (DETOX) grows toward the number that could potentially be in such programs. Potential enrollment in detox programs is a function of their nominal capacity (DETCAP), but may be more than that nominal capacity if conditions on the street are undesirable for addicts. Potential enrollment can equal as much as two times nominal capacity when drug availability is extremely low (LDAF = 1 when AAP = -1) and police harassment is intensive (PHE = 1 when AVARR = 0.1). Low drug availability has an effect three times as great as the police harassment effect in determining potential enrollment. This reflects the addict's urgent desire to reduce habit size when heroin is scarce.

Adjustment of actual enrollment to its potential size is restricted by a susceptibility factor (DSUS). This factor is structured somewhat differently from the susceptibility factors affecting entry to other programs. The detox susceptibility factor is a function of the ratio of addicts already in detox programs (DETOX) to the maximum number that might be expected to enter. That theoretical maximum is the fraction of the street addict population engaged in some sort of crime (ADDICT*CRIMF) multiplied by as much as two (LDAF = 1 at maximum) to reflect the effect of low drug availability on susceptibility to detoxification programs. Low values of the ratio allow most of the indicated adjustment in DETOX to take place (1 and 0.8 in DSUSTB). When DETOX equals this theoretical maximum, only half the indicated adjustment takes place (0.5 in DSUSTB). When DETOX is twice the theoretical maximum enrollment, hardly any further change in DETOX takes place because DSUS = 0.1.

The growth of DETOX toward potential enrollment takes 3 months (TTEDX). Detox programs are included in simulations by setting SWD to 1 rather than zero.

```
DETCAP.K=DETCAP.J+(DT) (CAPCHG.JK)                               279, L
DETCAP=0                                                         279.1, N
       DETCAP  —  DETOX CAPACITY
       CAPCHG  —  CAPACITY CHANGE RATE

CAPCHG.KL=( (ADDICT.K) (DETRES)–DETCAP.K)*DETATF.K*              280, R
   SWD/TCDXC
TCDXC=8                                                          280.1, C
DETRES=.5                                                        280.2, C
       CAPCHG  —  CAPACITY CHANGE RATE
       ADDICT  —  ADDICTS
       DETRES  —  DETOX RESPONSIBILITY
       DETCAP  —  DETOX CAPACITY
       DETATF  —  DETOX ATTITUDE FACTOR
       SWD     —  SWITCH FOR DETOX PROGRAM
       TCDXC   —  TIME TO CHANGE DETOX CAPACITY

DETATF.K=TABHL(DETATB,CATT.K,0,1,.2)                             281, A
DETATB=0,.1,.2,.5,.9,1                                           281.1, T
       DETATF  —  DETOX ATTITUDE FACTOR
       DETATB  —  DETOX ATTITUDE TABLE
       CATT    —  COMMUNITY ATTITUDE
```

Capacity of detox programs (DETCAP) grows to a level that can accommodate a specified fraction of the street addict population (DETRES). That fraction, in simulations including detox programs, is set initially to encompass 50 percent of the street addicts. Growth of capacity to this level is restricted by the effect of community attitude (DETATF). Because detox programs are not a "cure", but merely a way of making addiction easier to live with, a "medically-oriented" attitude toward addiction (high level of CATT) is assumed necessary. A value of CATT equal to 0.6 allows DETCAP to grow to its indicated level (ADDICT*DETRES) at only half the rate possible when CATT is at its highest value of 1. Development of detox capacity takes place only if SWD = 1 rather than zero and occurs over a period of 8 months (TCDXC).

```
DRCU.K=DRCU.J+(DT) (GDRCU.JK–DDRCU.JK)                           282, L
DRCU=0                                                           282.1, N
       DRCU   —  DETOX REDUCTION OF CRIME AND USAGE
       GDRCU  —  GROWTH OF DETOX REDUCTION
       DDRCU  —  DECLINE OF DETOX REDUCTION EFFECT

GDRCU.KL=(REDUC*(DETOX.K/(ADDICT.K+DETOX.K) )–                   283, R
   DRCU.K)/TADRCU
REDUC=.5                                                         283.1, C
TADRCU=2                                                         283.2, C
       GDRCU  —  GROWTH OF DETOX REDUCTION
       REDUC  —  REDUCTION FACTOR
```

```
       DETOX   – ADDICTS IN DETOX PROGRAM
       ADDICT  – ADDICTS
       DRCU    – DETOX REDUCTION OF CRIME AND USAGE
       TADRCU – TIME TO ADJUST REDUCTION
```

DDRCU.KL=DERED.K/3   284, R
      DDRCU   – DECLINE OF DETOX REDUCTION EFFECT
      DERED   – DELAYED EFFECT ON REDUCTION

DERED.K=DLINF3(DRCU.K,TDERED)   285, A
TDERED=6   285.1, C
      DERED   – DELAYED EFFECT ON REDUCTION
      DRCU   – DETOX REDUCTION OF CRIME AND USAGE
      TDERED – TIME FOR DELAYED EFF ON RED

DEMRED.K=DRCU.K   286, A
      DEMRED– STREET DEMAND EFFECT OF REDUCTION
      DRCU   – DETOX REDUCTION OF CRIME AND USAGE

The fractional reduction in crime and usage, enabled by detox programs and their effect on habit size, is affected by the fraction of street addicts going through detox programs and by the impact detox has on each of those addicts. The reduction of habit size and required crime for each addict is assumed initially to be 50 percent (REDUC). Impact on the average habit and crime requirements of the overall addict population is that 50 percent multiplied by the fraction of street addicts going through detox programs. Actual reduction in crime and usage (DRCU) grows to this value after a delay of 2 months (TADCRU).

This effect "wears off" gradually unless addicts continue to go through detox programs. The reduction in crime and usage is assumed to last for 6 months (TDERED) before beginning to deteriorate. After 6 months, the delayed effect (DERED) deteriorates over a period of 3 months.

The fractional reduction in crime and usage due to detox programs (DRCU) is the net result of these rates of growth (GDRCU) and decline (DDRCU). DRCU impacts directly on the crime rate. DEMRED, equal to DRCU, impacts on the usage rate per addict (URA).

Narcotic Antagonist Program

ANTAG.K=ANTAG.J+(DT) (GANTAG.JK–ANTAGD.JK–ANTRHB.JK)   287, L
ANTAG=0   287.1, N
      ANTAG   – ADDICTS IN ANTAGONIST PROGRAMS
      GANTAG – GROWTH OF ANTAGONIST LEVEL
      ANTAGD – ANTAGONIST DROPOUT RATE
      ANTRHB – ANTAGONIST REHABILITATION RATE

GANTAG.KL=((ANTCAP.K) (PAFICA.K)-ANTAG.K)*ASUS.K*   288, R
    SWA/TTANT
TTANT=6   288.1, C
    GANTAG — GROWTH OF ANTAGONIST LEVEL
    ANTCAP — ANTAGONIST PROGRAM CAPACITY
    PAFICA   — POLICE AND AVAILABILITY FACTORS-ANTAGONISTS
    ANTAG   — ADDICTS IN ANTAGONIST PROGRAMS
    ASUS   — ANTAGONIST SUSCEPTIBILITY
    SWA   — SWITCH FOR ANTAGONIST PROGRAM
    TTANT   — TIME TO ENTER ANTAGONIST PROGRAM

PAFICA.K=PAFIC.K*.75   289, A
    PAFICA   — POLICE AND AVAILABILITY FACTORS-ANTAGONISTS
    PAFIC   — POLICE AND AVAILABILITY FACTORS IN
                 COMMUNITY

ASUS.K=TABHL(ASUSTB,ASUSCP.K,0,.4,.1)   290, A
ASUSTB=.01,.3,.7,.9,1   290.1, T
    ASUS   — ANTAGONIST SUSCEPTIBILITY
    ASUSTB   — ANTAGONIST SUSCEPTIBILITY TABLE
    ASUSCP   — ANT SUSC PRCT

ASUSCP.K=(ALFRAC*ALLADP.K-ANTAG.K)/ALLADP.K   291, A
ALFRAC=.4   291.1, C
    ASUSCP   — ANT SUSC PRCT
    ALFRAC   — ANTAGONIST LIMITING FRACTION
    ALLADP   — ALL ADDICTS, INCL. MAINT. PROG.
    ANTAG   — ADDICTS IN ANTAGONIST PROGRAMS

    Narcotic antagonist programs maintain addicts on drugs that block the pleasurable effects of heroin and produce unpleasant side effects when heroin is used. The number of addicts in such program (ANTAG) grows as addicts enter from the street (GANTAG) and decline as addicts drop out (ANTAGD) or are rehabilitated (ANTRHB). The growth rate for antagonist programs is formulated in the same manner as the detox growth rate. A potential number of addicts in anatagonist programs is formed by the product of nominal program capacity (ANTCAP) and police and availability factors (PAFICA). PAFICA equals PAFIC*.75 which means that it can reach as high a value as 1.5 when the community has very low heroin availability and a very high arrest rate. Low drug availability and police harassment are assumed to have equal weights in affecting the potential number in antagonist programs.

    The number of addicts actually in antagonist programs (ANTAG) can adjust to this potential number in 6 months (TTANT). This adjustment is, however, affected by a susceptibility factor (ASUS) that is based on the remaining fraction of the addict population susceptible to antagonist programs (ASUSCP). Here, a maximum susceptible fraction of 40 percent is assumed (ALFRAC = 0.4) and the remaining fraction susceptible is simply that segment of the addict population less those already in anatagonist programs divided by the total addict population. Values of ASUSCP less than 20 percent have a serious inhibiting effect (lower values in ASUSTB) on antagonist program growth. SWA must be set to 1 rather than zero to include antagonist programs in a simulation.

```
ANTCAP.K=ANTCAP.J+(DT) (CANTCP.JK)                    292, L
ANTCAP=1                                             292.1, N
     ANTCAP  - ANTAGONIST PROGRAM CAPACITY
     CANTCP  - CHANGE IN ANTAGONIST CAPACITY

CANTCP.KL=( (ADDICT.K) (ANTRES) (LTMF.K)-ANTCAP.K)*   293, R
     ANTATF.K*SWA/TCANTC
TCANTC=8                                             293.1, C
ANTRES=.4                                            293.2, C
     CANTCP  - CHANGE IN ANTAGONIST CAPACITY
     ADDICT  - ADDICTS
     ANTRES  - ANTAGONIST RESPONSIBILITY
     LTMF    - LONG-TERM MAINTENANCE FACTOR
     ANTCAP  - ANTAGONIST PROGRAM CAPACITY
     ANTATF  - ANTAGONIST ATTITUDE FACTOR
     SWA     - SWITCH FOR ANTAGONIST PROGRAM
     TCANTC  - TIME TO CHANGE CAPACITY

ANTATF.K=TABHL(ANTATB,CATT.K,0,.5,.1)                 294, A
ANTATB=0,.2,.5,.8,.9,1                               294.1, T
     ANTATF  - ANTAGONIST ATTITUDE FACTOR
     ANTATB  - ANTAGONIST ATTITUDE TABLE
     CATT    - COMMUNITY ATTITUDE

LTMF.K=TABHL(LTMFTB,(METHDN.K+MMP.K+HERMNT.K)/        295, A
     YOUPOP.K,0,.05,.01)
LTMFTB=1,1.05,1.1,1.3,1.4,1.5                         295.1, T
SWA=0                                                295.2, C
     LTMF    - LONG-TERM MAINTENANCE FACTOR
     LTMFTB  - LONG-TERM MAINTENANCE FAC TABLE
     METHDN  - ADDICTS IN METHADONE PROGRAMS
     MMP     - EX-ADDICTS IN METHADONE MAINTENANCE PROG
     HERMNT  - ADDICTS IN HER MAINT
     YOUPOP  - YOUTH POPULATION
     SWA     - SWITCH FOR ANTAGONIST PROGRAM
```

Antagonist program capacity grows to a level sufficient to care for a certain fraction of the street addict population (ADDICT*ANTRES). That fraction is generally set at 0.4, but can be increased by as much as 50 percent by a long-term maintenance factor (LTMF) that is produced when the total number of addicts in methadone, long-term methadone maintenance, and heroin maintenance programs exceeds 5 percent of a community's youthful population. Lesser increases result when smaller fractions of the youthful population are in long-term maintenance. This factor reflects a presumed desire for an alternative treatment modality by a community with many of its young people enrolled in legal narcotics programs.

The attitude factor affecting growth of antagonist programs (ANTATF) is a relatively "lenient" one. It permits the full rate of growth when CATT equals 0.5 and substantial growth when CATT is as low as 0.3. Actual capacity adjusts to its desired value over a period of 8 months (TCANTC) if ANTATF has a neutral effect (equals 1). SWA must equal 1 rather than zero if antagonist capacity is to develop.

```
ANTAGD.KL=PDFANT.K/TTDOA                                        296, R
TTDOA=12                                                        296.1, C
     ANTAGD  — ANTAGONIST DROPOUT RATE
     PDFANT  — POTENTIAL DROPOUTS FROM ANATAGONIST PROGRAMS
     TTDOA   — TIME TO DROP OUT OF ANTAGONIST PROGRAM


PDFANT.K=PDFANT.J+(DT) ( (GANTAG.JK*FTDOA.J)-                   297, L
     ANTAGD.JK)
PDFANT=0                                                        297.1, N
     PDFANT  — POTENTIAL DROPOUTS FROM ANTAGONIST PROGRAMS
     GANTAG  — GROWTH OF ANTAGONIST LEVEL
     FTDOA   — FRACTION TO DROP OUT OF ANTAGONIST PROGRAM
     ANTAGD  — ANTAGONIST DROPOUT RATE


FTDOA.K=TABHL(DOATB,ASUSCP.K*(ANTAG.K/ANTCAP.K),0,.6,.1)        298, A
DOATB=.3,.4,.5,.7,.9,.95,1                                      298.1, T
     FTDOA   — FRACTION TO DROP OUT OF ANTAGONIST PROGRAM
     DOATB   — DROPOUT FROM ANTAGONIST TABLE
     ASUSCP  — ANT SUSC PRCT
     ANTAG   — ADDICTS IN ANTAGONIST PROGRAMS
     ANTCAP  — ANTAGONIST PROGRAM CAPACITY


ANTRHB.KL=PSANT.K/TTBRA                                         299, R
TTBRA=36                                                        299.1, C
     ANTRHB  — ANTAGONIST REHABILITATION RATE
     PSANT   — POTENTIAL SUCCESSES IN ANTAGONIST TREATMENT
     TTBRA   — TIME TO BE REHABILITATED-ANTAG


PSANT.K=PSANT.J+(DT) ( (GANTAG.JK*FTBRA.J)-ANTRHB.JK)           300, L
PSANT=0                                                         300.1, N
     PSANT   — POTENTIAL SUCCESSES IN ANTAGONIST TREATMENT
     GANTAG  — GROWTH OF ANTAGONIST LEVEL
     FTBRA   — FRACTION TO BE REHABILITATED-ANTAGONISTS
     ANTRHB  — ANTAGONIST REHABILITATION RATE
```

```
FTBRA.K=TABHL(FRATB,ASUSCP.K*(ANTAG.K/ANTCAP.K),0,.6,.1)        301, A
FRATB=.4,.35,.3,.2,.1,.05,0                                     301.1, T
     FTBRA    — FRACTION TO BE REHABILITATED-ANTAGONISTS
     FRATB    — REHABILITATION-ANTAG TABLE
     ASUSCP   — ANT SUSC PRCT
     ANTAG    — ADDICTS IN ANTAGONIST PROGRAMS
     ANTCAP   — ANTAGONIST PROGRAM CAPACITY
```

Dropout and rehabilitation rates are structured the same way for antagonist programs as they are for other forms of rehabilitation such as methadone. Fractions of the addicts entering antagonist programs (GANTAG) are diverted into potential dropout (PDFANT) and potential rehabilitation (PSANT) groups depending on the adequacy of the programs' resources [ratio of number in program to program capacity and the fraction of the addict population remaining susceptible to antagonist treatment (ASUSCP)]. In the dropout fraction (FTDOA), a lower ratio of addicts in antagonist treatment to program capacity indicates greater resources per addict and can reduce the dropout rate to as low as 30 percent. Similarly, a low ratio of addicts in antagonist treatment to program capacity produces a higher rehabilitation (FTBRA) rate, up to 40 percent for very low ratios.

Addicts who drop out of antagonist programs (ANTAGD) are assumed to do so over a 12-month period (TTDOA). Rehabilitation to the point where narcotic antagonists are no longer needed to avoid readdiction (ANTRHB) is assumed to require 36 months (TTBRA) on average. Addicts who neither drop out nor are rehabilitated remain in antagonist programs indefinitely, according to the model's assumptions.

Cost Sector

```
PLCOST.K=(PCOST+POC.K)*CAPE.K                                   302, A
     PLCOST   — TOTAL POLICE COST
     PCOST    — POLICEMAN COST
     POC      — POLICE OVH COST
     CAPE     — CUMULATIVE ADDITIONAL POLICE EFFORT


POC.K=TABHL(POCTB,CAPE.K,0,100,20)                              303, A
POCTB=1500,1000,600,500,450,400                                303.1, T
PCOST=1000                                                     303.2, C
     POC      — POLICE OVH COST
     POCTB    — POLICE OVH COST TABLE
     CAPE     — CUMULATIVE ADDITIONAL POLICE EFFORT
     PCOST    — POLICEMAN COST


PRCOST.K=PRISON.K*CPRCST                                        304, A
CPRCST=250                                                     304.1, C
     PRCOST   — PRISON COST
```

```
        PRISON    — PRISON ADDICTS
        CPRCST    — PER CONVICT PRISON COST


CRCOST.K=RCPA.K*COMRHB.K                                           305, A
        CRCOST   — COMM REHAB COST
        RCPA     — TOTAL REHAB COST PER ADDICT
        COMRHB   — COMMUNITY REHABILITATION


ROC.K=TABHL(ROCTB,COMRHB,K,0,800,200)                             306, A
ROCTB=400,200,100,70,60                                           306.1, T
        ROC      — REHAB OVH COST
        ROCTB    — REHAB OVH COST TABLE
        COMRHB   — COMMUNITY REHABILITATION


MPCOST.K=CMPA.K*METHDN.K                                          307, A
        MPCOST   — METH PROGRAM COST
        CMPA     — TOTAL COST OF METHADONE MAINTENANCE PER
                    ADDICT
        METHDN   — ADDICTS IN METHADONE PROGRAMS


ROM.K=TABHL(ROMTB,METHDN.K,0,8000,1600)                           308, A
ROMTB=100,80,60,40,30,20                                          308.1, T
        ROM      — RATE OF OVH FOR METH
        ROMTB    — RATE OF OVH–METH TAB
        METHDN   — ADDICTS IN METHADONE PROGRAMS


CMM.K=MMP.K*MAINTC                                                309, A
MAINTC=40                                                         309.1, C
        CMM      — COST OF METH MAINT
        MMP      — EX-ADDICTS IN METHADONE MAINTENANCE PROG
        MAINTC   — MAINTENANCE COST


ORCOST.K=OCPA.K*RBOCOM.K                                          310, A
        ORCOST   — OUTS REHAB COST
        OCPA     — OUTSIDE REHAB COST PER ADDICT/MO.
        RBOCOM   — ADDICTS IN REHABILITATION OUTSIDE THE
                    COMMUNITY


ROO.K=TABHL(ROOTB,RBOCOM.K,0,800,200)                             311, A
ROOTB=500,300,150,70,50                                           311.1, T
        ROO      — RATE OF OVH–OUTSIDE
        ROOTB    — RATE OF OVH–OUTS TABLE
        RBOCOM   — ADDICTS IN REHABILITATION OUTSIDE THE
                    COMMUNITY


EDCOST.K=EDEF.K                                                   312, A
        EDCOST   — EDUCATIONAL COST
        EDEF     — EDUCATION EFFORT
```

```
OCEPU.K=TABHL(OEPTB,PU.K,0,50E3,10E3)                    313, A
OEPTB=1,.6,.4,.3,.2,.2                                   313.1, T
      OCEPU   — OVH COST TO EDUC POTL USERS
      OEPTB   — OVH TO EDUC POTL USERS TABLE
      PU      — POTENTIAL USERS


OCEU.K=TABHL(OEUTB,USERS.K,0,40E3,10E3)                  314, A
OEUTB=2.5,2,1.7,1.4,1.3                                  314.1, T
      OCEU    — OVH COST TO EDUC USERS
      OEUTB   — OVH TO EDUC USERS TABLE
      USERS   — USERS


CECOST.K=CEC*COMMED.K                                    315, A
CEC=(400) (100)                                          315.1, N
      CECOST  — COMM EDUC COST
      CEC     — COMM EDUC COST FACTOR
      COMMED  — COMMUNITY EDUCATION EFFORT


CDCOST.K=CDC*COMDEV.K                                    316, A
CDC=1000                                                 316.1, C
      CDCOST  — COMM DEV COST
      CDC     — COMM DEV COST FACTOR
      COMDEV  — COMMUNITY DEVELOPMENT EFFORT


MHCOST.K=CMHCPR.K                                        317, A
      MHCOST  — MENTAL HEALTH COST
      CMHCPR  — COMM MENTAL HEALTH CENTER PROGRAM


MHOCST.K=TABHL(MHOTB,TFRAC.K*(PU.K*USERS.K),0,15E3,      318, A
   3E3)
MHOTB=40,30,25,20,17,15                                  318.1, A
      MHOCST  — MH OH COST
      MHOTB   — MENTAL HEALTH OVH TABLE
      TFRAC   — TROUBLED FRACTION
      PU      — POTENTIAL USERS
      USERS   — USERS


RECOST.K=RENEFF.K                                        319, A
      RECOST  — RE-ENTRY COST
      RENEFF  — RE-ENTRY EFFORT


RENOH.K=TABHL(REOHTB,REENT.K,0,1000,250)                 320, A
REOHTB=40,30,25,20,16                                    320.1, T
      RENOH   — RE-ENTRY OVH
      REOHTB  — RE-ENTRY OVH TABLE
      REENT   — ADDICTS IN RE-ENTRY PROCESS


HMTCST.K=HERMNT.K*CHPA.K                                 321, A
      HMTCST  — HEROIN MAINT COST
      HERMNT  — ADDICTS IN HER MAINT
      CHPA    — TOTAL COST OF HEROIN MAINTENANCE PER ADDICT
```

```
CDETOX.K=DETOX.K*CDTX                                          322, A
CDTX=450                                                       322.1, C
     CDETOX  — COST OF DETOX
     DETOX   — ADDICTS IN DETOX PROGRAM
     CDTX    — COST OF DETOX PER ADDICT


ANTCST.K=ANTAG.K*ANCOST                                        323, A
ANCOST=200                                                     323.1, C
     ANTCST  — ANTAGONIST COST
     ANTAG   — ADDICTS IN ANTAGONIST PROGRAMS
     ANCOST  — ANTAGONIST COST PER ADDICT


TPCOST.KL=PLCOST.K+CRCOST.K+ORCOST.K+EDCOST.K+                 324, R
   CECOST.K+CDCOST.K+MHCOST.K+RECOST.K+MPCOST.K+
   CMM.K+PRCOST.K+HMTCST.K+CDETOX.K+ANTCST.K
     TPCOST  — TOTAL PROGRAM COST/MO.
     PLCOST  — TOTAL POLICE COST
     CRCOST  — COMM REHAB COST
     ORCOST  — OUTS REHAB COST
     EDCOST  — EDUCATIONAL COST
     CECOST  — COMM EDUC COST
     CDCOST  — COMM DEV COST
     MHCOST  — MENTAL HEALTH COST
     RECOST  — RE-ENTRY COST
     MPCOST  — METH PROGRAM COST
     CMM     — COST OF METH MAINT
     PRCOST  — PRISON COST
     HMTCST  — HEROIN MAINT COST
     CDETOX  — COST OF DETOX
     ANTCST  — ANTAGONIST COST
```

The various cost equations shown above are self-explanatory. The cost of each program element is made up of a direct component and an indirect component that varies inversely with program magnitude. Costs for a particular program not found in this sector can be found in the sector describing that program element. Equation 324 provides a total program cost (**TPCOST**) for comparison among simulations with different program mixes.

Index

addiction: addict sector in model simulation, 149; associated factors, 42; burn-out phenomenon, 163; concept of addict, 14; creaming phenomenon and rehabilitation, 193; definition, 29; definition and categories, 21; dynamics, 19; economics, 56; entry, 35; heroin maintenance strategy, 112; model simulation, 91; New York City population, 53; peer interaction, 37; personality profile, 44; population, 142; population distribution, 122; population figures, 93, 94; prevention strategy, 68; projected population, 118; rate, 3; redefinition of problem, 62; rehabilitation strategy, 75–80; −scarcity effect on arrests, 171; and supply, 96

alienation, 39, 40; addiction as outlets, 153
antagonists, 79, 132, 219

Black Muslums, 44
Black Panthers, 44
BNDD (Bureau of Narcotics and Dangerous Drugs), 31
Britain, 68; heroin maintenance program, 80

California, 61
Chein, K., 43; addict personality, 44; education, 47
Chicago, 41
civil commitment: definition, 60
community: alarm and crime rate, 26; black response, 75; change sector, 180; constant state of change, 119; definition of heroin problem, 78, 169; education policy, 173; education and strategy, 101; influence on police, 8; model simulation,

92; prevention strategy, 69; response, 56; response sector, 163; soft-drug availability, 146
Connecticut Mental Health Center, 80
Crawley, England, 41
crime: and addiction, 6; data collecting, 52; drug-free rehabilitation, 114; education programs, 100; heroin price, 26; heroin price effect, 165; maintenance programs, 124; and methadone, 106; prison, 208; in simulation, 108;
cyclazocine, 80

Dangerous Drug Act, 1968, 81
Daytop Village, 76
decriminalization, 130; attitude of, 14; and community attitude, 28; and heroin maintenance, 83; redefinition of addiction, 63; sociomedical solutions, 169
detoxification, 21, 70, 133; defined, 79; impact, 216
distribution: heroin availability, 159; methadone, 74; network, 56; price, 136; price and crime, 9; and Rockefeller policy, 98; scale of, 42
Dole and Nyswanger, 70
drug culture: cost for community, 51; durg availability, 24; model simulation, 94; multiple factor, 145; phenomenon of, 35; prevention programs, 69
DuPont, Robert, 70, 74

education: as deterrent, 45; dissuasive, 135; impact on use, 143; need, cost and credibility factor, 153; prevention program, 68; scare tactics, 24; strategy as deterrent, 85

About the Authors

Gilbert Levin is associate professor of psychiatry and community health at the Albert Einstein College of Medicine. He graduated from the University of Michigan and received a Ph.D. in clinical and social psychology from Boston University. He has conducted research at the Harvard Medical School and taught at Carnegie-Mellon University. At Einstein since 1963, he teaches and conducts research on social and community psychiatry and consults to industrial and health organizations. He is best known for his contributions to the development and evaluation of community mental health practices and has published many articles in this field.

Edward B. Roberts is the David Sarnoff Professor of the Management of Technology at the M.I.T. Alfred P. Sloan School of Management. He received his degrees from M.I.T., including a Ph.D. in economics. On the M.I.T. faculty since 1961, Dr. Roberts was a founding member of what is now the System Dynamics Group. He helped organize and direct the M.I.T. Research Program on the Management of Science and Technology, and now chairs the Technology and Health Management area at the Sloan School.

Dr. Roberts has been active as a consultant and lecturer to government and industry. He is co-founder and president of Pugh-Roberts Associates, Inc., and a director of several other firms. For several years he was a member of the U.S. Air Force Scientific Advisory Board and the Commerce Technical Advisory Board, and also served as a consultant to the President's Advisory Council on Management Improvement. An author of several books and numerous articles, Dr. Roberts has also consulted to the Association of American Medical Colleges and the American College of Physicians.

Gary B. Hirsch is Senior Consultant at Pugh-Roberts Associates, Inc., a Cambridge-based management consulting firm, and directs the firm's activities in the areas of health and social systems. Recipient of the bachelor's and master's degrees from the M.I.T. Sloan School of Management, Hirsch has led major projects on human service delivery systems, including criminal justice, welfare and health care. His extensive publications in the health field include works on manpower planning, medical education, dental care, mental health, and HMO planning.